Educational Leadership

Changing Schools, Changing Roles

Judy Reinhartz
The University of Texas at Arlington

Don M. Beach
Tarleton State University

D0144675

PEARSON

A and *B*

Boston   New York   San Francisco
Mexico City   Montreal   Toronto   London   Madrid   Munich   Paris
Hong Kong   Singapore   Tokyo   Cape Town   Sydney

Series Editor: *Arnis E. Burvikovs*
Editorial Assistant: *Christine Lyons*
Marketing Manager: *Tara Whorf*
Production Administrator: *Marissa Falco*
Production Service: *Colophon*
Electronic Composition: *Galley Graphics*
Composition and Prepress Buyer: *Linda Cox*
Manufacturing Buyer: *Andrew Turso*
Cover Administrator: *Kristina Mose-Libon*

For related titles and support materials, visit our online catalog at www.ablongman.com

Between the time Web site information is gathered and then published, it is not unusual for some sites to have closed. Also, the transcription of URLs can result in typographical errors. The publisher would appreciate notification where these errors occur so that they may be corrected in subsequent editions.

Library of Congress Cataloging-in-Publication Data

Reinhartz, Judy.
  Educational leadership: changing schools, changing roles / Judy Reinhartz, Don M. Beach.
    p. cm.
  Includes bibliographical references and index.
  ISBN 0-205-34103-9 (alk. paper)
   1. School management and organization. 2. Educational leadership. I. Beach, Don M.
  II. Title.

LB2805.R435 2004
371.2—dc21

2003043729

Printed in the United States of America

10 9 8 7 6 5 4 3 2   HAM 08 07 06 05 04

This book is dedicated to leaders—
who are the foundation and cornerstone of education—
and to two special educators, our spouses, Dennis and Linda,
who provided love, encouragement, and support
that made this book possible.

Contents

3 *Values and Ethics of Leadership*   46

4 *Legal Issues and School Leadership*   65

Mark Littleton

9   *Accountability: Using Data for School Improvement*   184

Trinidad San Miguel

10   *Professional Development for School Leaders: Reflection, Growth, and Change*   212

Preface

The purpose of this book, *Educational Leadership: Changing Schools, Changing Roles*, is to provide school leaders with the concepts and skills needed to be dynamic, creative, and adaptive in an ever changing environment. The book seeks to promote the development of leaders who are able to create school cultures in which teachers, students, and parents work together collaboratively toward the common goal of learner-centered schools. In a contemporary context, school leaders must have the necessary knowledge and skills to be able to make a difference in the lives of those they serve, by promoting the success of all students. **The Interstate School Leader Licensure Consortium (ISLLC) standards have been used as a framework to support professional practice.** These standards are introduced in Chapter 1 and each chapter addresses one or more of these school leader standards. Figure 1.2 provides a rubric for each standard which documents the knowledge and skills needed for leadership in changing schools of the twenty-first century.

The following questions have guided our thinking in the development of the book: What knowledge and skills do principals and other school leaders need in order to promote the success of all students while creating learner-centered schools? What can leaders do to promote the best professional practice? How can school leaders build a school climate that results in the highest quality of teaching and learning? In responding to these questions, we view school leaders as critical to developing and articulating a vision that empowers all constituencies so that their collective talents and actions result in academic success for all students. We view school leaders as key facilitators for the success of students and schools, and we view campus leadership positions as essential to school renewal and improvement.

Educational Leadership: Changing Schools, Changing Roles provides an overview of best practices related to effective school leadership. The theoretical and research base of the field of leadership has been cited and synthesized as it relates particularly to the principalship. The phrase *school leaders* is used throughout the book and refers to building and district-level administrators such as principals, assistant principals, teacher specialists, superintendents, and associate superintendents for instruction and curriculum.

The major topics that confront school leaders in their day-to-day roles include exhibiting positive leadership behaviors; following ethical and legal guidelines; building school cultures; fostering curriculum development and alignment; enhancing organizational leadership and decision making; building collaborative work teams; promoting action research; and using student data to guide school improvement efforts. These topics address the national standards related to school licensure or certification, particularly the ISLLC of the Council of Chief State School Officers.

Unique to this book are chapters that provide an overview of legal issues, action research, and learner accountability standards. The text also emphasizes the importance of creating a vision and mission in the development of a campus culture and the importance of ethical leadership in promoting success for all students from diverse populations. Additional resources are available on the Allyn & Bacon Educational Leadership SuperSite, www.ablongman.com/edleadership.

Educational Leadership: Changing Schools, Changing Roles is divided into three major parts. Part I, Setting the Stage for School Leadership, provides an introduction to schools as the context for leadership. The chapters in Part I discuss the evolving nature of leadership and the preparation of school leaders within the context of national standards and address the importance of leadership paradigms, trust building, campus cultures, and values and ethics. Part I also describes legal implications in school operations and concludes with an examination of the role of school leaders in building culture and community on school campuses. These beginning chapters establish a framework for leaders to use as they establish a collaborative learning culture in their schools.

The chapters in Part II, Foundations of Organizational Leadership, are more pragmatic in their orientation. Where Part I includes the general knowledge and understanding of leadership, Part II is more pragmatic and stresses the application of appropriate leadership behaviors and attendant technical skills. These chapters address the importance of action research in school improvement efforts. The chapters also emphasize the importance of organizational leadership including decision making and management in problem solving through effective communication. Finally, Part II discusses the importance of leadership in managing and developing human and fiscal resources and promoting instructional excellence. The importance of technology in the management/leadership process is also discussed including technology standards for school leaders.

Part III discusses the Foundations of Curriculum and Instruction: Implications for School Leaders. The emphasis in these chapters is on the teaching–learning process and the role of school leaders in working with teachers to achieve quality instruction through analysis and alignment. Part III discusses the processes by which schools truly become learning organizations, by stressing the importance of curriculum development and instruction and accountability and data driven decisions. This section ends with a discussion of the need for continuing professional development of school leaders.

Throughout the book, growth, change, and reflection are discussed as integral to the development of school leaders. Reflection is central to making decisions that support school leaders in establishing a culture that is more collaborative in initiating and sustaining school improvement efforts. Each chapter has opportunities for the readers to apply what they have learned. These application sections include both Case Studies and the Your Turn sections, which provide opportunities for the reader to interact with, reflect on, and apply the concepts and skills presented in the chapter. The application step nurtures reflective thinking in school leaders and provides opportunities for them to assess their understanding of the leadership process in real-world situations.

Educational Leadership: Changing Schools, Changing Roles has evolved from the combined experiences of the authors and contributors who have held administrative and leadership positions in a variety of educational settings. These leadership experiences include building and district level administration, state board of education, head of state educator certification agency, member of local and state school boards, district and classroom supervisory positions, as well as dean and department head at the university level. Perhaps more importantly, the sections called View from the Field are the stories and experiences from educational leaders in a variety of campus settings. Their stories provide real-life voices that reinforce the topics discussed. This book has been a collaborative effort, and we therefore believe that the result is a unique blend of our multiple experiences and perspectives. All the contributors to the text have *lived leadership* and are in unique positions to speak with relevant voices as they address leadership issues and concepts. Contributors to the book include: Dr. Elaine Wilmore, Associate Professor, The University of Texas at Arlington (Chapter 2), Dr. Mark Littleton, Professor, Tarleton State University (Chapter 4), Dr. Diane Porter Patrick, Assistant Professor (Chapter 7), and Dr. Trindad San Miguel, Director of the Administrator Assessment Center, ESC Region 13 (Chapter 9).

This book has been a labor of love and most, if not all, of the suggestions offered by reviewers and students who have used it have been incorporated. In a sense, one could say the information has been *field tested*. Practices and procedures have been presented that can guide school leaders in being more effective in renewing and transforming schools so that all students learn and achieve. It is hoped that this book promotes a clearer understanding of the complexities of the roles and responsibilities of school leaders.

Acknowledgements

We want to thank the following individuals who kindly reviewed our manuscript and provided valuable suggestions and insights that guided the final outcome: Rose Cameron, Tarleton State University; Dr. Michael Cunningham, Marshall University; Richard A. Fluck, Northern Illinois University; and Kip Sullivan, Sul Ross State University.

We also want to acknowledge the staff at Borders Bookstore in Fort Worth, Texas for their hospitality, support, and interest; they provided a place to think, write, and edit as this book moved from conception to reality.

About the Authors

Judy Reinhartz is currently professor of education in the School of Education and the Director for the Center for Research at The University of Texas at Arlington. She received her Ph.D. from the University of New Mexico in the area of science education, curriculum, and instructional leadership. Her master's degree was conferred by Seton Hall University. In her more than thirty-five years of experience in education, Dr. Reinhartz has served in various teaching assignments and supervisory leadership positions at all levels of education in New Jersey, Virginia, New Mexico, and Texas. In 1985, she was the recipient of the Amoco Foundation Outstanding Teaching Award at The University of Texas at Arlington. She has received numerous grants in the areas of teacher research and promoting excellence in science teaching. Dr. Reinhartz is actively involved in professional organizations, including the American Educational Research Association, the National Science Teachers Association, the Association of Teacher Educators, and the Association for Supervision and Curriculum Development. With her varied educational experiences, Judy has published extensively and has frequently served as a consultant to a number of school districts and publishers on topics such as effective teaching, inquiry science, supervisory leadership, and instructional assessment.

Don M. Beach is currently professor of educational administration at Tarleton State University, Texas A&M University System. He received his Ph.D. in Curriculum and Educational Leadership from George Peabody College of Vanderbilt University. His master's in secondary education and administration is from Texas Tech University. He has taught at both the elementary and secondary levels in the schools of Texas and Tennessee and served in numerous supervisory positions in education. He is an active writer, researcher, and teacher and has served a variety of leadership roles in numerous professional organizations, including the Association of Teacher Educators, the Association for Supervision and Curriculum Development, and the Council of Professors of Instructional Supervision. He continues to conduct workshops at the state and national levels and publish in professional journals. Don is the author of numerous textbooks and monographs concerning supervision, leadership, and elementary and secondary curricula.

1

School Leadership for the Twenty-First Century

Standard 1: A school administrator is an educational leader who promotes the success of all students by facilitating the development, articulation, implementation, and stewardship of a vision of learning that is shared and supported by the school community.

Standard 2: A school administrator is an educational leader who promotes the success of all students by advocating, nurturing, and sustaining a school culture and instructional program conducive to student learning and staff professional growth.

Standard 3: A school administrator is an educational leader who promotes the success of all students by ensuring management of the organization, operations, and resources for a safe, effective, and efficient learning environment.

Standard 5: A school administrator is an educational leader who promotes the success of all students by acting with integrity, fairness, and in an ethical manner.

Chapter Objectives

The objectives of this chapter are:

- Describe the importance of preparing school leaders.
- Identify and describe standards for school leader development.
- Discuss the changing context of schools and the changing roles of school leaders.
- Describe the leadership process and the importance of trust building.

Educational systems nationwide are transforming themselves to meet the needs of students of the twenty-first century and seldom has being an educational leader been as exciting as well as challenging. Part of the transformation involves "heart, hope, and faith, [which is] rooted in soul and spirit . . . Leading . . . requires giving gifts from the heart that breathe spirit and passion into your life and [school]" (Bolman & Deal, 1995, p. 12). The real challenge for school leaders in the coming decades, according to Neil Shipman, director of the Interstate School Leaders Licensure Consortium (ISLLC), is remaining focused on teaching and learning, rather than resorting to being managers (Franklin, 2000). School leaders must strike a balance in managing buildings, holding to higher accountability standards for student achievement, promoting teacher professional development, and involving parents and community members in campus and district decisions.

School leadership has become increasingly more complicated and vital to ensuring school success and soliciting substantial participation from faculty, staff, and students. In responding to higher standards of increased student progress, school leaders recognize that they alone cannot be the sole instructional leaders but must coach, mentor, and empower faculty and staff in the common pursuit of reform and renewal. As school leaders continue to adapt to their changing roles, effective leadership skills will be essential, and for Green (2001), the real challenge ". . . is providing the type of leadership necessary to assist schools in expanding their traditional boundaries" (p. 5). As Lambert (2002) notes, "For decades, educators have understood that we are all responsible for student learning. More recently, educators have come to realize that we are responsible for our own learning as well. But . . . I am also responsible for the learning of my colleagues" (pp. 37–38).

Deal and Peterson (1999) have observed, "Students deserve the best schools we can give them—schools full of heart, soul, and ample opportunities to learn and grow. . . . Leadership from throughout the school will be needed to build and maintain such positive, purposeful places to learn and grow" (p. 137).

The study of leaders and leadership has a long history that can be traced from nomadic tribes to today's multicultural corporations. The very concept of *effective leadership* prompts the question, By whose standards? Research on the concept of leadership using scientific methods is relatively new, and Orozco (1999) notes that, as in other organizations, school leadership can be viewed from the perspective of teachers ". . . students, parents, the community, and government agencies [which] complicates the process of dissecting and confirming the most important qualities of leadership" (p. 1). Greenberg and Baron (1997) further describe the complexities of leadership when they note that ". . . leadership resembles love. It is something most people believe they can recognize but often find difficult to define" (p. 433). Leadership is partially based on the positive feelings that exist between leaders and subordinates and involves noncoercive influence (Greenberg & Baron, 2000). For Cashman (2000), "leadership is authentic self-expression that creates value . . . [it] is not seen as hierarchical—it exists everywhere in organizations" (p. 20). For Bolman and Deal (1994), leadership is about giving and spirit. Ultimately, leadership is like a dance in which partners signal to one another as they engage in the ongoing give and take, involving mutual respect and trust.

Historically, school leaders have been portrayed as people *in charge* of a school who have the sole responsibility for leading the *troops* to success. This kind of a school leader has been likened to someone astride a horse with bugle in hand, sounding the charge with the expectation that all will follow. More recent views of leadership suggest that it is contextual and complex and involves more than yelling "Charge!" For Hogan, Curphy, and Hogan (1999), "leadership involves persuading other people to set aside for a period of time their individual concerns and to pursue a common goal that is important for the . . . group" (p. 33). They continue by saying that "leadership is persuasion, not domination; persons who can require others to do their bidding because of their power are not leaders. Leadership only occurs when others willingly adopt, for a period of time the goals of a group as their own" (p. 33).

Leadership involves building cohesive and goal oriented teams that are capable of working together to accomplish objectives and fulfill the mission. A causal and definitional link exists between leadership and team performance. Blanchard, Hybels, and Hodges (1999) note that leadership is about serving and starts on the inside and moves outward to serve others. Such leadership has the interest of others in mind, nurtures growth and development in others, is willing to listen, and thinks less about self while being held accountable for performance. Lambert (1998) suggests that leadership involves "learning together and constructing meaning and knowledge collectively and collaboratively to reflect on and make sense of work in the light of shared beliefs and create actions that grow out of these new understandings" (pp. 5–6).

Research from the last two decades has also shown a strong link between effective leadership and effective organizations (Lezotte, 1997; Sergiovanni, 1995; Bolman & Deal, 1994; Boyan, 1988; Griffiths, 1988). Hogan, Curphy, and Hogan (1999) assert that ". . . a growing body of evidence supports the common sense belief that leadership matters" (p. 34). Fullan (2002) says that schools need leaders who can change "what people in the organization value and how they work together to accomplish it" (p. 19). Fullan (2002) continues by saying that schools "need leaders who can create a

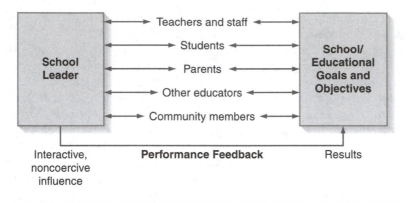

FIGURE 1.1   *The Leadership Process*

fundamental transformation in the learning cultures of schools and of the teaching professional itself" (p. 18). Beach and Reinhartz (2000) note that ". . . leadership is essential to promoting student achievement and creating a vision of success for the total educational program" (p. 72). For us, educational leadership is an interactive, noncoercive process whereby an individual influences the behavior of various constituencies, including teachers and staff, students, parents, other educators, and community members, to attain the goals and objectives of the school or district. The interactive relationship between leadership and effective schools can be seen in Figure 1.1 and is essential in accomplishing the school's mission and objectives.

As Figure 1.1 illustrates, the school leader must interact in noncoercive ways with various constituencies (teachers and staff, students, parents, other educators, and community members) to accomplish the educational goals and objectives of the school or district. The results of these efforts provide feedback so that the leader can modify interactions or goals as needed.

This book, and more specifically this chapter, provides leaders with views regarding school leadership and discusses key concepts of effective leadership at the campus and district levels. The chapter presents the new licensure standards for school leaders, and these standards emphasize not only the skills and behavior of leadership but are grounded in the belief that school leaders must promote the success of all students. As Lezotte (1997) notes, today school leaders must be concerned with academic success for all students. Within the context of change, school leaders must deal with the reality of their work while building trust at all levels. For Fullan (2002), "Leaders have a deeper and more lasting influence . . . and provide more comprehensive leadership of their focus extends beyond maintaining high standards . . . [to establishing] the conditions for 'enduring greatness'" (p. 17).

Within the changing context of school, old leadership models are proving ineffective and new paradigms of leadership are required. The chapter concludes with a discussion of the importance of trust building and the questions that school leaders must answer to be effective. For students to be successful, they need teachers who are successful and in turn they need effective leaders.

School Leadership and Standards

Any discussion of school leadership must include the standards by which school personnel are certified or licensed. Standards for the preparation of school administrators reflect contemporary views of leadership theory and serve not only to guide professional programs but also serve as job descriptions for school leaders. Although each state may have a set of standards to guide school leader preparation, the Interstate School Leaders Licensure Consortium (ISLLC) of the Council of Chief State School Officers (1997) recognized the importance of leadership in the teaching–learning process and proposed the six standards. A school administrator is an educational leader who promotes the success of all students by:

- facilitating the development, articulation, implementation, and stewardship of a vision of learning that is shared and supported by the school community.
- advocating, nurturing, and sustaining a school culture and instructional program conducive to student learning and staff professional growth.
- ensuring management of the organization, operations, and resources for a safe, effective, and efficient learning environment.
- collaborating with families and community members, responding to the diverse community interests and needs, and mobilizing community resources.
- acting with integrity, fairness, and in an ethical manner.
- understanding, responding to, and influencing the larger political, social, and economic, legal, and cultural context. (ISLLC, 1997, np)

Figure 1.2 presents a framework for understanding and applying each standard. The figure identifies the standard, the chapter and the evidence of where and how the standard is applied or addressed in the chapter. For example, the stories of school leaders that are captured in the "View from the Field" illustrate how campus leaders apply concepts presented in the appropriate standard. Each standard has one or more chapters with several applications. Figure 1.2 shows how the standard is addressed and what the requisite knowledge and skills look like.

As emphasized in the ISLLC standards, school leaders must be committed to promoting the success of all students, not just some. Each standard begins with this commitment to learning for all. School leaders must also be able to generate a shared vision for the school as well as obtaining a commitment to the vision from all members of the school community. Along with the creation of a shared vision, leaders must also advocate, nurture, and sustain a campus culture that values and validates student learning while also promoting staff development. Through resource management, leaders help to create a safe, effective, and efficient learning environment. School leaders must also collaborate with all constituencies in responding to diverse needs and interests in the learning community. Perhaps one of the most important areas for school leaders to address is the need to treat everyone in an ethical manner, with fairness and integrity. Finally, school leaders must recognize their political roles by

Standard	Chapter	Evidence of how Standard is presented or applied in the chapter
Standard 1 Facilitating the development, articulation, implementation, and stewardship of a vision of learning that is shared and supported by the school community.	1	• The View from the Field illustrates how one campus leader applies the concepts and skills needed to be effective. • "Leadership Paradigms" presents the traits, behaviors, and qualities of effective leaders.
	2	• "Developing a Campus Culture" describes the development of a campus culture. • "Creating a Community of Learners" describes the process of facilitating the development and implementation of a vision of learning for the campus.
	4	• In the View from the Field, one campus leader provides an analysis of a legal situation involving community values. • The Case Study provides the readers with the opportunity to apply legal principles to address community concerns.
	5	• The View from the Field provides an example of how a school leader used action research to inform the implementation of a vision of learning. • The Case Study has readers apply the principles of action research to better understand how it can be used to inform teaching practice.
	6	• "Building School Work Groups and Teams" describes the process of building school work groups and teams to implement the campus vision of learning. • "Communication" discusses the importance of the communication process in articulating and building support for a vision.
	8	• "Curriculum and Curriculum Development" section provides key questions to guide curricular decisions in the development and implementation of a vision of learning. • Figure 8.2 provides the components of the curriculum alignment process which helps in the articulation and implementation of the vision of learning. • The View from the Field illustrates how one school leader uses the alignment process to keep the school focused on its vision and mission regarding student learning.
	9	• "Accountability Models" provides five questions to guide learners in their efforts to improve educational accountability and ensure learning for all. • The View from the Field illustrates how one campus uses data to implement and monitor the success of the campus plan and vision of learning. • "Improving Student Performance: Campus Improvement Plan" describes the components of an improvement plan and how it becomes the action plan for the vision. • The View from the Field illustrates how one campus uses data to implement and monitor the success of the campus plan and vision of learning.

FIGURE 1.2   *Rubric Illustrating Applications of ILLSC Standards by Chapter*

Standard	Chapter	Evidence of how Standard is presented or applied in the chapter
Standard 2 Advocating, nurturing, and sustaining a school culture and instructional program conductive to student learning and staff professional growth.	1	• In the View from the Field, Sam Sterner describes the evolution of becoming an instructional leader who can advocate, nurture, and sustain a learning community. • "Learning Paradigms" identifies and describes various leadership qualities and principles. • "Becoming a Leader" provides a series of questions to help establish a leadership profile.
	2	• "Developing a Campus Culture" describes the process of culture building. • In the View from the Field, the principal describes ways in which leaders can create a school culture that values collaboration and collegiality and list strategies to develop a learning community. • "Involvement of Community Members" emphasizes the need to include the broader community in culture building and gives examples on how to include others. • "Building Transformational Leadership" identifies seven traits of transformational leaders and discusses its importance in culture building. • "Leading Campus Improvement" identifies three things leaders can and should do to advocate, nurture, and maintain the culture of a learning community. • In the View from the Field, Dr. Leigh describes the process of guiding and transforming a campus into a learning community by implementing celebrations to reinforce successes. • The Case Study has readers synthesize data and make plans for transforming Norwood Middle School into a community of learners.
	5	• Figure 5.2 identifies the steps in action research that can lead to improved student achievement and school success. • In the View from the Field, Mrs. Mesa describes how she used action research to increase student learning on her campus.
	6	• "Organizational Membership" describes the importance of organizational behaviors as indicators of the degree to which teachers and students are sustained and nurtured on the school campus. • "Building School Work Groups and Teams" and Figure 6.1 present ways that groups can organize to enhance the learning of students and reinforce the nature of school community. • In the View from the Field, Ms. Lavone describes how she used grade level teams to build a learning community.
	8	• In the View from the Field, Judd Graves describes how he involved the faculty in curriculum issues which demonstrates ways to support and sustain a learning community. • "Best Practices and Curriculum Standards" describes 13 principles that can guide leaders as they seek to advocate and enhance the teaching–learning process.

(continued)

Standard	Chapter	Evidence of how Standard is presented or applied in the chapter
Standard 2 *(cont.)*	10	• "Professional Development for School Leaders" describes the importance of engaging in professional growth experiences for all members of the school community, especially the leader which begins with a series of reflective questions. • "Reflective Journals" discusses the role and importance of journalizing in promoting reflection as a strategy for enhancing professional development. • "Leader Assessment and Professional Development" links the assessment process to professional development and identifies several assessment models. • Figure 10.3 provides sample guidelines to follow in developing a professional growth plan. • Figure 10.5 provides a Self Report using the ISLLC standards to assess skills for each standard.
Standard 3 Ensuring management of the organization, operations, and resources for a safe, effective, and efficient learning environment.	1	• "Becoming a School Leader" provides questions for readers to ask themselves about becoming a leader. • The Case Study has readers apply principles that successful school leaders will need with regard to improving performance at an elementary school.
	2	• "Creating a Community of Learners" provides strategies for leaders to use in developing an effective learning community.
	4	• "School Safety" discusses legal issues that must be addressed in providing a safe learning environment. • Figures 4.3 and 4.4 provide checklists to guide school leaders as they make decisoins related to school safety and school operations. • The View from the Field illustrates the issues school leaders must address in promoting school safety. • Figure 4.5, Legal Guidelines, provides a quick and easy reference for school leaders of things to do in promoting safety and efficient operations.
	5	• The View from the Field provides an example of how action research can be used to examine the effectiveness of the classroom learning environment. • "Three Sources of Data Collection" provides examples of data relative to creating an efficient learning environment.
	6	• "Organizational Membership" discusses the complex dynamics of behavior in organizations and presents ways of organizing work groups or teams for more efficient operations. • In the View from the Field Jerry Stone, a district instructional specialist describes the use of work groups to align the science curriculum for more efficient learning. • "Strategies to Improve Group Effectiveness" discusses four approaches leaders can use to increase the efficiency and effectiveness of work groups in a school setting. • The Case Study has the readers apply principles of organizational work and decision making in implementing a new curriculum.

FIGURE 1.2   *Continued*

Standard	Chapter	Evidence of how Standard is presented or applied in the chapter
Standard 3 *(cont.)*	7	• "The Budgeting Process" describes the process of allocating resources for a safe, effective, efficient learning environment. • Figures 7.1 and 7.2 identify the steps in the budgeting process and how the budget process provides the opportunity for leaders to align fiscal, curricular, and human resources to support the needs and goals of a campus. • Figures 7.3 and 7.4 illustrate possible sources of income and common categories leaders can use to track budget expenditure to make maximum use of available resources. • The Case Study requires the readers to anticipate funding issues to maximum learning for a campus that is in transition.
	9	• "Accountability Models" illustrate various ways school leaders must take responsibility for the management and operation of an effective and efficient learning environment. • "Using and Analyzing Data for School Improvement" presents strategies for leaders to use in collecting and disaggregating data to improve the effectiveness of the campus teaching learning process. • Figures 9.1 and 9.2 present various kinds of data that leaders can use to make decisions that enhance the effectiveness and efficiency of the school campus. • The View from the Field illustrates how one campus leader involved faculty in data analysis regarding learning outcomes and goals.
Standard 4 Collaborating with families and community members, responding to the diverse community interests and needs, and mobilizing community resources.	2	• "Developing a Campus Culture" discusses ways that school leaders are actively involved in the events of the daily life of the community. • "Involvement of Community Members" describes new roles for parents and community members and identifies strategies for involving them in planning activities and securing resources. • "Celebrations that Reinforce the Campus Community" provides examples of celebrations involving the entire community that reinforce school success. • The Case Study requires that readers plan ways to involve the community in addressing the issues presented by a school in a transitional neighborhood.
Standard 5 Acting with integrity, fairness, and in an ethical manner.	1 3	• "Trust Building" discusses the importance of building trust as a foundation for ethical leadership behavior. • "Ethical Actions and Behaviors" presents questions leaders can ask themselves in addressing ethical issues. • Figure 3.1 presents a code of conduct for school leaders to guide ethical behavior. • The View from the Field provides an ethical dilemma for the readers to address regarding confidentiality issues relative to fairness and equity.

(continued)

Standard	*Chapter*	*Evidence of how Standard is presented or applied in the chapter*
Standard 5 *(cont.)*	4	• "What Is Your Ethical IQ" provides an inventory to assess the leader's ethical behavior. • The Case Study presents an ethical dilemma for the readers to frame an appropriate ethical response. • Figure 4.2 provides a checklist to use for determining the legality of hiring practices. • In the View from the Field, one leader describes the legal issues involving interview questions and the interview process at his school. • Figure 4.5 presents legal guidelines as to what to do and not do to help leaders act in a legal and ethical manner.
Standard 6 Understanding, responding to, and influencing the larger political, social, and economic, legal, and cultural context.	4 7	• Court cases provide leaders with the background for the legality of school actions within the larger context. • "Foundational Aspects of Fiscal Resource Management" discusses the funding of education within the larger socio-political context. • "Public School Finance and Equalization Models" provide the background for leaders to understand the mechanisms states use to distribute revenue for the support of education. • Figure 7.2 provides a description of how the budget process can be used to address fiscal, curricular, and human resource issues to support the teaching–learning process. • The View from the Field describes one campus leader's process of soliciting information from a diverse group in the budget development process.

FIGURE 1.2 *Continued*

understanding, responding, and influencing the larger area of politics, economics, and society in general.

Each of these standards is addressed by one or more of the chapters in this book. The chapters address the need for school leaders to promote the success of all students. Leadership in the past has too often been seen as more of a managerial function, rather than as a visionary function. These new standards set the tone, not only for the book, but for the profession itself. According to Murphy (2001), these standards:

> (1) reflect the centrality of student learning; (2) acknowledge the changing role of the school leader; (3) recognize the collaborative nature of school leadership; (4) . . . upgrad[e] the quality of the profession; (5) inform performance-based systems of assessment and evaluation for school leaders; (6) . . . [are] integrated and coherent; and (7) . . . [are] predicated on the concepts of access, opportunity, and empowerment for all members of the school community. (p. 4)

In the following View from the Field, Sam Sterner discusses his role as a principal of a middle school. The concepts and skills needed by a school leader emerge in the discussion Mr. Sterner provides as he reflects on the changes that have occurred as his

View from the Field

In his third year as a middle school principal, Sam Sterner says, "I finally feel that I have a handle on the job as a school leader. I have noticed a change from my first year when I spent much of my time taking care of organizational priorities such as budgets, maintenance, substitute teachers, and the day-to-day operation of the school. Initially, I was frustrated because I felt I had little time to be an instructional leader, much less one who promoted the success of all the students in his middle school." When the results of the state mandated tests, which were administered in the early spring, were returned to his campus, the students on his campus performed well enough for his campus to receive recognition. Reflecting on their results he says, "I had hoped they would achieve the highest rating, but they fell short in a number of areas. In each level, a handful of students on each test seem to be the difference in obtaining the highest rating."

Over the last eighteen months, Sam Sterner has gradually begun to develop strategies to address the needs of this small group of students. Sam says, "I am beginning to feel like an instructional leader. I have had the teachers at each grade level examine the test scores and make recommendations for addressing the learning needs of each student who did not perform well on the test." One thing that all of these students seem to have in common is a lack of self-confidence. Sam has asked the counselor to administer a self-concept test to this group of students. The teachers have also noted that these students seemed to have limited life experiences. Based on these observations, the assistant principal has written a grant that would allow these students to travel to various places. Sam comments, "I have taken the initiative to promote the success of all students on my campus. I have worked with the teachers to establish a 'culture of excellence,' and I have worked to secure funding for several projects by contacting community organizations."

According to Sam, "My role as an administrator is no longer about paddling kids and keeping order. My role is to make sure that no kid is left behind. My role is one of facilitator, who not only helps to obtain the necessary resources for my campus, but I strive to maintain a high morale among the faculty by constantly encouraging growth and development. I even try to model this life-long learning myself."

own leadership has evolved from being a manager to being more of a leader on his campus so that all children learn.

Leadership Paradigms: Traits, Behaviors, and Qualities

Historically, the study of leadership has focused on traits, behavior, and more recently qualities that create leadership. The trait views of leadership focus on having the *right stuff* and are concerned with who leaders are. Another perspective examines leader behavior, for as Greenberg and Baron (2000) note, we "... may not be born with the 'right stuff,' but we certainly strive to do the the 'right things'—that is, to do what it takes to *become* a leader" (p. 449). More recently, studies have looked more holistically at leader behavior and examined various qualities related to interaction dynamics between leaders and followers.

Leadership Traits

The trait view of leadership suggests that individuals become leaders because of the traits they possess. "In short, people become leaders because, in some special ways, they are different from others" (Greenberg & Baron, 2000, p. 447). These traits can be clearly identified and defined. Green (2001) notes that, "Such traits or characteristics [can be] classified under the headings of capacity, friendliness, achievement, responsibility, participation, and status" (p. 7). House, Shane, and Herold (1996) have found that successful leaders possess many of the following traits: drive, honesty and integrity, leadership motivation, self-confidence, cognitive ability, creativity, and flexibility. Individuals who possess these traits are thought to be good leaders, especially if they are successful in accomplishing tasks and are generally effective in getting results. The more successful "the organization [is] in achieving its goals, the more effective the leader" (Green, 2001, p. 7). For Kirkpatrick and Locke (1991), the research is clear

> that leaders are not like other people . . . they do need to have the 'right stuff' and this stuff is not equally present in all people. Leadership is a demanding, unrelenting job . . . [and] it would be a profound disservice to leaders to suggest that they are ordinary people. . . . In the realm of leadership . . . the individual does matter. (p. 58)

Trait theory also suggests that the more traits a leader possesses, the more effective the leader. As leaders demonstrate the requisite traits, they are promoted within the organization. Trait theory also matches the hierarchical organizational structure, and successful leaders, those with the key traits, are placed in top positions within the organization.

Leadership Behaviors

When discussing leadership behavior, it is helpful to use a continuum that illustrates the degree of influence leaders exert over followers. This continuum is illustrated in Figure 1.3 and has autocratic/authoritarian behaviors at one end and democratic/participative behaviors at the other.

As seen in Figure 1.3, autocratic/authoritarian behaviors tend to be controlling, with the sole responsibility for decision making and action resting with the leader. Such people tend to be directive and controlling in their actions toward others, and leaders with the behaviors that cluster at this end of the continuum tend to run the show, tell people when and where to do things, and do not like their authority or decisions and actions questioned. Leaders at the democratic/participative end of the continuum tend to share in decision making and courses of action. They encourage others to participate in the what, when, and how questions they confront daily and are therefore seen as collegial and collaborative in their behavior.

This leadership behavior continuum is sometimes expressed as a dichotomy with concern for task pitted against concern for people. House (1971) suggests that leaders can engage in four different kinds of behavior that, depending on the situation, help accomplish the goal or task. These leader behaviors are presented here:

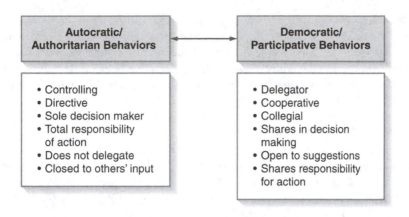

FIGURE 1.3 *Leadership Continuum Behavior*

1. *Supportive leadership*, which seeks to maintain a supportive relationship in the workplace and demonstrates consideration and awareness of the needs of others.
2. *Directive leadership*, which sets standards for success, communicates performance standards, schedules the work, and provides specific directions for accomplishing the task.
3. *Participative leadership*, which involves consulting with others and seeking opinions of others concerning task completion or other work-related activities.
4. *Achievement-oriented leadership*, which emphasizes excellence in task completion and sets goals that are challenging, yet attainable.

Greenberg and Baron (2000) note that there is a movement in many organizations today toward self-managed teams. Such a move clearly would be beyond the demo-cratic/participative behaviors. In such a view, "... leaders are less likely than ever to be responsible for getting others to implement their orders to fulfill their vision. ... Instead ... [they] may be called upon to provide ... resources to groups. ... These leaders do not call the shots; rather they help [others] take responsibility for their own work" (p. 452).

In developing high-performance self-managed teams, Blanchard, Carew, and Parisi-Carew (2000) and Zenger, Musselwhite, Hurson, and Perrin (1994) have sug-gested the following guidelines to help leaders in building these teams.

- Build trust, inspire teamwork, and empower others—"empowerment is all about letting go so that others can get going" (Blanchard et al., 2000, p. 104).
- Clarify team purpose and values—"more of us is as smart as all of us" (Blanchard et al., 2000, p. 15).
- Expand team capability by recognizing and affirming optimal performance.
- Create team identity through relationship building and communication.
- Be flexible and make the most of team differences.

Perhaps schools, more than any other organizations can implement the self-managed teams. As seen in these guidelines for building high-performance self-managed teams, the leader's role is very different. The special nature of these teams requires leaders to make adjustments in their behavior because, "Leading new teams using old [behaviors] is a sure formula for failure" (Greenberg & Baron, 2000, p. 453).

Leadership Qualities

Another frame of reference for viewing leaders involves their overall qualities and focuses on the interactive nature of leadership. Qualities develop as individuals interact within the context of the organization and reflect the give and take aspect of the leadership process. Drawing on the literature, Beach and Reinhartz (2000) have identified the following leadership qualities:

- The ability to create a culture that guides all members of the organization
- The ability to use interpersonal skills in building trust and working with others
- The ability to communicate and articulate the mission, goals, and strategies
- The ability to model personal integrity and responsibility in interacting with others
- The ability to diagnose problems, select protocols and procedures based on equity, and take risks
- The ability to unite effort with purpose to obtain results

On the surface, these qualities have the appearance of being related to traits or behaviors, but the key difference is the interpersonal application as leaders interact with various constituencies of the school organization. The nature of this interaction between leaders and others can be characterized as charismatic or transformational leadership. Charismatic leaders have that *something special* about them and ". . . exert especially powerful effects on followers . . ." (Greenberg & Baron, 2000, p. 460). When the qualities are incorporated in their behavior, a special kind of leader–follower relationship develops that results in higher than normal performance, a greater sense of commitment and loyalty, and a higher level of enthusiasm and excitement (Bass, 1985; House, 1977). As Conger (1991) says, charismatic leaders can "make ordinary people do extra-ordinary things . . ." (p. 32).

Transformational leaders also have charisma, but are able to incorporate the leader qualities in such a way that they are able to transform and renew their organizations. Transformational leaders not only inspire, but captivate strong emotions to teach and change followers (House & Podaskoff, 1995). They tap into cognitive processes by helping others to be problem solvers while providing support to individuals by giving them attention and encouragement. In one study (Koh, Steers, & Terborg, 1995), teachers indicated that the more transformational their principal was, the greater the satisfaction of teachers with their jobs and the stronger the commitment to their schools. Transformational leadership is discussed in greater detail in Chapter 2.

Contemporary leadership theory involves an eclectic approach to leadership and emphasizes the need to create a cooperative vision within nonthreatening learning environments. Such strategies as participatory decision making, reflection, and self-awareness are important to this leadership view. These strategies have promoted a leadership theory that suggests that the authoritarian ways of the past will no longer work. People today have the need to feel empowered in their work and function best when they are continuously learning.

Perhaps the new view of leadership is best summarized by Lambert (1998), who talks about building leadership capacity in schools. For Lambert, there are key assumptions that drive the capacity for building leadership in schools today. These assumptions include the following:

- Leadership and leader are not the same, and leadership is not based on traits;
- Leadership is a reciprocal learning process that allows individuals to construct and validate meanings that result in shared school goals and purposes;
- Leadership results in constructive change, and learning is a critical part of the process;
- Leadership is a process that everyone in the school community can engage in and involves skilled and complicated work;
- Leadership involves sharing decision making with others and is a collective endeavor, and the journey of learning leadership must be appreciated in order for the purpose and action to be shared; and
- Leadership is collaborative in nature and involves the sharing or power and authority in order to empower others.

For Lambert (2002), "The days of the principal as the lone instructional leader are over. We no longer believe that one administrator can serve as the instructional leader for an entire school without the substantial participation of other educators" (p. 37).

Concepts involving leadership continue to change as organizations and society change. A culture is needed that nourishes leadership and fosters the continuous development of people in the school organization. For Barth (2002), "Changing a toxic school culture into a healthy school culture that inspires lifelong learning among students and adults is the greatest challenge of instructional leadership" (p. 6). Pigford (1999) and Carrow-Moffett (1993) have identified the following principles that school leaders of the twenty-first century need to follow in order to be successful:

- Leadership is a sacred trust, not a bestowed right, and involves knowing our core values;
- Leadership is about hearing all the voices—teachers, students, staff, parents, and others;
- Leadership is about creating a "surplus of vision"—yours, mine, and ours;
- Leadership is about being uncomfortable—looking for data that disconfirms what we believe to be true;
- Leadership is about a journey that begins with introspection and reflection;
- Leadership is about empowering ourselves and others—sharing information and decision making; and

- Leadership involves identifying and dealing with personal barriers to change, both personal and organizational.

While the title *building principal* conveys a certain position of leadership, that title alone will not be sufficient to achieve success in school. No longer is maintaining an orderly environment sufficient for the school to be judged a success. As Fullan (2000) notes, "Never before has leadership in education been more critical for public school systems. . . . When systems are complex and when the tendencies of such systems are toward overload and fragmentation, the need for leadership to forge synergy and coherence is paramount" (p. xix).

Trust Building

The level of trust created by a leader is the foundation on which success is built. Kerfoot (1999) suggests that leaders who ". . . can create trust among their members can create a high-performing, synergistic environment that will produce exceptional . . . outcomes" (p. 79). For Bennis and Townsend (1995), the ability of a leader to be congruent, consistent, caring, and competent is essential to building trust. They note that these four C's are the energy that creates a sense of teamwork that holds the group together and moves them toward the goal. As Levering (1988) described it, trust is the glue that holds organizations and groups together. When school faculties have a sense of commitment to each other, as well as commitment to a common goal, they can produce greater results. Glaser (1999) describes trust as ". . . the cement that binds together all relationships, and provides the foundation from which society operates, leadership flourishes, and changes occur" (p. 82). Trust is the quality that gives followers the security to be themselves and take risks. Bennis and Goldsmith (1994) note that leaders generate and sustain trust when they demonstrate constancy, congruity, reliability, and integrity. School leaders need to be available and accessible to create an environment of trust, and they must be willing to communicate with candor and compassion and be willing to invest in others.

Glaser (1999) describes ways leaders can build trust. First, they should model what they say they believe by narrowing the gap between their intentions and their behavior; trust is enhanced when behavior is congruent with intentions. Second, leaders should make their intentions known to others and solicit feedback. Such feedback helps all parties to be more consistent and behave in trusting and compassionate ways. Leaders should also look for solutions to problems, rather than fixing blame on others. They should see problems as learning opportunities and reflect on their role or part in the process. It is critical that leaders keep all confidential information as a sacred trust and share it with no one. Nothing undermines trust building more than gossip or sharing confidential information. Leaders should share their values and goals with others by letting people know what they stand for and what they wish to accomplish. This sharing of values and hopes helps to establish a school vision and culture.

Leaders must also create a safe environment so that others feel comfortable sharing and taking risks. In the process, leaders must be good listeners and avoid being judgmental. School leaders must also be able to demonstrate their professional skills and competence as leaders and team members. It is vital that school leaders demonstrate a high level of integrity by being honest and keeping commitments made to others. Perhaps more than ever, leadership must be grounded in integrity and ethical behaviors. Leaders should know themselves and the biases and personality traits that form and inform them. Finally, leaders must demonstrate their credibility and reliability, consistently delivering on commitments that have been made.

Technology and School Leadership

When school leaders are confronted with the word *technology* they are often fearful, but as Slowinski (2000) points out, technology has permeated public schools and more than 90% of all public schools have access to the Internet. Donovan (1999) emphasizes an appropriate use of technology is in promoting school improvement and notes that administrators must be willing to invest the time to move technology from an add-on to a fully implemented curriculum tool. As of 2000, forty-five states have standards in the area of technology-related exit examination for graduates (Slowinski, 2000). As of 2001, North Carolina and Idaho require teachers to demonstate proficiency in technology for certification (Slowinski, 2000). Because technology is as much a part of school life, school leaders must not fear it, but realize that technology is simply the activities, equipment, and knowledge used to get things done (Greenberg & Baron, 2000). Technology involves the physical and mental processes used to transform data into usable information. With this view in mind, technology becomes a valuable tool to help school leaders get things done.

For Lezotte (1992), school improvement "is probably unattainable (or even unapproachable) without a major commitment to the use of computers and other related information-processing technologies" (p. 72). Technology is an essential tool for school leaders to monitor and adjust processes, collect and analyze data, and communicate with a wide variety of constituents. Technology is critical to develop and maintain a database relative to students and teachers as they engage in the teaching–learning process. Lezotte (1992) goes on to say that, "Such information systems are essential if school leaders are going to be able to monitor the instructional system and make appropriate adjustments in a timely fashion" (p. 72).

The ability to analyze data is important to school improvement efforts. Creighton (2001) notes that technology, especially in the form of computer software programs, allows school leaders to analyze campus data by (1) tabulating the number of students according to categories (i.e., by subgroups); (2) reporting grade distributions by subject and grade level; (3) comparing test scores by category (i.e., grade level, gender, ethnicity); and (4) determining significant differences between or among different categories of students (i.e., athletes versus nonathletes, males versus female students). School leaders must be able to use data to guide decision making, and ". . . technical support in gathering and analyzing data and access to individuals with the expertise for statistical analysis are essential" (Holcomb, 2001, p. 133).

In addition to the management aspects of data collection and analysis, technology also supports instruction. School leaders must help teachers recognize that rather than competing ". . . with the blips, beeps, and dazzle of electronic equipment, [they must] bring the information age into the classroom" (Gross, 1997, p. 105). Curriculum and learning implications of technology also include distance learning in which "vision, drive, and tenacity convert new modes of transmitting information into new approaches to constructing knowledge" (Gross, 1997, 105). In supporting technology as an instructional tool, school leaders should be cognizant of ". . . technology's potential for increasing students' achievement [which] goes largely untapped" (Allen, 2001, p. 2). Allen (2001) continues by saying, "In order for technology to truly transform learning and student achievement, . . . school systems will have to embrace it as a reform that's as important as any other, with buy-in from the top tier of school leaders" (p. 6). Technology also adds to the instructional improvement efforts of teachers by allowing them to post "class assignments, web lessons, grading rubrics, school memos, and student grades" on a web page, which also helps "parents stay better informed of what their students are learning" (Allen, 2001, p. 7).

Finally, technology can support teachers and leaders in their own growth and development as educators. By taking advantage of on-line professional development networks, they can ". . . advance their own professional growth without leaving . . . their classroom or [school]" (Slowinski, 2000, p. 4). The 21st Century Teachers Network is an online support system "organized by state as well as content areas, allowing for both virtual interactions on a national level and actual collegial opportunities on a local level" (Slowinski, 2000, p. 4).

Becoming a School Leader

As this chapter has indicated, the world of school leadership is evolving, and there are new paradigms, standards, and expectations for school leaders. Gates (1999) has posed several questions for teachers, but when modified they can serve as prompts for school leaders as they reflect on the complexities of their jobs. As you read this book, use the following questions to guide you in your thinking about being or becoming a school leader. As you read each question, think about yourself in the role of a school leader.

Do I Have the Right Stuff or What It Takes to Be a School Leader?

Good school leaders believe they have what it takes to make a difference in their schools. School leaders who have this desire to make a difference have one basic goal: success for all students.

Do I Like Teachers and Students?

Can I work with them effectively? Do I enjoy working with all stakeholders in the teaching–learning process? What can I do to not only empower my faculty and staff, but improve the learning and success of students at my school?

Do I Have a Strong Work Ethic and Like Challenges?

Being a school leader requires a time commitment; it is not a 9-to-5 job as many school functions occur after school or in the evening. Being a school leader is not just a role; it involves many hours beyond the *regular* school day. Am I willing to invest or dedicate the requisite hours?

Do I Engage in and Encourage Continuous Improvement?

Effective school administrators reflect on their work and seek to continuously learn from their experiences and improve their professional practices. Not only do they constantly seek ways to improve what they do, they encourage others to improve as well.

Do I Know How to Handle Conflict?

As a school leader, you have to deal with conflicts that arise between and among various constituencies including teachers, students, parents, and even community members. As these conflicts arise, school leaders need to maintain a positive working relationship with all the parties involved. You have to practice effective listening skills, the art of compromise, flexibility in thinking by suspending judgment, and consensus building so that the agendas or issues that prompted the conflict are addressed and resolved satisfactorily.

Do I Have a Commitment to the Community?

Effective school leaders build bridges to the community and encourage community members to participate in helping the school achieve its goals. School leaders establish strong relationships with parents by using every opportunity to involve them actively in the education of their children. Administrators must seek to interact and communicate often with the community, especially parents, and solicit support for the overall goal of the campus—success for all students.

Do I Have the Management and Organizational Skills to Create a Positive School Culture that Values Teaching and Learning?

Effective school leaders create a culture that values teaching and learning. To implement such a culture, a leader should have those skills that support others in being successful. Support for teachers may involve not only appropriate resources for teaching and classroom research, but praise, recognition, and encouragement. For students, opportunities are needed to help them develop self-discipline and an attitude of life-long learning that means putting in place policies and procedures that encourage self-directed learning.

Do I Have a Sense of Humor?

As a school leader, you need not only to develop a *thick skin*, but the ability to laugh at yourself and difficult situations. The role of school leader is demanding and can be both frustrating and exhilarating. As a leader, you need to be able to keep your perspective and not take your role or position personally. The ability to smile and see the humor in daily frustrations will help you survive a crisis.

Now that you have read these questions, begin by starting your professional growth by jotting down the responses to each question. Periodically, reread these questions and entries and rate yourself on a scale of one (outstanding) to seven (needs work). As you read this book, continue to refer back to these questions and ratings. Have your ratings changed? Why? Why not? These self-ratings are an attempt to determine your perceptions of who you are as a school leader—the degree to which you have kept your perspective, responded to issues in an ethical manner, and so on.

Case Study

Read the following case of Mr. R. J. Couple and be prepared to discuss your ideas with colleagues and respond in writing in your journals to the questions that follow.

Mr. Couple is a new principal who was reassigned from his central office position to the principalship of an elementary school (pre-K to 6th grade). He did not ask for the new position and was told he could take this position or "look elsewhere." He has been a principal for only three years. He is replacing a retiring principal who has only been at this campus for several years and had an extremely nondirective approach. This campus has had little or no faculty turnover in the last ten years. In addition, this school is viewed by the administration and the parents as one of the top elementary schools in the district. Mandated state test scores have been good, but there is room for improvement. Parents are extremely involved with their children and the activities that take place on the school campus.

Mr. Couple calls a faculty meeting two days before the end of school to discuss what will be taking place in September. At the faculty meeting, he informs the staff of the following changes that he will be making for the new school year:

- Six teachers will be changing grade assignments (most of these have been at the same grade level for over fifteen years)
- No recess will be scheduled for 3rd and 4th grade students so that tutoring sessions can be held for students with low scores on the state achievement test
- Field trips will be suspended so that more time is spent on academic pursuits
- Grade levels will no longer be housed together (classroom location)
- There will be four families or pods consisting of a 1st, 2nd, 3rd, and 4th grade classes and two families or pods consisting of 5th and 6th grade classes
- Families will eat and have recess together instead of by grade levels
- The school day will be increased by twenty-five minutes.

These changes have been discussed with the central administration, particularly the superintendent and director of curriculum. There has been virtually no faculty or parent input. Mr. Couple has taken a directive approach in an attempt to have teachers change grade levels and to improve test scores. He essentially made these decisions on his own, reassuring everyone that they will have to trust him. He informed everyone that he was a professional and had a much better picture of what needed to be done. What the central administration was not aware of was the degree to which Mr. Couple did not seek feedback in determining the capacity for change among the staff and the parents.

Questions to Consider

1. How do you think the teachers responded?
2. How do you think the parents responded?
3. Will the changes occur as smoothly as Mr. Couple anticipated? Will the faculty trust him as he requested? Why? Why not?
4. What could Mr. Couple do differently to model a more effective leadership in his school?
5. If you were Mr. Couple and could start over again, what would you do to successfully bring about change at this school campus in the coming school year?

Summary

This chapter has introduced the concept of leadership and its importance in schools. Leadership has deep historical roots and leadership paradigms have changed over time as social, cultural, political, and economic conditions. School leadership has become more important as it has been linked to school success. The challenge for educational leaders today is to remain focused on being a leader, rather than on being a manager. School leadership has become more complex as pressure mounts for all schools to maintain a positive, purposeful environment in which all students are academically successful. The chapter presented a view of educational leadership that emphasized the use of interactive, noncoercive influence to move teachers, staff, students, and members of the larger educational community to accomplish the goals and objectives of the school.

New standards have been established by the ISLLC of the Council of Chief State Officers that serve as guidelines for licensing school administrators. These standards emphasize the need to promote the success of all students by developing and articulating a vision, creating and nurturing a positive school culture, establishing policies and procedures that ensure a safe and effective learning environment, responding to the diversity of student and community needs, acting in an ethical manner, and understanding and influencing the larger sociopolitical context. The standards also serve as job descriptions for individuals seeking leadership positions.

There are changing expectations for school leaders, and the old authoritarian and autocratic ways are ineffective. New paradigms of leadership are required. The chapter discussed the various views of leadership including traits, behaviors, and qualities. To be successful, school leaders must establish a climate of collaboration and collegiality. Finally leaders must invest in trust building. Trust is the emotion that holds groups together and empowers them to work together toward common goals and objectives.

Your Turn

1.1. Interview a building level administrator (principal or assistant principal). Write four to six questions that focus on the key leadership behaviors that the administrator considers critical to success. For example, ask this school leader to put these behaviors in a context as they apply them at the school campus level. One question related to curriculum might be, What leadership behaviors are needed to ensure that the curriculum is meeting the needs of all students? A follow-up question might be, What are you doing to ensure that your curriculum is working for your student population? Have a system to record responses, complete with date of meeting in the event you interview more than one administrator.

1.2. Look at the school leader licensure standards in the chapter. Select one or two that you find to be of special interest to you. If you had to write a profile of how this leader would act relative to these standards, what would that leader behavior look like? The end product will be a case study of that standard, describing how a school leader would *live it* at the campus and community levels. (Note: For more information about case studies, refer to Chapter 5.)

1.3. With one or two classmates or peers, brainstorm five ways that school leaders can build trust when given the following situation. A teacher comes to the school leader with information about a department chair. In order to tell her story about the department chair, the administrator hears information that is controversial and undermines the authority of the chair. How can the administrator remain trustworthy to the teacher and at the same time maintain the authority as the department chair? What should the administrator say and do as he is meeting with the teacher? What, if anything, should he do with the information he has regarding the chair because the information was given to him in confidence about the chair?

1.4. In an interview for an assistant principal position, you are asked about your view or philosophy of leadership. How would you respond? Outline your key thoughts about leadership in schools.

References

Allen, R. (2001 Fall). Technology and learning: How can schools map routes to technology's promised land? *Curriculum Update*. Alexandria, VA: Association of Supervision and Curriculum Development.

Barth, R. (2002). The culture builder. *Educational Leadership, 50*, 8, 6–11.

Bass, B. M. (1985). *Leadership and performance beyond expectations*. New York: Free Press.

Beach, D. M., & Reinhartz, J. (2000). *Supervisory leadership: Focus on instruction*. Boston: Allyn & Bacon.

Bennis, W., & Goldsmith, J. (1994). *Learning to lead.* Reading, MA: Addison-Wesley.

Bennis, W., & Townsend, R. (1995). *Reinventing leadership.* New York: William Morrow.

Blanchard, K., Carew, D., & Parisi-Carew, E. (2000). *The one minute manager builds high performing teams.* New York: William Morrow.

Blanchard, K., Hybels, B., & Hodges, P. (1999). *Leadership by the book.* New York: William Morrow.

Bolman, L., & Deal, T. E. (1995). *Leading with soul.* San Francisco: Jossey-Bass.

Bolman, L., & Deal, T. E. (1994). Looking for leadership: Another search party's report. *Educational Administration Quarterly, 30,* 1, 77–96.

Boyan, N. J. (1988). Describing and explaining administrative behavior. In N. J. Boyan (ed), *Handbook of research on educational administration.* New York: Longman.

Carrow-Moffett, P. A. (1993). Change agent skills: Creating leadership for school renewal. *NASSP Bulletin, 77,* 57–62.

Cashman, K. (2000). *Leadership form the inside out.* Provo, UT: Executive Excellence Publishing.

Conger, J. A. (1991). Inspiring others: The language of leadership. *Academy of Management Executive, 5,* 31–45.

Creighton, T. B. (2001). *Schools and data.* Thousand Oaks, CA: Corwin Press.

Deal, T. E., & Peterson, K. D. (1999). *Shaping school culture: The heart of leadership.* San Francisco: Jossey-Bass.

Donovan, M. (1999 Sept/Oct). Rethinking faculty support. *The Technology Source.* Publication of the Michigan Virtual University.

Franklin, J. (2000). Evaluating the principal. In *Education update.* Alexandria, VA: Association for Supervision and Curriculum Development. *42,* 8, 1, 4, 8.

Fullan, M. (2000). Introduction. In *Educational leadership.* San Francisco: Jossey-Bass.

Fullan, M. (2002). The change leader. *Educational Leadership, 50,* 8, 16–20.

Gates, R. (1999). *Classroom leadership.* Alexandria, VA: Association for Supervision and Curriculum Development.

Glaser, R. (1999). Paving the road to trust. In L. Orozco (ed), *Educational leadership.* Bellevue, WA: Coursewise.

Green, R. L. (2001). *Practicing the art of leadership.* Upper Saddle River, NJ: Prentice-Hall.

Greenberg, R. A., & Baron, J. (2000). *Behavior in organizations* (7th ed). Upper Saddle River, NJ: Prentice-Hall.

Greenberg, R. A., & Baron, J. (1997). *Behavior in organizations* (6th ed.). Upper Saddle River, NJ: Prentice-Hall.

Griffiths, D. (1988). Administrative theory. In N. J. Boyan (ed), *Handbook of research on educational administration.* New York: Longman.

Gross, P. A. (1997). *Joint curriculum design.* Mahwah, NJ: Lawrence Erlbaum Associates.

Hogan, R., Curphy, G. J., & Hogan, J. (1999). What we know about leadership: Effectiveness and personality. In L. Orozco (ed), *Educational leadership.* Bellevue, WA: Coursewise.

Holcomb, E. L. (2001). *Asking the right questions: Techniques for collaboration and school change* (2nd ed). Thousand Oaks, CA: Corwin Press.

House, R. J. (1977). A 1976 theory of charismatic leadership. In J. G. Hunt & L. L. Larson (eds), *Leadership: The cutting edge.* pp. 189–207. Carbondale, IL: Southern Illinois University Press.

House, R. J. (1971). A path-goal theory of leader effectiveness. *Administrative Science Quarterly, 16,* 331–333.

House, R. J., & Podaskoff, P. M. (1995). In J. Greenberg (ed), *Leadership effectiveness: Past perspectives and future directions for research.* Hillsdale, NJ: Erlbaum.

House, R. J., Shane, S. A., & Herold, D. M. (1996). Rumors of the death of dispositional research are vastly exaggerated. *Academy of Management Review, 21,* 203–224.

Interstate School Leaders Licensure Consortium (ISLLC) of the Council of Chief State School Officers (1997). Candidate Information Bulletin for School Leaders Assessment. Princeton, NJ: Educational Testing Service.

Kerfoot, K. (1999). Creating trust. In L. Orozco (ed), *Educational leadership.* Bellevue, WA: Coursewise.

Kirkpatrick, S. A., & Locke, E. A. (1991). Leadership: Do traits matter? *Academy of Management Executive, 5,* 48–60.

Koh, W. L., Steers, R., & Terborg, J. R. (1995). The effects of transformational leadership on teacher attitudes and student performance in Singapore. *Journal of Organizational Behavior, 16*, 319–333.

Lambert, L. (2002). A framework for shared leadership. *Educational Leadership, 50*, 8, 37–40.

Lambert, L. (1998). *Building leadership capacity in schools.* Alexandria, VA: Association for Supervision and Curriculum Development.

Levering, R. (1988). *A great place to work.* New York: Avon Books.

Lezotte, L. W. (1997). *Learning for all.* Okemos, MI: Effective Schools Products.

Lezotte, L. W. (1992). *Creating the total quality effective school.* Okemos, MI: Effective Schools Products.

Murphy, J. (2001). The interstate school leaders licensure consortium—Standards for school leaders. *The AASA Professor, 24*, 2, 2–4.

Orozco, L. (1999). *Educational leadership.* Bellevue, WA: Coursewise.

Pigford, A. (1999). Leadership: A journey that begins within. In L. Orozco (ed), *Educational leadership.* Bellevue, WA: Coursewise.

Sergiovanni, T. J. (1995). *The principalship: A reflective practice perspective.* Boston: Allyn & Bacon.

Slowinski, J. (2000). Becoming a technological savvy administrator. ERIC ED 438593. ERIC Digest Number 135.

Texas Education Agency. (2000). *Instructional leadership development manual.* Austin, TX: Texas Education Agency.

Zenger, J. H., Musselwhite, E., Hurson, K., & Perrin, C. (1994). *Leading teams: Mastering the new role.* Homewood, IL: Business One Irwin.

2

Leadership and the Campus Culture

ISLLC Standards

Standard 1: A school administrator is an educational leader who promotes the success of all students by facilitating the development, articulation, implementation, and stewardship of a vision of learning that is shared and supported by the school community.

Standard 2: A school administrator is an educational leader who promotes the success of all students by advocating, nurturing, and sustaining a school culture and instructional program conducive to student learning and staff professional growth.

Standard 3: A school administrator is an educational leader who promotes the success of all students by ensuring management of the organization, operations, and resources for a safe, effective, and efficient learning environment.

Standard 4: A school administrator is an educational leader who promotes the success of all students by collaborating with families and community members, responding to the diverse community interests and needs, and mobilizing community resources.

Chapter Objectives

The objectives of this chapter are:

- Describe the development of campus culture through the establishment of high expectations and valuing learning.
- Create a community of learners with the involvement of multiple stakeholders.
- Discuss transformational leadership and its role in collegial relationships and collaborative groups.
- Define and analyze the function of facilitating and implementing campus improvement plans for shared vision, effective use of resources, and risk taking.
- Explore celebration as a tool for building campus culture and collegiality.

When people walk into any school or other organization, within moments they can perceive its *feel*. This feel is often intangible and based purely on perception and other times it can be identified through a variety of factors from a warm friendly attitude to camaraderie among the people who work there. The climate or feel of a place is shown in the way things are done such as routines, rituals, celebrations, and discouragements (Deal & Peterson, 1990; Deal & Kennedy, 1982). Regardless, individuals sense the nuance of an organization, and archeologists and social scientists alike refer to this as *organizational culture and climate*. In their work on school culture, Peterson and Deal (1998) call this feeling the *ethos* of the school.

School leaders must be able to advocate, nurture, and sustain a school culture that is conducive to student learning and promotes professional growth among teachers and staff. The development of a healthy organizational climate and culture are essential to ultimate campus productivity (Newmann, 1996; Schien, 1991). Organizations that have members who (1) have collaboratively developed and clearly articulated a mission, (2) have worked closely together to develop and implement goals, and (3) share the same values are more successful than those that do not (Covey, 1995). When educators become change agents, they can cultivate powerful cultures and learning communities that make a difference for students (Fullan, 1996). Making these changes is often easier said than done. Finding common ground for agreement on goals and strategies among teachers of various grades or content areas is often difficult to achieve. School leaders must not only help individuals on their campus find the common ground and basic tenets all can agree on, but they must then help them take risks by stepping out on *groundless ground*, which is essential to campus success (Palestini, 1999; Schmieder & Cairns, 1996).

Some schools appear to be successful based on test scores or attendance rates. However, they are not as successful as they could be if they had a common bond, with everyone working from the same set of values, and where a collaborative team effort is established among students, school, family, and community (Sergiovanni, 1995, 1992). More specifically, culture is how a school or an organization does things, climate is the way it feels, and the two are interwined (Peterson & Deal, 1998; Bolman & Deal, 1993; Deal & Peterson, 1994). To achieve maximum results, both a collaborative culture and a positive climate are imperative (Hoyle, English, & Steffy, 1998). Success by an individual or any one segment of the school should be celebrated by everyone (Daresh & Playko, 1997; Deal & Peterson, 1990). By like measure, concerns or weaknesses within any segment of the school should also be addressed by all (Creighton, 2000; Holcomb, 1998). By winning or losing together, this bonding and ethos become key components in developing a campus culture. The leader's role in the development and nurturance of a positive campus ethos is imperative in promoting the academic success of all students (Lunenburg & Ornstein, 2000; Palestini, 1999; Owens, 1995; Robbins & Alvy, 1995; Hoy & Miskel, 1996).

This chapter discusses the development of a campus culture by emphasizing the need for high expectations, valuing learning, and creating a community of learners that includes the involvement of multiple stakeholders. The chapter also describes transformational leadership and its role in fostering collegial relationships and collaborative groups. The chapter also explores the importance of the development and implementation of campus improvement plans that involve developing and implementing a shared vision, effective use of resources, and a willingness to take risks. Last, the role of celebration as a tool for building campus culture and climate is considered.

Developing a Campus Culture

The underlying values, beliefs, and traditions that are imbedded in the relationships among school leaders, teachers, students, parents, staff, and community members are reflected in school culture (Deal & Peterson, 1990). It is important for new and current campus leaders to watch and listen to the faculty, staff, and members of the school community with regard to traditions, rituals, and other nuances concerning the way the campus functions, particularly in light of school improvement and reform efforts. When seeking to change or initiate new programs, leaders must be careful making changes to the ethos of the school without significant input and involvement from all stakeholders. For example, when additional space was needed, one new administrator cleaned out a storage room and threw away things considered to be junk. Although the leader was proud of the resulting new space, the faculty did not react the same way. They felt that important campus artifacts had been thrown away, thus devaluing their heritage (Bolman & Deal, 1993).

Every school or organization has its own traditions, rituals, ceremonies, and symbols that represent the way things are done at that school and even in that district. Although they may not make sense or be valued by new people coming in, their decisions are important to the people already there. Traditions and rituals may seem entirely trivial to new people or outsiders, but are symbolic of time-honored traditions within the school organization and are a central part of the campus culture.

The cultural dimensions of the leader's job become important. The leader assumes other roles in addition to being a resource manager and an instructional leader. According to Deal and Peterson (1994), the effective leader becomes:

- A symbol who models campus values through routines, dress, and behavior
- One who shapes the school's heroes, rituals, ceremonies, and symbols, and who is shaped by them
- A poet who uses language to reinforce values and sustain the school's best image of itself
- An actor who improvises in the drama of school life
- A healer who oversees transitions and changes in school events

The leader sets the standards and models the values, routines, dress, and behavior that are acceptable in the school by practicing what the leader advocates. At one school, for example, the principal lit a candle as a symbol of the "lamp of learning" at the beginning of the school year (Deal & Peterson, 1990). By articulating the values and demonstrating such behaviors, leaders become models of the values and attitudes that are incorporated into the life of the school and become an integral part of the campus culture.

The leader also plays an important role in defining and shaping the heroes and heroines, rituals, ceremonies, and symbols of the school. For example, in one school, the principal, who was loved and respected by all, took a central administration position. She had been the only principal this campus had ever had, and her name had become synonymous with this school. Although there was joy and pride within the campus for her promotion, there was also a sense of loss. The following year, she was in the difficult position of maintaining close ties with the campus while also giving the new leader time and autonomy to begin to create a new culture and climate within the school.

The use of language and words are also important tools in facilitating the campus culture. The words leaders use convey powerful messages to the learning community. For example, the Grizzly Bear was the mascot of one elementary school, and using this symbol, the principal took the image a step further by generating a motto that the campus was home of the "beary best." By consistently using language to connect the mascot to levels of academic performance, attendance, and behavior, the principal set a fun standard of high expectations in all areas of campus life. While a simple slogan may seem trite, the process of linking language to symbols is at the heart of campus culture building.

School leaders are also actively involved in events of daily life that occur within the school and community. In one school, the assistant principal responded to a dare by some of the students, parents, and staff. The assistant principal, who was in charge of tardies and absences at a middle school, kissed a pig when attendance averaged 95 percent or higher for the six weeks. In his active participation in the life of the school by agreeing to kiss a pig, he helped to improve overall attendance and set a high standard for students. Admittedly, kissing a pig is not for everyone, but the critical element is that leaders must be willing to do whatever it takes to foster a culture of success. By engaging in fun activities in the daily life of the school, leaders help to set the *cake of custom* on that campus.

School leaders also oversee transitions within a school. Sometimes the transitions are caused by changing demographics within the community and other times they may be due to dramatic, sudden changes in the learning community. At one school, the sudden death of a respected principal in an accident created an emotional vacuum. The new leader, who served as acting principal had to oversee the transition and change in campus life, climate, and culture, while also respecting the campus's grief and healing. The new leader had to keep the school running smoothly and proactively during a time of shock and pain. Such actions have been likened to steering through permanent white water.

Campuses also reflect the values, beliefs, and management and leadership styles of their principals. While the previous illustrations of lighting a candle or kissing a pig may seem insignificant, in the larger context they serve to illustrate the cultural and symbolic roles that school leaders play at their schools. Building a campus culture takes more than campus mascots and slogans or kissing pigs. It is difficult work that occurs over time as faculty, staff, students, and parents come to know and most importantly trust the school leader.

Leaders, then, are essential in the development and nurturance of school culture (Lunenburg & Ornstein, 2000; Hoyle, English, & Steffy, 1998; Hoy & Miskel, 1996; Owens, 1995). Different leaders handle the development of school culture in different ways based on their own personalities and leadership styles. Some leaders are more like cheerleaders for every facet of their schools (Reavis, Vinson, & Fox, 1999). Others are low key, being methodically and deliberate in their actions. It is an art to be able to blend personal traits with a vision to bring about needed change (Leithwood, Leonard, & Sharratt, 1998; Peterson & Deal, 1998; Hoyle, 1995; Starratt, 1995; Wallace, 1995; Deal & Peterson, 1994; DePree, 1989; Peters & Waterman, 1982).

Transforming a school culture requires that the entire learning community of faculty, parents, students, and staff come to an internal realization that they need a new direction. Unless the campus has this realization, any new ideas the school leader proposes will likely be partially accepted at best. If a leader comes to a school with a personal mission of fixing it, when the school staff does not perceive the school as needing fixing, there is often a problem, and the leader's efforts can be thwarted or doomed to failure (Daresh & Playko, 1997; Bolman & Deal, 1993). The challenge for the leader is to bring the school needs to a conscious level and have the school

View from the Field

For two years researchers tracked the behavior of a high school principal in a rural area using open-ended teacher questionnaires; school document analysis; observations of student and teacher advisory group meetings; shadowing of the principal; focus groups of teachers and students; and interviews with the assistant principal, principal, and superintendent. The school was poor, isolated, and had a history of low academic performance. As the principal tells his story, "I tried to create a school culture that emphasized high expectations for all members of the learning community including teachers, staff, and volunteers as well as the students themselves. In the three years I have been here, I have seen the school go from a 38% to 93% passing rate for tenth graders on the state-mandated achievement tests over this short time period. Recently, I invited the local media to a special assembly for the announcement about our school's success and being designated as a blue-ribbon school. I had the teachers stand for recognition and applause, and then I had the students stand and applaud their own success. I bragged on everyone for their effort, stressing that they had accomplished something they thought they would not be able to do. They had tried, persevered, and been successful. I was indeed proud." For a small, rural school this leader created a campus culture that personified high expectations that led to success.

community discover them, rather than telling them what should be done (Short & Greer, 1997). Autonomy throughout the process of developing goals and in developing the campus improvement plan is essential to success and an important part of the school culture (Short & Greer, 1997; Hoyle & Crenshaw, 1997).

The leadership style of the administrator is inextricably linked to the values and beliefs of the school and helps to shape the campus culture. Goldman's (1998) study of leaders who vary their leadership styles supports the need to acknowledge each person's different gifts, strengths, and concerns and then use them appropriately. Finding the right fit that links individual strengths to campus needs is important to campus and individual productivity and task satisfaction. The View from the Field illustrates the importance of creating a campus culture with high expectations.

Covey (1989) says that as long as we keep on doing what we have always done, we will keep on getting what we have always gotten. Unless we are satisfied with what we have, it is time to change, and change is not easy (Owens, 1995; Hershey & Blanchard, 1993; Goldring & Rallis, 1993). Difficult decisions often involve personnel, programmatic, and philosophical issues (Lunenburg & Ornstein, 2000; Palestini, 1999; Reavis, Vinson, & Fox, 1999). Many of these changes may not be popular, but the leader must be the standard bearer of the new culture that emphasizes high achievement for all students. It is up to the leader to keep the school focused on its goals and to evaluate consistently what is going on. The reflective leader keeps the school community constantly asking, "How can we do things better?" As DuFour and Eaker (1999) note, the campus leaders

should be fixated on results. Principals of learning communities work with their staff members to articulate clear and measurable goals, identify indicators that offer evidence of progress, and develop systems for monitoring those indicators on a continuous basis. They use the evidence to inform practice, celebrate successes, and identify areas that need further attention. (p. 47)

This becomes the foundation of action research and evaluation projects that are designed for school improvement (Glanz, 1998). Additional information on the role of action research and school improvement is found in Chapter 5.

The values of a school are a critical part of the campus culture. The values of the school directly relate to its mission and purpose; how school leaders conduct themselves during their initial period will have a direct relationship on their ultimate effectiveness (King & Blumer, 2000; Deal & Peterson, 1999; Hoyle, 1995; Bolman & Deal, 1993, 1995). Thoughtful and appropriate decision making is important during these transitional periods because it is often difficult to get past early mistakes.

It is particularly important for a new leader to take advantage of the significant power players on the campus, whether these are grade level or content chairpersons, site-based decision-making team members, parents, or others (Bolman & Deal, 1993). These informal leaders know the history and context of why things and people are the way they are. Simply put, they also know where the bodies are buried. They understand the history of the culture and climate of the school, and their assistance can be critical to success.

Societal pressures and attitudes affect schools as well as any other organization. Society thus influences the values and norms that shape human behavior and as a result, leadership of groups of people varies from culture to culture and school to school. Because of these differing cultural norms, a leader who has used a basic set of leadership constructs successfully in one school can move to another and use the same applications with vastly different results. Hallinger and Leithwood (1998) note that social culture and values are impacted by school leadership through observed and unobserved forces and suggest that the practical side of school leadership is as important as the academic. Therefore, leaders should view their faculty, staff, and students as microsystems of the society that reflect the values and culture of the community in which they exist. The values of the community have a direct effect on the values of the school itself and must be studied and used as a part of the total heritage and culture of the school. As O'Neill (2000) suggests, "Telling stories about the past can help schools understand where they have been and chart where they are going" (p. 63).

Creating a Community of Learners

Successful leaders learn to create a community of learners that extends beyond the school itself. Fullan (1994) notes that educators, in partnership with all community agencies, must initiate the creation of learning communities as part of a larger social agenda. The learning community consists of families, neighborhoods, businesses, and churches in addition to students, faculty, and staff. In such a view, every person who works in the kitchen, cleans the buildings, tends to the grounds, or drives a bus is a part of the school's learning community. As McChesney and Hertling (2000) note, "Many reform efforts neglect to gain the support of families and the community. Parents and teachers should have an active role on any committees investigating . . . programs" (p. 13).

For the school to be as productive as possible, every person in the community must have a vested interest in its welfare. As such, each person has a role and responsibility to be proactive in initiating activities on the campus. The learning community then develops an attitude of teamwork to create the best school possible. Kugelmass (2000) says that school leaders are not solely responsible for creating a culture of success, but by supporting instructional initiatives, and "providing staff development opportunities to empower teachers [they help] create new organizational structures and encourage collaboration and . . . innovation" (p. 26). When the school is successful, the entire community, as well as society as a whole, is successful. Conversely, when the school is less than successful, every other component suffers as well. It is the role of school leaders to develop a bond among several facets of the school to build the learning community. Leaders who are able to create, sustain, and nurture this bond generate successful school cultures (Schmieder & Cairns, 1996). With a strengthened sense of interdependency, the school can become the center and focus of community life (Cartwright & D'Orso, 1993).

Although there is no recipe for developing a sense of learning community, common strategies include

- Creating a vision of what the school should be
- Selecting staff with corresponding values
- Addressing conflict rather than avoiding it
- Setting a consistent example of core values in daily routines
- Nurturing the traditions, rituals, ceremonies, and symbols that reinforce a community of learning (Deal & Peterson, 1999, 1994)

A leader should facilitate, not dictate, the development of a common school vision. The strength of the vision comes in its development from the grassroots level. It should consist of a collective vision of what everyone agrees the school can and should become.

Personnel decisions are obviously important. In building the learning community, selection of a staff that shares the common vision and values of the school is a critical component. Kugelmass (2000) suggests that school leaders should recruit new teachers who support the shared beliefs already at the school. Over time, opportunities should be provided for contemplation, discussion, and analysis of campus needs, hopes, and dreams before the campus vision and mission can be identified, developed, and articulated. After discussion, input, and analysis, if there are existing staff members who do not agree, they should be given the opportunity to move to a different campus where their vision, personal mission, and values would be a better fit. In the process of articulating the core values of the school some people may decide to leave, although this is in the long-term best interest of the organization (Collins & Porras, 1996).

Collins and Porras (1996) recommend a process called *Mars Group* for developing and articulating the core values in an organization. Members are asked to imagine that they have to recreate the best attributes of their organization on another planet. Whom would they send on a rocket ship that can only seat five to seven people? Most likely, they would choose the people who understand the core values of the organization, and who are highly credible and highly competent. In developing these values for faculty and staff, the leader should work from the individual to the organization. Each individual should answer several questions such as: What core values do you bring to work? Will they be as valid for you in several years as they are today? What core values would you build into a new organization regardless of its industry?

There are leaders who know the appropriate things to say and the philosophy to articulate, but they do not consistently apply what they claim to believe. In times of stress or fatigue, these individuals revert to their inner leadership and management styles that may or may not be aligned with the culture of a specific school. People in leadership positions who are afraid of decision making, discourse, and conflict that challenge their core values hold the organization back. Peters (1987) says vibrant, growing organizations should thrive on the chaos that develops as creative people develop new ideas and are not afraid to take risks—a birth of innovation. Today's change-oriented schools need a birth of innovation as people work together to develop and articulate their common core values.

When seeking to create change and reform within a school, the leader must keep a constant focus on how and what students learn (Leithwood, Leonard, & Sharratt, 1998). This focus on learning requires a new way of looking at instruction as well as the concept of leadership itself (Elmore, 1999–2000). The entire learning community, with the support and encouragement of the leader must seek to determine student needs, engage in action research, and assess and evaluate everything that takes place within and affecting the school (Brainard, 1996; Creighton, 2000; Walford, 1998). When these pieces are in place, then appropriate and informed decisions can be made that promote a community of learners. Too often nonproductive academic programs continue simply because they are in place, not because they are effective. Without well-planned and reflective evaluations, schools can never truly know if programs are productive or cost effective. By conducting proper and appropriate action and evaluative research, campus improvement decisions become data driven (Creighton, 2000; Holcomb, 1998). Decisions and change are thus based on facts, rather than perceptions and biases. Chapter 9 discusses in detail the collection and use of data within the context of accountability.

Inspired leadership toward a common cause also can do much for the needs of individuals. As teachers, staff, parents, and community develop and share a common vision, each person, as well as the group, develops goals for individual and school improvement. People become empowered in goal development, implementation, and evaluation, thus maximizing effort and results. Individual and group strengths and weaknesses are aligned with campus goals, objectives, and strategies. Individuals are empowered to be creative and take risks in all components of the campus improvement plan. Satisfaction and gratification occur in being a part of a winning endeavor (Blanchard & Johnson, 1982). Individuals are empowered to know that what they do matters to the greater good of the long-term and short-term campus goals. People and organizations grow by doing and being a part of a successful process. In this manner, all members of the learning community, as well as the school itself, grow personally and professionally.

Involvement of Community Members

When school communities bond together around a mutually developed set of goals they become more effective (Wilmore & Thomas, 2001; Hoyle, English, & Steffy, 1998). Community forums and parent leadership training are two strategies that can assist in successful project planning, implementation, and evaluation (Buysse, Wesley, & Skinner, 1999). The community must be actively involved in school improvement and campus planning efforts. For Fege (2000), "Educational improvement needs to rally the community around a common vision and purpose" (p. 42). Parents and other community members should have input in setting campus goals and objectives; planning strategies to reach them; and in the approval, implementation, and evaluation of the campus improvement plan.

Fege (2000) describes new roles for parents noting that, a "results-oriented curriculum with accountability for learning means that parents become a strategic instructional resource" (p. 39). He continues by suggesting that "school leaders can no longer view parents as appendages to schooling or meddlers in their work. They can no longer ignore parents or treat them with disdain. Without community support, [school improvement] will not survive . . ." (p. 39). Edmondson, Thorson, and Fluegel (2000) describe the situation in a school district in Minnesota by saying, "Sustainable change could only occur with significant public involvement . . . [and] the strong sense of community ownership in the district's strategic plan set the stage for long-term sustainable change" (p. 52).

For any program to have sustained success, empowerment and ownership must occur in all stakeholders within the entire learning community (Palestini, 1999; Short & Greer, 1997; Starratt, 1995; Covey, 1992). Stakeholders consist of everyone at the school, in the surrounding neighborhood, families, caregivers, businesses, civic groups, and churches. Members of the school community will do what they have to do when they are made aware of a need (Heskett & Schlesinger, 1996; Taylor, 1947). For Edmondson, Thorson, and Fluegel (2000), town meetings provide a forum to build consensus as "teachers, principals, retirees, . . . students and parents voiced their opinions about what would be best for the school" (p. 52). Over time, though, these efforts will cease to be as productive unless the people involved have put their heads and their hearts into what they are doing (Palestini, 1999; Deal & Kennedy, 1982). Ultimate productivity occurs when both head and heart are committed to success for all.

Individuals support what they help build. When the learning community has worked together to develop goals, they have ownership in them and work toward their success. If members do not feel that the goals or programs are truly theirs, but rather superimposed on them in a hierarchical manner, they will not fully support them. Moffett (2000) says that, "More than any other factor, the sense of a professional community in schools enhances student achievement" (p. 36). Further, individuals may subvert the efforts toward change, which creates problems. For programs or ideas to be ultimately successful, they must be developed and implemented from the ground up (Helgesen, 1996). This does not mean that the campus leader cannot facilitate or help shape curriculum development, instructional strategies, or program designs. It does mean that the leader should be a member of the team, not the dictatorial top of a pyramid, shouting ideas downward for others to implement (Short & Greer, 1997).

An example of community engagement in schools can be seen in organized volunteer programs. For example, one school district has multiple programs, resources, and cocurricular and extracurricular activities for students to participate in. Scores on state achievement tests are high, and the district is often looked to as a model. Others might look at this district and wish their schools had its money. However, what they should wish for are the volunteers that this district has developed, along with an effective parent and community program that help teachers teach, students learn, and all succeed.

Volunteer programs are not limited to wealthy districts. One school district has won awards for its VIP: Volunteers in Education program. Through a systematic parent, civic club, and business program, thousands of hours are contributed yearly at each campus, including the alternative high school. Volunteers do everything from listening to children read, to tutoring, running off papers, and laminating for teachers. Some volunteers help put up bulletin boards while others serve as bilingual interpreters. Businesses have provided paid released time for employees to volunteer in the schools and still others provide needed resources. Perhaps most notable are the efforts of the women's club, which annually provides one-year renewable scholarships to every applying graduate from the alternative high school. Other districts have Adopt a School partners who provide volunteers; they are honored at special luncheons or in front of the school board during an open session when the media are present. Developing and using volunteers can become a source of pride for the businesses and the individuals.

By involving the community in as many ways as possible, schools engage a vast resource of low- or no-cost assistance. Parents and other community members can bring knowledge, skills, and goodwill into the schools. The more they are actively involved in the schools and observing the teaching–learning process, the more they will feel a part of the school culture and work toward its success. The greater the community involvement, the more supportive individuals will be of the school in the wider community. The more schools incorporate community members and volunteers in decision making, planning, goal setting, budgeting, and evaluation, the more empowered the schools will become (Carr, 1997; Starratt, 1995). People like being an appreciated part of a successful team. The schools and community reap the ultimate benefits as many people feel pride, ownership, and empowerment in the schools. As Fege (2000) describes this process, "Without a public behind us, without parental ownership of its schools, and without a clear and articulate vision about what binds parents and the community of all colors, races and languages in a common purpose, individualism will render obsolete our hope that all children receive a quality public education" (p. 43).

Building Transformational Leadership

The concept of transformational leadership is an outgrowth of an earlier theory, transactional leadership, often credited to James MacGregor Burns (1978). Burns's theory viewed leadership as being primarily designed around some transaction, such as exchanging money for work (Riggio, 2000) or giving people something in exchange for something in return (Kuhnert & Lewis, 1987).

Transformational leadership moves beyond this form of motivation and focuses on "the leader's ability to provide shared values and a vision for the future" (Riggio, 2000, p. 362). Bass (1985) and Bennis and Nanus (1985) describe transformational leaders as visionary and inspirational. For Hoy and Miskel (1996), transformational leaders exhibit the following traits:

- Define the need for change
- Create new visions and muster commitment to the visions
- Concentrate on long-term goals
- Inspire followers to transcend their own interests for higher order goals
- Change the organization to accommodate a new vision, rather than work within the existing one
- Mentor followers to take greater responsibility for their own development and that of others. Followers become leaders and leaders become change agents, and ultimately transform the organization (p. 393)

Day (2000) suggests that transformational leaders are able "to manage the boundaries of autocratic and democratic decision making [and are] . . . values led, people centered, achievement oriented, and able to manage a number of ongoing tensions and dilemmas" (p. 56). He goes on to say that effective leaders are able to manage "changes with integrity and skill, integrating them into the vision, values, and practices of their schools" (p. 59). Greenberg and Baron (2000) define transformational leadership as "leadership in which leaders use their charisma to transform and revitalize their organizations" (p. 462). However, as these authors point out, charisma alone is not enough to change an organization; as part of the change process leaders must provide intellectual stimulation, individualized consideration, and inspirational motivation as they work with faculty, staff, students, and all members of the learning community. Individualized consideration means providing support, attention, encouragement, and resources so that members of the learning community can perform at their best. Finally, educational leaders must clearly articulate the school's mission and goals to focus efforts on student learning and success for all.

Transformational leaders are at the heart of the learning community. They are change agents who look beyond immediate needs of the organization and focus on long-term goals (Wilmore & Thomas, 2001; Starratt, 1995; Leithwood, 1992). Transformational leadership is based on a strong personal belief system of the leader and their ability to inspire others to work for common, long-term goals. A sense of common culture and stories, along with an intrinsic, positive climate, are essential development tools for such leaders. Within this context, people change their work ethos and belief systems to achieve higher goals and expectations previously thought impossible. This model of transformational leadership supports all members of the learning community in a common quest toward the same vision of how things can and should be instead of the current status (Starratt, 1995).

Becoming a transformational leader is not easy; however, individuals should seek to follow these suggestions: (1) develop and articulate a clear and appealing vision;

(2) describe the process for bringing that vision to reality; (3) build confidence in others' ability to achieve the vision; (4) provide inspiration and motivation; (5) provide appropriate models and set an example; (6) look for opportunities to celebrate successes; and (7) be intellectually honest (Podsakof, MacKenzie, Moorman, & Fetter, 1990; House & Podasakof, 1995; Yukl, 1998). Transformational leaders seek to inspire internal, intrinsic change within an organization, and such a leadership model requires hard work, persistence, and a passionate commitment to a common cause. Although difficult to achieve, given the situation in some schools, the results can be dynamic (Wilmore & Thomas, 2001; Starratt, 1995).

The development of collegial relationships among faculty and staff and the ability to foster work within collaborative groups is important to organizational culture and climate. Transformational leaders help to provide both meaning and challenge to the work of others as individuals and as members of a team. Such leaders have the ability to empower teachers, staff, parents, and community members in their work and in the collective efforts of the group. Such school leaders are excellent at developing consensus on a common vision, then empowering the team to set high goals, objectives, and strategies for how to reach them (Leithwood, 1992).

Transformational leaders begin with what Covey (1989) calls the end in mind. They empower all stakeholders to visualize and set goals over a longer period of time than one school year. They work as a team to create a campus improvement plan that is developmental in nature and has support from all stakeholders. They devote time to relationship building and create opportunities for others to think about and envision what the school can become, how well the students can learn, and how great an environment the campus could be. Providing the time to facilitate collegial relationships and collaborative group action leads to an intrinsic motivation to achieve the goals and ultimately greater success. The subsequent effect becomes *transformational* or changes the nature of the organization. The inspired commitment to a common cause creates a strong bond among all members of the school, which results in higher academic performance for all students.

Leading Campus Improvement

Campus planning for improvement is essential to the ultimate enhancement of a school or district. The process of developing a campus improvement plan is described in detail in Chapter 9. However, campus leaders have the responsibility to develop a campus culture that continuously seeks to be better. To develop a campus culture for continuous improvement school leaders can do the following suggestions:

- The leader can involve the entire learning community in the development of campus goals. These goals must be collaboratively developed, mutually agreed upon, and committed to. They should be high enough for schools to reach. When goals are attained they should be celebrated and then used as a baseline for success in subsequent years. Each year the goals should challenge both teachers and students, as well as others in the learning community, resulting in cumulative individual and campus growth and improvement.

• The leader can develop specific strategies for each goal that are collaboratively supported. The strategies identify the activities that the campus will undertake to reach each identified goal. Resources needed to implement or assess the strategies should be directly tied to the campus budget. Campus resources must be tied to both campus goals and the budget. Subsequently, leaders should avoid budgeting anything that is not also tied to campus goals and strategies for their implementation. Leaders should continuously ask, "Is this linked to our campus improvement goals?"

• The leader can establish a specific timeline for the planning, implementation, and assessment of goals. Because strategies are directly linked to specific goals, continuous formative and summative assessment with resulting modifications of campus goals is the primary responsibility of the campus leader in guiding the learning community toward continuous improvement.

In the process of continuous improvement, goals should be reexamined throughout the school year. As goals are met, new ones can be developed. If evaluative studies show that goals have been set too high or are no longer appropriate, they should be modified. At a minimum, systematic needs assessments, surveys, interviews, and extensive discussion within and outside the campus community should be undertaken regularly as the campus leaders focus on ways to improve and grow.

School goals and the process of continuous improvement are roadmaps for success. Without appropriate discussion, development, implementation, and evaluation of campus goals, campuses are often fragmented and lack a clear focus regarding specific objectives. Goals are the outgrowth of a collaboratively developed campus vision and mission that can lead to greater productivity in teaching, learning, and school achievement. The campus leader must be instrumental in creating a positive culture and linking the campus vision to specific goals and strategies improvement for all, so the campus can achieve ultimate productivity.

Celebrations That Reinforce the Campus Community

Celebrations are an important element in reinforcing the campus culture and sense of community (Hoyle, English, & Steffy, 1998; Starratt, 1995). Celebrations focus on things, events, and people that the school values and sees as important, and credit should be given where credit is due. Too often leaders and parents are quick to reprimand and slow to praise (Podesta, 1993; Blanchard & Johnson, 1982). By looking for as many chances as possible to celebrate people or events, school leaders have the opportunity to reinforce positive behavior. Costa and Kallick (2000) suggest that, "In teaching maximizing meaning from experiences requires reflection," and celebrations can be generated from these reflections (p. 61).

Everyone needs to feel accepted, appreciated, and recognized. Common needs identified by Maslow are represented in Figure 2.1. The top three levels of Maslow's hierarchy represent social needs, self-esteem needs, and self-fulfillment needs (Maslow, 1954). According to Maslow (1998), the "higher needs are precisely what enlightened management policy paints itself toward. That is to say, enlightened management policy may be defined as an attempt to satisfy higher needs . . . to have the work situation give intrinsically higher need satisfaction" (p. 239).

Celebrating people, things, and events within the context of the heritage of a campus can result in greater creativity, human self-actualization, and a clearer sense of personal and organizational success. Cunningham (1991) believes that encouragement is like empowerment because it helps people to focus on their assets that build self-confidence and self-esteem. Opportunities for affirmation and encouragement help faculty, staff, and students believe in themselves and their own abilities and are important in establishing a culture of success.

Today's schools should never be content with the status quo; they should constantly be seeking ways to improve teaching and learning. As all members of the learning community strive to become self-actualized, school leaders have to be more creative and take risks as they seek new ways of addressing school improvement and generating a climate and culture where everyone succeeds.

It is easy to find things to celebrate in schools. Leaders can celebrate the successes of students, staff, and teachers who do well, improve, and bring positive recognition to the school or community. The culture of the school can be further emphasized when former school leaders and community leaders are included in the celebration (Hoyle, English, & Steffy, 1998; Daresh & Playko, 1997; Bolman & Deal, 1993, 1995). O'Neill (2000) says that by including others in such celebrations, we can use this as a time "to reflect together to understand the patterns, cycles, and trends of our collective organizational history" (p. 64). Assembly programs, parent conferences, community events, school board meetings, dinners, parties, pep rallies, school marquees, posters, public address announcements, newspaper articles, and certificates are all examples of ways a campus can celebrate the many things, large or small, that have happened. As in campus planning, success breeds success, and celebrations applaud success.

Resources for celebrations should be built into the campus budget and tied to campus goals. Many celebrations cost little or nothing, such as enthusiastic praise over

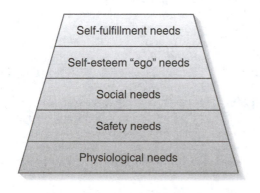

FIGURE 2.1 *Maslow's Needs Hierarchy.*

the public address system for the whole school. A great *pat on the back*, through notes in boxes or banners in the hall, cost very little. Submitting noteworthy events into the media costs little or nothing if it is done as a public service announcement or news release. Many other celebratory tools, such as certificates, assemblies, or pep rallies have minimal cost. Larger events such as dinners can cost more, but community resources such as contributions, grants, sponsorships, and underwriting can be solicited. Businesses love a good cause that celebrates success in the schools, so leaders should use them. In the View from the Field, the principal created a celebration that did not cost any money, but generated joy, pride, and success within the school and community.

By creating a spontaneous celebration of a successful endeavor with sincere joy and excitement, this school leader helps to create a strong bond within the school community. The bar of excellence was raised a step higher, academic achievement went up, and people were acknowledged for a job well done. The campus culture of success for all was reinforced, as was the emphasis on continuous improvement. Celebrations create goodwill and allow people to feel good. In today's world, where there is often much *doom and gloom*, schools should be safe places where every person can come, be successful, feel good about themselves, and be appreciated and recognized. Through celebrations leaders develop and facilitate a positive campus culture and climate.

View from the Field

Dr. Leigh is the principal of a high-performing but unrecognized elementary school. Recently, the students participated in a series of highly stressful state mandated achievement tests. There was a lapse of several months before the results were reported to the district and Dr. Leigh's campus.

The day Dr. Leigh and other school leaders were called to the district office to pick up their test scores was anxiously anticipated. Before passing out the campus results, the superintendent challenged all the principals by saying, "These scores need to improve significantly!" No exceptions were noted; needless to say, all school leaders were nervous about receiving their campus results.

As Dr. Leigh tells the story, "When I received my campus scores I was delighted to see that the school had indeed done very well. I later learned that we were the highest performing campus in the district. The third grade scores

were particularly high and were, in fact, the highest in the history of the school and the district. I was surprised that the superintendent made no mention of this accomplishment."

"When I got back to my campus, I rushed directly to the third grade corridor, drawing each teacher into the hallway where I told them the results of the test, praised the school, praised the third graders, and, then I praised each third grade teacher by name. We were all so excited over our success the teachers celebrated by jumping up and down and hugging each other. The whole endeavor took less then five minutes and cost no money at all. I could see from this experience that the teachers were proud of themselves, their students, and their accomplishments. I had the secretary generate a computer-printed banner and the next morning I hung the banner on the front door proclaiming our success."

Case Study

As the new principal of Norwood Middle School, Ms. Watson realized she had a difficult job ahead. The school is known for being a tough campus located in a transitional area of the city that had a wide array of discipline problems, little community support, and students with marginal academic performance. Students are generally unmotivated and do poorly on class academic measures as well as state-mandated achievement tests. The dropout rate for the school has averaged as high as 35% during the past three years. Few students plan to pursue the academic high school diploma path. Over half of the student body comes from homes that are classified as low socioeconomic status. What has evolved over time is a climate of low expectations with regard to behavior and academic achievement. Less than 30% of the students are involved in any cocurricular activities or sports programs. Turnover rate among the faculty is between averaging 40% to 50% for the last three years. The last two principals resigned because of various disagreements with the administration, the school board, or stress-related health problems.

As the first female principal of the middle school, Ms. Watson hears that the teachers are taking bets to see if she will last till Thanksgiving or Winter Break. Ms. Watson is determined to both prove them wrong and provide the leadership that will transform the culture at Norwood.

Ms. Watson knows the first step must be to change the image of the school. During the first faculty meeting, she speaks openly and freely with the faculty and staff about the school's image, history, academic performance, and future. The teachers respond to her candor, warmth, frankness, and genuine concern. Together they are beginning to develop a plan to make changes in the mission and goals of the school. Working with teachers in the first days of staff development, they collaboratively develop a vision of excellence as a way to positively impact the culture and climate of the school as well as address the academic performance of the students.

Over time Ms. Watson hopes that teachers and staff members will begin to meet with parents to develop a new vision for the school that is relevant to the current circumstances. Working together, they will develop specific goals and strategies to attain their vision of Norwood.

As the school leader, Ms. Watson is the steward of the new school vision and maintains a high visibility within the school and community, constantly serving as the voice and catalyst of the new can-do attitude of high expectations, positive achievement, and community involvement. New ideas have been encouraged and some old ideas have been revisited.

One new idea was to host a fall open house. Although some opposed the idea, saying no parents would come, Ms. Watson and the campus leadership team refused to be deterred. Ms. Watson knew that if the students were engaged and excited about the open house, there was a stronger likelihood that their parents would come. A specific format of the items each teacher would discuss with parents during their brief *mini-classes* was developed. The school's new mission, vision, and goals were to be given to the parents with time to talk about them. Class issues and policies including curriculum, homework, and assessment were to be addressed. If you are Ms. Watson, how would you address the following questions?

- What transformational leadership skills will you need to employ?
- What specific strategies can be used to make the open house a success?
- What pitfalls would you anticipate in generating attendance and support?
- How can the school visually present its new mission and goals?
- How can parents and teachers keep the commitment to continuous improvement alive throughout the school year?
- How can open house become an opportunity for a celebration?

Summary

The culture and climate of any organization are important criteria for its success. Leaders should pay specific attention to fostering and developing rites, rituals, and celebrations that nurture the values and ethos of the entire learning community. The school is a microsystem of the community in which it exists and manifests the values and culture of this community.

Leaders should be role models of high expectations for everyone, including themselves. Their walk must match their talk. Every person within and around the school should be invested and empowered in the campus's vision, mission, planning, goal setting, and decision making. Directives of vision should not come from the leader downward, but should be developed and articulated with input from all constituencies.

Effective school leaders who exhibit characteristics of transformational leadership inspire a passion and commitment toward long-term, collaborative goals and create a culture of school and community empowerment. The development and nurturance of collegial relationships and collaborative groups including all stakeholders in the learning community are essential to a positive and developing school climate. Lastly, risk taking and creativity are important as schools constantly look for ways to improve teaching and learning. Leaders must seek to encourage all people to be involved and interested in the school by developing a culture of empowerment, shared decision making, continuous improvement, and true learning within a school. School leaders must be committed to the development of a school culture that facilitates growth, warmth, and success for everyone and provides opportunities for celebration.

Your Turn

2.1. You have recently been appointed as principal of a low-performing school. Test scores are low, and campus morale is lower. Using Deal and Peterson's (1994) cultural dimensions, develop a plan for how you as the campus leader will facilitate the development of an improved campus culture.

2.2. You have recently been transferred as principal to a successful school where the previous highly respected principal has been suddenly killed in an automobile accident. The faculty, staff, students, and community are grieving. What do you do first?

2.3. You have accepted a position on a successful, though not cutting edge, campus. On your arrival you learn that the faculty, staff, and community are committed to excellence. They want to push the boundaries of their current successes. What would - do you first to facilitate this?

2.4. After several years in your current position as campus leader, your campus culture seems to be growing stale. While still hard working, the faculty and staff seem to be losing their enthusiasm and vitality toward the vast goals ahead of them. Using tenets of transformational leadership, what would you do to invigorate your school toward long-term success and productivity?

2.5. Although your faculty and staff are diligent and dependable, they do not volunteer to sponsor extracurricular activities or other student events. The prevailing attitude seems to be that they will do what needs to be done during the school day, but nothing more. What could you do to try to spark their interest and commitment beyond the basic needs of the school day?

2.6. Little parental or community involvement occurs at your school. Parent conferences are sparsely attended. The parent–teacher organization is about to dissolve due to lack of interest and poor attendance. What can you do as a campus leader to reinvigorate the parent–teacher organization?

References

Bass, B. M. (1985). *Leadership and performance beyond expectation*. New York: Free Press.

Bennis, W. G., & Nanus, B. (1985). *On becoming a leader*. New York: Harper & Row.

Blanchard, K., & Johnson, S. (1982). *The one minute manager*. New York: William Morrow.

Bolman, L. G., & Deal, T. (1991/1995). *Leading with soul*. San Francisco: Jossey-Bass.

Bolman, L. G., & Deal, T. E. (1993). *The path to school leadership*. Thousand Oaks, CA: Corwin Press.

Brainard, E. A. (1996). *A hands-on guide to school program evaluation*. Bloomington, IN: Phi Delta Kappa.

Burns, J. M. (1978). *Leadership*. New York: Harper Torchbooks.

Buysse, V., Wesley, P., & Skinner, D. (1999). Community development approaches for early intervention. *Topics in Early Childhood Special Education, 19*, 4, 236–243.

Carr, A. A. (1997). Leadership and community participation: Four case studies. *Journal of Curriculum and Supervision, 12*, 2, 152–168.

Cartwright, M., & D'Orso, M. (1993). *For the children*. New York: Doubleday.

Collins, J. C., & Porras, J. I. (1996). Building your company's vision. *Harvard Business Review*, 65–77.

Costa, A., & Kallick, B. (2000). Getting into the habit of reflection. *Educational Leadership, 57*, 7, 60–62.

Covey, S. R. (1995). *First things first*. New York: Fireside.

Covey, S. R. (1992). *Principle-centered leadership*. New York: Fireside.

Covey, S. R. (1989). *The 7 habits of highly effective people*. New York: Simon & Schuster.

Creighton, T. B. (2000). *The educator's guide for using data to improve decision making*. Thousand Oaks, CA: Corwin Press.

Cunningham, W. (1991). *Empowerment: Vitalizing personal energy*. Atlanta, GA: New Age Press.

Daresh, J. C., & Playko, M. A. (1997). *Beginning the principalship: A practical guide for new school leaders*. Thousand Oaks, CA: Corwin Press.

Day, C. (2000). Beyond transformational leadership. *Educational Leadership, 57,* 7, 56–59.

Deal, T. E., & Kennedy, A. (1982). *Corporate cultures: The rites and rituals of corporate life.* Reading, MA: Addison-Wesley.

Deal, T. E., & Peterson, K. D. (1999). *Shaping school culture: The heart of leadership.* San Francisco: Jossey-Bass.

Deal, T. E., & Peterson, K. D. (1994). *The leadership paradox: Balancing logic and artistry in schools.* San Francisco: Jossey-Bass.

Deal, T. E., & Peterson, K. D. (1990). *The principal's role in shaping school culture.* Washington, DC: U.S. Department of Education, Office of Educational Research and Improvement.

DePree, M. (1989). *Leadership is an art.* New York: Dell.

DuFour, R., & Eaker, R. (1999). *Professional learning communities at work: Best practices for enhancing student achievement.* Alexandria, VA: Association for Supervision and Curriculum Development.

Edmonson, J., Thorson, G., & Fluegel, D. (2000). Big school change in a small town. *Educational Leadership, 57,* 7, 51–53.

Elmore, R. F. (1999–2000). Building a new structure for school leadership. *American Educator, 23,* 4, 6–13.

Fege, A. F. (2000). From fund raising to hell raising: New roles for parents. *Educational Leadership, 57,* 7, 63–65.

Fullan, M. (1994). Change forces: Probing the depths of educational reform. school development and the management of change series: 10. ERIC Document Reproduction Service No. ED373391.

Fullan, M. (1996). Professional culture and educational change. *School Psychology Review, 55,* (4), 496–500.

Glanz, J. (1998). *Action research: An educational leader's guide to school improvement.* Norwood, MA: Christopher-Gordon Publishers.

Goldman, E. (1998). The significance of leadership style. *Educational Leadership, 55,* 7, 20–22.

Goldring, E. B., & Rallis, S. F. (1993). *Principals of dynamic schools.* Thousand Oaks, CA: Corwin Press.

Greenberg, J., & Baron, R. A. (2000). *Behavior in organizations* (7th ed). Upper Saddle River, NJ: Prentice-Hall.

Hallinger, P., & Leithwood, K. (1998). Unseen forces: The impact of social culture on school leadership. *Peabody Journal of Education, 73,* 2, 126–151.

Helgesen, S. (1996). Leading from the grass roots. In F. Hesselbein, M. Goldsmith, & R. Beckhard (eds), *The leader of the future,* pp. 19–24. San Francisco: Jossey-Bass.

Hershey, P., & Blanchard, K. H. (1993). *Management of organizational behavior.* Englewood Cliffs, NJ: Prentice-Hall.

Heskett, J. L., & Schlesinger, L. A. (1996). Leaders who shape and keep performance-oriented culture. In F. Hesselbein, M. Goldsmith, & R. Beckhard (eds), *The leader of the future.* pp. 111–119. San Francisco: Jossey-Bass.

Holcomb, E. L. (1998). *Getting excited about data: How to combine people, passion, and proof.* Thousand Oaks, CA: Corwin Press.

House, R. J., & Podsakof, P. M. (1995). Leadership effectiveness: Past perspectives and future directions for research. In J. Greenberg (ed), *Organizational behavior: The state of the science.* Hillsdale, NJ: Erlbaum.

Hoy, W. K., & Miskel, C. G. (1996). *Educational administration: Theory, research, and practice* (5th ed). New York: McGraw-Hill.

Hoyle, J. R., English, F. W., & Steffy, B. E. (1998). *Skills for successful 21st century school leaders.* Arlington, VA: American Association of School Administrators.

Hoyle, J. R. (1995). *Leadership and futuring: Making visions happen.* Thousand Oaks, CA: Corwin Press.

Hoyle, J. R., & Crenshaw, H. (1997). *Interpersonal sensitivity.* Princeton, NJ: Eye on Education.

King, M., & Blumer, I. (2000). A good start. *Phi Delta Kappan, 81,* 5, 356–361.

Kugelmass, J. W. (2000). Not made for defeat. *Educational Leadership, 57,* 7, 25–28.

Kuhnert, K. W., & Lewis, P. (1987). Transactional and transformational leadership: A constructive/developmental analysis. *Academy of Management Review, 12,* 4, 648–657.

Leithwood, K. (1992). The move toward transformational leadership. *Educational Leadership, 49,* 5, 8–12.

Leithwood, K., Leonard, L., & Sharratt, L. (1998). Conditions fostering organizational learning in schools. *Educational Administration Quarterly, 34,* 2, 243–276.

Lunenburg, F. C., & Ornstein, A. C. (2000). *Educational administration: Concepts and practices.* Belmont, CA: Wadsworth/Thomson Learning.

Maslow, A. H. (1998). *Maslow on management.* New York: John Wiley & Sons, Inc.

Maslow, A. H. (1954). *Motivation and personality.* New York: Harper & Row.

McChesney, J., & Hertling, E. (2000). The path to comprehensive school reform. *Educational Leadership, 57,* 7, 10–15.

Moffett, C. A. (2000). Sustaining change: The answers are blowing in the wind. *Educational Leadership, 57,* 7, 35–38.

Newmann, F., & Associates. (1996). *Authentic achievement: Restructuring schools for intellectual quality.* San Francisco: Jossey-Bass.

O'Neill, J. (2000). Capturing an organization's oral history. *Educational Leadership, 57,* 7, 63–65.

Owens, R. G. (1995). *Organizational behavior in education* (5th ed). Boston: Allyn & Bacon.

Palestini, R. H. (1999). *Educational administration: Leading with mind and heart.* Lancaster, PA: Technomic Publishing Co.

Peters, T. J. (1987). *Thriving on chaos: Handbook for a management revolution.* New York: Alfred A. Knopf.

Peters, T. J., & Waterman, R. H. (1982). *In search of excellence: Lessons from America's best-run companies.* New York: Harper & Row.

Peterson, K. D., & Deal, T. E. (1998). How leaders influence the culture of schools. *Educational Leadership, 56,* 1, 28–30.

Podesta, C. (1993). *Self-esteem and the six-second secret.* Thousand Oaks, CA: Corwin Press.

Podsakof, P. M., MacKenzie, S. B., Moorman, R. H., & Fetter, R. (1990). Transformational leader behaviors and their effects on followers' trust in leader, satisfaction, and organizational citizenship behaviors. *Leadership Quarterly, 1,* 107–142.

Reavis, C. A., Vinson, D., & Fox, R. (1999). Importing a culture of success via a strong principal. *Clearing House, 72,* 4, 199–202.

Riggio, R. E. (2000). *Introduction to industrial/organizational psychology* (3rd ed). Upper Saddle River, NJ: Prentice-Hall.

Robbins, P., & Alvy, H. (1995). *The principal's companion.* Thousand Oaks, CA: Corwin Press.

Schien, E. H. (1991). *Organizational culture and leadership.* San Francisco: Jossey-Bass.

Schmieder, J. H., & Cairns, D. (1996). *Ten skills of highly effective principals.* Lancaster, PA: Technomic Publishing Co.

Sergiovanni, T. (1995). *The principalship: A reflective practice perspective.* Boston: Allyn & Bacon.

Sergiovanni, T. (1992). *Moral leadership: Getting to the heart of school improvement.* San Francisco: Jossey-Bass.

Short, P., & Greer, J. (1997). *Leadership in empowered schools.* Columbus, OH: Merrill, Prentice-Hall.

Starratt, R. J. (1995). *Leaders with vision: The quest for school renewal.* Thousand Oaks, CA: Corwin Press.

Taylor, F. (1947). *Scientific management.* New York: Harper & Row.

Walford, G. (1998). *Doing research about education.* Bristol, PA: Falmer Press, Taylor & Francis.

Wallace, R. (1995). *From vision to practice.* Thousand Oaks, CA: Corwin Press.

Wilmore, E. L., & Thomas, C. (2001). The new century: Is it too late for transformational leadership? *Educational Horizons, 79,* 3, 115–123.

Yukl, G. (1998). *Leadership in organizations* (4th ed). Upper Saddle River, NJ: Prentice-Hall.

3

Values and Ethics of Leadership

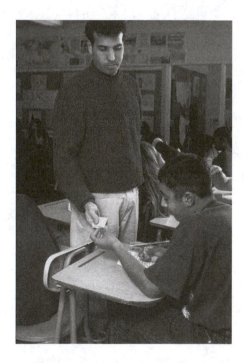

ISLLC Standard

Standard 5: A school administrator is an educational leader who promotes the success of all students by acting with integrity, fairness, and in an ethical manner.

46

Chapter Objectives

The objectives of this chapter are:

- Discuss the importance of ethical behavior for school leaders.
- Identify key concepts in codes of ethics for school leaders.
- Describe ethical leadership behavior.
- Develop, clarify, and reflect on ethical practice as it relates to personal and professional behavior.
- Discuss implications of ethical dilemmas for school leaders.

In today's educational setting leadership and ethics go hand in hand as many administrators are confronted daily with ethical dilemmas that call for decisions. With greater scrutiny given to the actions of leaders, especially those who hold the public's trust, ethical behavior has become an area of greater focus. The headlines proclaiming the need for greater ethical behavior in corporate America after the fall of Enron, World Com, and the accounting firm of Arthur Anderson, have resulted in greater scrutiny of leader behavior. Ethical behavior is nested in values and is related to the conduct and motives of leaders in the organization. For school leaders, ethical behavior involves providing not only vision and inspiration, but a purpose or meaning to the educational process. Yates (2000) says, "Good leaders must first be good people" (p. 57); they are virtuous and not only take the high ground by modeling values such as truthfulness, integrity, commitment, and compassion, but they have character as well. For Maxwell (1999), "The development of character is at the heart of our development not just as leaders, but as human beings" (p. 4). Such leadership has often been called *value-centered*, and Behr (1998) notes that it helps to create a sense of community and organizational integrity that is centered on shared goals, values, and commitments.

Successful school leaders must possess specific ethics-related skills including vision, character, values, empowerment, and persistence. Ethical behavior is the result of a combination of a number of factors that include knowledge and a clear understanding of the underlying philosophical principles embedded in a code of conduct (Bersoff, 1996). Ethical conduct is the cumulative effect of mature thinking, careful judgment, wise observations, and prudent thinking. "Values are motivating determinants of behaviors . . . [and] shared values define the basic character of an organization and give it meaning" (Razik & Swanson, 2001, pp. 366–367). Sometimes values and ethics are used interchangeably, but according to Corey, Corey, and Callanan (1998), ". . . the two terms are not identical; values pertain to beliefs and attitudes that provide direction to everyday living, whereas ethics pertain to the beliefs we hold about what constitutes right conduct" (p. 3). School leaders need values and attitudes that guide their daily behavior, and they also need ethics to give them a moral compass for right conduct.

Until recently, little attention has been given to the study of ethical issues (Beck & Murphy, 1994), and historically, few school leaders have been formally trained to deal with ethical questions. Czaja and Lowe (2000) suggest that a new or renewed interest in teaching ethics has come from the realization that the behavior of school leaders must be governed by moral and ethical guidelines or imperatives. Others acknowledge the need for persons in positions of responsibility to know their own values and model ethical behavior. Perhaps more than ever, leaders are required to not only understand the consequences of their behavior from an ethical standpoint, but be able to articulate their values and beliefs. Creighton (1999) says that "One of the major lessons [for leaders] . . . is the importance of . . . moral values as they are embedded in the circumstances of everyday life" (p. 3). As Henderson (1992) notes,

> Ethical standards, whether formal or informal have changed tremendously in the last century. Boldly stated, no one can make the case that ethical standards have fallen in the latter decades of the twentieth century. The reverse is true . . . [people] expect more sensitive behavior in conduct. . . . The issue is not just having the standards, however. It is living up to them. (p. 24)

Although often viewed as esoteric rather than pragmatic, ethical principles must guide everyday thought and action as school leaders deal with the realities of school communities. Czaja and Lowe (2000) note that, "The experience of practicing ethics literally changes lives" (p. 10). The importance of ethical behavior cannot be over-stated: "How one thinks and what one believes about leadership are translated into institutional values and practices" (McKerrow, 1997, p. 214). Clearly, the values to which leaders ascribe are related to how they function at the campus level, and as Campbell (1997) notes, much of the literature suggests ". . . that educational leaders must develop and articulate a much greater awareness of the ethical significance of their actions and decisions" (p. 288). Organizations that seek to encourage ethical behavior communicate the expectations that individuals will behave according to ethically defined standards. These organizations also hire leaders who model such behavior and discourage and punish unethical behavior, while teaching everyone the basic tools of ethical decision making by encouraging dialogue and discussion of ethical issues (Osland, Kolb, & Rubin, 2001).

This chapter discusses the importance of ethical behavior by examining a code of ethics for school leaders and provides guidelines that can shape ethical decision making. The chapter also explores possible options to ethical dilemmas school leaders face. The View from the Field highlights the reality of ethical decisions school leaders confront regularly. For us, ethical school leaders advocate and promote success of all students and act according to a value system that reflects character and a sense of equity, fairness, and integrity. Ethical leaders also model the highest standards of conduct as they work with the school and community members.

Ethical Code of Conduct

Most professions and organizations have a code of behaviors that guides their actions. Osland, Kolb, and Rubin (2001) note that "ethics refers to standards of conduct that indicate how one should behave based on moral duties and virtues arising principles about right and wrong" (p. 111). For Corey, Corey, and Callanan (1998), ". . . ethics, values, morality, community standards, laws and professionalism are critical components in any discussion of professional ethic" (p. 3). Leaders must be aware of these codes of conduct for they provide a possible course of action when confronted with problems or dilemmas. For Maxwell (1999), "How a leader deals with the circumstances of life tells you many things about his character" (p. 3). Although ethical codes are important in guiding leaders in making decisions, codes alone are not sufficient for demonstrating ethical responsibility. In fact, other professions have found that there are problems and limitations in various professional codes (Lanning, 1997; Herlihy & Remley, 1995; Bersoff, 1996). Problems that leaders may encounter as they seek to apply codes to practice include:

- Some dilemmas or situations may not be specifically addressed in an ethical code.
- Some areas of ethical codes may lack specificity or clarity.
- Simply knowing the code does not ensure ethical practice.
- The ethical code may be in conflict with organizational policies and practices.
- A code of ethics should be considered within the context of various cultures.

Kitchener (1984) and Meara, Schmidt, and Day (1996) have described six fundamental principles for counselors, but they can provide direction for school leaders in making the highest ethical decisions. These principles are autonomy, nonmalificence, beneficence, justice, fidelity, and veracity. Autonomy involves respecting the rights of others and allowing them to choose and act according to their own values and beliefs. In some ways, this is closely related to academic freedom and the delicate balance of freedom to choose versus what is prescribed in the curriculum. Nonmalificence basically involves doing no harm. As leaders make decisions, they must ask themselves if the decision will do harm to others. Beneficence involves promoting the well-being of others. School leaders should not only do no harm, they must seek to make decisions that promote the well-being of others. Justice involves fairness and equity in the treatment of individuals regardless of gender, age, race or ethnicity, or socioeconomic status. In building a culture that emphasizes success for all, leaders must demonstrate justice in working with all members of the learning community. Fidelity requires leaders to be honest and honor commitment to others and is fostered by the development of trust with the organization. As noted in Chapter 1, trust is the glue that holds the organization together and fidelity is crucial to creating trust. Veracity is required as leaders interact with faculty, staff, students, parents, and community members. It is important that leaders be able to speak the truth with compassion as they give feedback to teachers or talk to parents.

In order to be principle-centered, Blanchard and Peale (1988) have also proposed general principles that can serve to guide their behavior. These principles are purpose, pride, patience, persistence, and perspective and also provide guidelines for individuals seeking to make quality ethical decisions. Purpose involves seeing ourselves as operating with a conscience so that we can face ourselves in the mirror each morning and feel good about who we are. Pride is based on a healthy or balanced self-esteem that does not need acceptance from others in order to make decisions. Patience is the result of a sense of peace and an understanding that things will eventually work out. Persistence involves the ability to stay with a person or project even when inconvenient. Finally, perspective allows leaders to examine their day and to focus on seeing people as well as issues more clearly.

As leaders function within organizations, most have a set of values and principles that shapes and guides their behaviors. Various organizations have established their own sets of principles or values related to employee behavior. For school administrators, the American Association of School Administrators has adopted a code of ethics that serves to guide school leaders and shape their professional behaviors. The code is in many ways idealistic, but at the same time practical so that it applies to school leaders in a variety of roles and settings. Administrators acknowledge that the schools belong to the public they serve for the purpose of providing educational opportunities to all. However, educational leaders must assume responsibility for providing ethical leadership in the school and community. Such responsibility requires each individual to maintain standards of exemplary professional conduct for their actions, and the leader will be viewed and appraised by all within the school organization. Therefore, professionals subscribe to the statements or standards reflected in Table 3.1.

Although the administrators' code of ethics has been adopted for over two decades, many school leaders may not be aware of the specific behaviors identified in the document. School leaders must not only be aware of such behaviors, but integrate them into their everyday routines as they model the highest integrity for their learning communities.

TABLE 3.1 *Code of Ethics for Administrators*

---

1. Makes the well-being of students the fundamental value of all decision making and actions
2. Fulfills professional responsibilities with honesty and integrity
3. Supports the principle of due process and protects the civil and human rights of all individuals
4. Obeys local, state, and national laws and does not knowingly join or support organizations that advocate, directly or indirectly, the overthrow of the government
5. Implements the governing board of education's policies and administrative rules and regulations
6. Pursues appropriate measures to correct those laws, policies, and regulations that are not consistent with sound educational goals
7. Avoids using positions for personal gain through political, social, religious, economic, or other influences
8. Accepts academic degrees or professional certification only from duly accredited institutions
9. Maintains the standards and seeks to improve the effectiveness of the profession through research and continuing professional development
10. Honors all contracts until fulfillment, release, or dissolution mutually agreed upon by all parties to contract

---

Source: Adopted by American Association of School Administrators Executive Committee, 1981—American Association of School Administrators.

In addition to the school leader's code of ethics seen in Table 3.1, Kidder (1995) provides other strategies for addressing ethical issues. These include:

- Ends-based thinking: doing what is best for the greatest number of people and "relies heavily on assessing the consequences or ends of action" (p. 155)
- Rule-based thinking: following your highest sense or inner conscience and basing your ". . . action on a maxim or precept that could be universalized" (p. 157)
- Care-based thinking: doing what you would want others to do to you, which asks us ". . . to care enough about the others involved to put ourselves in their shoes" (p. 159)

These principles, as well as the code of ethics and other guidelines presented, can serve to guide leaders in making decisions, but as Kidder (1995) notes there is no panacea ". . . you don't stick in the dilemma at one end, turn the crank and pick up your answer at the other" (p. 163). Ultimately, ethical decision making requires individuals to exercise ". . . judgment, character, moral awareness, perception, discrimination—a whole host of imponderables" (p. 163). Living and modeling ethical behavior may be one of the most difficult aspects of school leadership.

Ethical Actions and Behaviors

School leaders face many difficult challenges in meeting the diverse needs of their school communities. Historically, society has struggled with the application of ethical behavior in ever changing environments in which the meaning of right and wrong may be clouded or unclear as a result of the times or the nature of the circumstances. Adams and Maine (1998) note that ethical behavior is the result of ". . . the standards and values that people use to judge what is right and good or worthwhile—their moral standards" (p. 1). When presented with ethical dilemmas or situations, leaders must critically examine their own beliefs about what is right and good and then use ethical codes and guiding principles to make a decision or resolve a problem.

As leaders negotiate through the complex and quickly changing circumstances that occur in schools, they must make decisions not only for the good of each student, but they must also consider the good of the campus and district as well. Adams and Maine (1998) suggest that an understanding of ethics provides a way to confront issues, understand the complexities of a situation, consider options in problem solving, and search for a solution. The solution must be equitable and fair and meet the many guideline parameters of ethical conduct.

How do school leaders make appropriate decisions that reflect ethical behavior? Blanchard and Peale (1988) offer the following questions that provide a quick ethics check when confronted with an ethical decision the leader should ask:

1. Is it legal?
2. Is it balanced?
3. How will it make me feel about myself? (p. 27)

In answering these questions, school leaders must first determine if their behavior will violate statute, code, or school policy. Next, they must determine if their actions are fair to all parties both in the short-term and long-term. Finally, leaders must ask themselves if they can live in peace with their decisions and actions. Would they feel good about themselves if their decisions were the focus of the evening news or a newspaper editorial?

Given the diverse beliefs, both cultural and religious, that are represented in the school community, school leaders often have to deal with conflicting value systems. While Kidder (1995) points out that ethical decisions begin with an acknowledgement of one's own value system, a school leader will be unable to act appropriately when an ethical dilemma occurs if the leader is unclear or uncertain of personal beliefs and lacks an internal compass. Leaders have a personal set of values that govern their thoughts and actions and gives them the ability to analyze the situations that occur in school settings. In the View from the Field, John, a campus leader, is placed in an ethical dilemma that requires that he make a series of decisions about what to do with budget information that he had access to. As you read through this scenario, think about how you might have responded if you had been in this situation.

As the scenario illustrates, John has been confronted with several options, all of which have consequences. Simply returning it can have consequences and just leaving it alone can also have consequences. To help resolve his dilemma, John needs to be able to apply the various guidelines in order to make ethical decisions.

View from the Field

Recently, John attended a budget briefing at the central office with all of the campus administrators in his district. Because of population shifts in the district, some schools would be losing funds while others would receive an increase in their budget. Although no decisions were *set in concrete*, John and other administrators were asked to review potential enrollments at their schools and review their budgets for the upcoming year.

As John tells the story, "When the meeting was over, people gathered informally to discuss the possible implications for their campuses. I was one of the last to leave, noticed a folder on the table that said Budget Recommendations for the next year. Evidently, the Director of Finance left the folder there after her presentation. I immediately realized the significance of this situation. With knowledge of the budget recommendations to be made to the board, I would be in a better position to defend my school's needs by comparing its budget with others. I could be in a position to either protect my budget or even gain some additional support. Suddenly, I realized my dilemma. Should I look at the budget document or not? Even though it was an *accident* that allowed me this possibility, was it wrong to look at it? Even if I didn't consult the document, but simply returned it to the Director of Finance, she might think I did look at it. Another dilemma I had to consider is should I just leave it and give someone else the advantage in the somewhat competitive budgeting process? I began to think that it was a no-win situation, and I wanted to be in a win-win situation. I realized that ethical behavior is not some abstract notion, but very real."

Kidder (1995) notes that few people have trouble with the big ethical questions such as lying, stealing, and killing. But the nuances of dilemmas, like the budget folder, can confront leaders daily. The really tough choices fall into four general categories or dilemma paradigms. These categories include truth versus loyalty; individual versus community; short-term versus long-term; and justice versus mercy (Kidder, 1995). The truth versus loyalty dilemma occurs when the school leaders withhold some aspect of *truth*. For example, recently in a school, a teacher was reassigned from a regular classroom to a special education position. The teacher was told the reassignment was based on the teacher's potential for working with special needs students. In reality, the teacher was reassigned partly because students in the regular classroom performed poorly on state achievement tests. The administrator was *loyal* to the teacher in protecting a position, but not totally truthful.

Leaders confront the individual versus community dilemma when the needs of one student conflict with the needs of the school. In one school, a student had such severe emotional behavior problems that he was assigned to one teacher all day. In terms of cost, it hardly seems fair and is not cost effective to have a one-on-one situation to meet the needs of a single student. More students could be served if they could be assigned to the teacher as well. To protect the learning of others, one student needed a single teacher, though it required greater resources.

The short-term and long-term dilemma results when expediency is an issue. School leaders may have to address an issue that is immediate and not a part of a long-range plan. For example, when confronted with an emergency (damage to a building), leaders often have to spend their budgeted money to fix a nonbudget problem, hoping to *recover* the money or find additional funds to complete the year without sacrificing more. Such a dilemma often calls for a quick fix at the expense of long-term goals or projects.

The justice versus mercy dilemma can also be common in schools. Leaders are confronted with the need to punish offenders and deliver justice while at the same time trying to show mercy. At a high school, a student was arrested and suspended from school because a gun was found in his vehicle during a routine parking lot search. That morning the student was running late to school, so his dad said "Take my truck." Because the vehicle belonged to his dad, the student did not know the gun was under the seat. Following a zero tolerance policy the board had adopted, the school leader had no choice but to suspend the student. The school leader was confronted with the dilemma of providing justice at the expense of mercy, and the student was punished even though there were extenuating circumstances.

Kidder (1995) also offers leaders steps to follow that may prove helpful in resolving such ethical dilemmas. These steps are based on the leader's ability and willingness to honestly and truthfully search for the right decision. First, determine if there truly is a moral or ethical dilemma. Some situations may initially appear to involve ethical issues when in reality, the issues are superficial and involve manners or social conventions or are based on economic, technological, or aesthetic concerns. For example, cutting in line may be more of a social convention than an ethical dilemma.

Second, after determining if an ethical conflict exists, then the individual should determine if there is a moral or ethical responsibility to do anything about the situation.

Honesty and integrity require the leader to assess the situation within the professional responsibilities of a school administrator rather than on what is personally or politically expedient. The fundamental question to answer is, "Do I have a responsibility here?" For example, a student confides to a school leader that she is afraid she is pregnant. The leader must determine what the leader's responsibility is.

The third step is to gather all relevant data or information. In making an ethical decision, leaders should have as many facts as possible and take the time to make the effort to obtain them. Only in extreme emergencies will leaders have to decide on an issue immediately. Making a decision without pertinent facts and relevant information can make the process seem arbitrary. School leaders must make and take the time to get all the data about the issue or situation before acting. This situation frequently occurs when a student is sent to the office for disciplinary action with only the sketchiest details. Before taking action, the school leader needs to get all the details.

Once a leader has the data or relevant information, the fourth step involves testing for right versus wrong and right versus right issues. In assessing right versus wrong first ask, Was it legal? Was a law broken? If the answer to the second question is yes, the decision then becomes one of enforcing the laws or code. If there is some uncertainty concerning the legal issues, Kidder (1995) provides three other useful tests. The first subtest, the *stench* test, involves asking, "Does this go against my internal moral principles, my own moral compass? If the first reaction is that 'something smells,' then you should go with your own sense of right and wrong." A second test is the *front-page* test and asks the question, "Would you want this decision to be on the headlines of the front page of the newspaper?" If you are concerned about embarrassment that might come from public scrutiny, then you should go with your feelings. The final test is the *mom* test, which asks, "Would you want your mother to know about your actions or decisions?" If the answer is no, then that serves as an internal guide for rightness.

To test the right versus right paradigm, leaders must analyze the situation using the four benchmarks discussed earlier: truth versus loyalty, self versus community, short-term versus long-term, and justice versus mercy. Not only must leaders determine rightness or wrongness, they must also determine if two deeply held core values are in conflict. A school counselor distributed condoms at school. Her motives were right in that she was trying to help prevent teenage pregnancies, but the conflict arose in the community when several parents believed that distributing condoms encouraged promiscuous sexual behavior. The school leader is confronted with two rights.

After the issues have been clarified and the school leader has determined that there is an ethical duty to act, the individual must adopt a line of reasoning that seems relevant and appropriate to the issue at hand. School leaders must realize that in many situations, no clear-cut answer will become apparent, and negotiations, compromise, or win-win agreements will need to be used to validate both sides of the issue.

Finally, school leaders must take action after an often exhaustive, intellectually tiring process. After undergoing this process, there is a danger to regress to what Kidder (1995) calls a "quasi-academic" mind-set that can result in the leader confusing analysis with action and not addressing the dilemma or situation in a practical way. It is obvious that each community requires school leaders to make decisions that are not only tough but have far-reaching consequences. Ethical decisions are not made in isolation, and

those in positions of responsibility must make decisions based on their best understanding of all concerned.

Think back to John and his moral dilemma concerning the budget folder. Faced
with this opportunity, what would you do? What values and beliefs would support your
reasoning? These questions represent the ethics of this situation and require that you
apply some standard of right and wrong as you wrestle with the decision of what to do.
As you critically examine your own beliefs and convictions, you engage in ethical
reasoning. You might reason that the other administrators would take the folder if they
had the opportunity. Or you might justify looking at the document with the good
intentions of trying to protect your faculty and staff from budget cuts. For Adams and
Maine (1998), "some of the most profound and challenging questions any of us can put
to ourselves involve such ethical [decisions]" (p. 2).

Ethical Decisions and Gender Differences

As educators in leadership positions seek to make ethical choices, they must also consider
the context and be sensitive to differences that exist in schools. School leaders must be
particularly aware of gender equity as it relates to both students and professional staff.
Often school leaders are confronted with the dilemma of providing equal opportunities
for male and female students and staff, but lack the rules to enforce such equity.

Gender Equity

Laws are currently in place that affirm the principles of equal rights and equal opportunities regardless of gender. However, progress in gender equity has been slow, and
stereotypical views about women and girls still exist and even prevail in many fields.
According to Kirkpatrick (1996), despite the gains in numbers, top management
positions continue to be dominated by men, with women holding 30 percent of
managerial positions, and only 2 percent of senior executive positions. Adams and Maine
(1998) comment that, "many women . . . perceive that their work is still under-valued
relative to that of men [and] traditional women's professions, such as . . . teaching . . .
have become targets of recent efforts to cut budgets . . ." (p. 285).

Despite an affirmation of equal rights for all, many women continue to suffer the
discouraging reality of discrimination. Educational leaders must be sensitive to all issues
in which gender discrimination exists and seek to make decisions or take action based
on fairness and equity. A continuous dilemma for school leaders is ensuring that in
fostering equal rights and opportunity for one group, the rights of another group are
not compromised. Supporting the cause of those who have been discriminated against
may sometimes give them an advantage. Administrators and board members should
adopt the policy of selecting the best-qualified person for a leadership position without
regard to gender or other subjective criteria.

Title IX, a landmark civil rights law passed in 1972, reinforced the belief that all
Americans should have equal rights and opportunities. The Title IX law prohibited sex
discrimination against all students and employees in federally assisted education pro-

grams, which included most public and private schools, from kindergarten through graduate or professional schools. This law was designed to ensure that policies and programs give boys and girls full and equal access to quality education (Ornstein, 1994). Title IX has impacted all aspects of schooling, achievement, and employment. For girls, passage of the law resulted in lowering the dropout rate among pregnant, high school girls, increased opportunities in math and science, and boosted completion of postsecondary, graduate, and professional degrees (Office of Civil Rights, 1990).

Although progress has resulted from the passage and implementation of Title IX, there are still areas of inequity between the sexes. School leaders must somehow make sense of the equity laws and strive to make ethical decisions concerning programs and policies related to gender bias. Clearly, ethical decisions with regard to gender equity also have legal implications, but a sense of rightness should guide decisions as well as legality.

Equal opportunity and fairness are two of the ethical principles that have been promoted within the broader culture and society. School children depend on educators to address ethical dilemmas related to gender issues with fairness and equity. For example, no easy way exists to determine relationship between self-image and the availability or lack of availability of gender-specific role models in schools. But in many schools, the teaching staff is predominantly female and the administration is predominantly male, and a silent, but powerful message is sent to students. That message suggests that a girl can aspire to be a teacher, but a boy can aspire to be an administrator (Nieto, 1996; Sanders, 1999).

Research has documented that schools are often unequal and unfriendly environments for girls in mathematics, science, and technology, and a growing achievement gap exists between male and female students (Lockheed, 1985; Lucidi, 1994; Sadker & Sadker, 1994). Along with the data that suggest gender preferences for academic subjects, cultural biases also perpetuate many sexist beliefs. According to Cardenas (1994), minority and disadvantaged girls are recipients of discrimination in several forms. Curriculum materials may also contain gender-biased language, content, and illustrations, with boys being portrayed as active and energetic and girls shown to be more passive in watching and waiting (Love, 1993). Gender-biased practices reinforce the idea that some fields are for boys and some are for girls (Colby & Foote, 1995). According to Flynn and Chambers (1994), boys and girls are treated differently in school, and many subtle and unintended culturally biased messages from adults create the idea among girls and boys that there are fields in which they cannot be successful because of gender. As a result, many girls often have lower self-esteem than boys and attribute their successes to luck rather than ability (Sanders, 1999).

An example of gender issues is illustrated in the next View from the Field. Susan Barnes, the new athletic Director, is confronted with several dilemmas in the athletic budget.

In the field of educational leadership, as in the corporate arena, it's still a man's world, especially in positions of CEO or school superintendents (Skrla, 2001). In the corporate world, women still constitute only 10 percent of the CEOs of major corporations (Himelstein, 1996). In education more women have college degrees and frequently more classroom experience, but fewer become school leaders, particularly

View from the Field

Susan Barnes has just accepted the position as Athletic Director for a large suburban school district. She is the first female athletic director in the district and is only one of five in the entire state. In her first week on the job, she has been approached by the girls' volleyball coach with a request for an additional $500 to her budget. This girls' volleyball team has been very successful in the past and is looking forward to another winning season.

As Susan tells the story, "In looking for additional money for the volleyball team, I reviewed the athletic budgets for the school district and discovered significant inequities. Although there were an equal number of girls' and boys' teams, the boys' athletic programs accounted for two-thirds of the total budget. I also discovered that in power lifting, the boys not only had a coach, but the district provided uniforms and travel money. The girls' power lifting team worked out with the boys, but they had to buy their own uniforms and pay their own way to power lifting meets." What started out as a simple request became a very real dilemma in trying to address the inequities in the athletic budget.

Although there are legal issues associated with the discrepancies, there are also ethical issues related to fairness and equity in the athletic programs. Ms. Barnes has been confronted with an ethical dilemma that, according to her, "Depending on the decision I make, could result in losing my job."

superintendents. According to Skrla (2001), "90 percent of all school superintendent jobs in the United States are held by men" (p. 1). Although teaching is a job historically done by women, somehow they hit a dead end with regard to leadership positions. Skrla (2001) offers this comment, "As far as education in the United States is concerned, the message is clear: women teach, but men manage" (p. 1). Clearly the universities that train school leaders and school boards who employ them are confronted with an ethical dilemma: How can they more effectively train and recruit women for leadership positions?

Ethical Decisions and Cultural Diversity

School leaders must be cognizant of the changes that have occurred within society and the wide range of cultural diversity that is represented in the general population. Greenberg and Baron (2000) have identified the following trends, which reflect diversity in the workforce and society:

- More women are in the workplace than ever before.
- Racial and ethnic diversity is a reality.
- People are living and working longer than ever before. (pp. 20–21)

In 1995, Carnevale and Stone observed, which was confirmed in the 2000 Census, that the relative percentage of Asians, Hispanics, and African Americans is rising and in many states and communities the term *minority* is obsolete. Today's schools reflect the cultural pluralism that is prevalent in today's society. For Smither (1998), as more minorities and people from other cultures have been employed, organizations have been faced with the reality that the old ways of working with traditional white men who constituted the workforce of earlier decades no longer are effective. He continues, "To the surprise of many, issues of race and gender . . . have proved to be too complex to be addressed simply through legislation" (p. 34). A society that once used schools as an instrument for creating a homogeneous culture must become a society that not only affirms cultural diversity, but affirms, accepts, and respects differences.

Everyday, school leaders must deal with ethical decisions that address issues of diversity in some way, and ethical dilemmas arise when one or more ethnic or racial groups are put at a disadvantage because of the school policies. Administrators and teachers constantly have to make academic decisions concerning the degree of inclusion into regular education, not only by handicapped students, but in the development of programs that address the needs of migrant, bilingual, low socioeconomic, and minority children. According to Smith, Moallem, and Sherrill (1997), four factors help educators initiate change in their beliefs. These include education, travel, experience with discrimination, and exposure to different cultures.

As school leaders wrestle with making ethical decisions that reflect equity and fairness, they must identify the culturally sensitive issues that impact or influence their thinking and then identify the cultural or equity principle that is being jeopardized or compromised.

What Is Your Ethical IQ?

Being a school leader requires individuals to make ethical decisions. White and Wooten (1986) have suggested that ethical behavior results from the intersection of four constructs: values, norms, science, and laws. They suggest that these constructs help to shape our responses to ethical dilemmas or problems. In the section that follows, there are ten real-life dilemmas from education. Each of the dilemmas requires a choice. Give your first reaction to each question by answering *no, depends,* or *yes.* Your responses should reflect what you believe you would actually do in the situation, not what you think you should do or believe is the best answer.

1. You have just been hired as the new curriculum director for a suburban school district, and you have been attending a conference sponsored by the state educational agency. You had planned to fly home on Saturday, but two friends from a neighboring school district that you met at the conference are driving back by car and have invited you to join them. They suggest that in riding together you can discuss the suggested curriculum changes that were presented at the conference. It would be a good opportunity to network with others on the four-hour trip instead of flying, which would take two hours. In addition, they would drop you off at home and your family would not have to make the thirty-minute drive to the airport to meet you. It would be stimulating to ride back with your new colleagues. You reason that the additional travel time would come out of your pocket, not the school district's. You drive back with your new colleagues, and give them $20.00 for gas at the midpoint of the trip.

    Question: Would you cash in the return ticket and keep the money?

No   Depends   Yes

2. The school district has a strict policy regarding personal appropriation of office supplies. The most competent and longest-tenured secretary is caught by you, her boss, taking boxes of computer disks home in a briefcase. There is a rule against this as well as a clearly defined protocol for securing supplies when working at home. The policy requires that you terminate the secretary.

    Question: Would you make an exception for this loyal worker?

No   Depends   Yes

3. Your school district has just purchased an expensive computer software program for tracking student achievement and your technology person asks if you would like a take-home copy. You know it is protected by copyright.

    Question: Would you let the person make a copy for you?

No   Depends   Yes

4. You are the Director of Assessment in your school district. One of the building principals, a friend of yours, confides to you that the Superintendent wants building level administrators to give vague and misleading information about student performance on state-mandated tests. Your friend is very concerned and wants your advice.

    Question: Would you encourage your friend to follow the Superintendent's suggestion?

No   Depends   Yes

5. Three months ago you established your own educational consulting company. Your first major client is a curriculum development firm that wants you to promote a new mathematics program that is "guaranteed to get immediate results!" Despite your repeated requests, neither the program developers nor the curriculum development company have given you data that support their claim.

    Question: Would you continue to serve as this firm's consultant without substantial proof?

No   Depends   Yes

6. You are the leader of a large school campus. The personnel office has identified two candidates for a math teaching position in your school. The better-qualified candidate could make a significant contribution to the math department but during the interview process appeared to be rather cold and aloof and will likely clash with your personality. The less-qualified candidate is your personal choice, even though the department will not be as well served.

    Question: Would you choose the less-qualified candidate?

No   Depends   Yes

7. You are the athletic director and one of your responsibilities is to oversee the eligibility of athletes. Your school's team has a good chance to make the state playoffs, but must get past this week's strong district rival. One of the starting players is in jeopardy of losing eligibility. One of the teachers comes to you and offers to "insure" that the student remains eligible.

Question: Would you take advantage of this teacher's offer to help keep this athlete eligible?

No   Depends   Yes

8. You recently accepted the position as principal at a large high school. One of your first assignments is to authorize an all expenses paid trip for the senior class sponsor. The four-day trip to Las Vegas is paid for by the vendor who sells senior class rings and invitations on your campus. The trip includes first-class tickets for the sponsor and a companion to stay at a luxury hotel with all meals paid and a $500 honorarium. You know the district policy does not expressly prohibit this and it has been routinely done in the past.

Question: Would you authorize the travel for the senior class sponsor?

No   Depends   Yes

9. You serve as a member of the school policy review committee. Despite attempts to reduce the number, the district has maintained a high rate of dropouts, especially girls. In conducting interviews with administrators in the district, you discover that the Superintendent, because of his "deep religious convictions" has implemented a policy that pregnant students must drop out of school.

Question: Would you let the Superintendent's personal beliefs go unchallenged?

No   Depends   Yes

10. You overhear two coaches in your building discussing the new equipment. While they are excited to have new equipment, they have voiced concerns that because of its design, it "may not adequately protect students"—although, the chance of any serious injury is remote.

Question: Since you are not directly responsible for the students in question, would you completely ignore the comment?

No   Depends   Yes

In scoring your ethical IQ, count the number of responses for No, Depends, or Yes. Take the highest number of your scores in the three categories and multiply it by 100, and then divide the results by 5. This is your Ethical IQ. The average is 100 and a perfect score is 200. If you scored higher than 160 in any of the three categories you are a person with a strong and consistent ethical decision-making pattern (modified from Greenberg & Baron, 2000; and Henderson, 1992).

Case Study

Return to the first dilemma on the ethical IQ. You were just hired as the new curriculum director for a suburban school district. You attended a conference, and you planned to fly home. Eager to make friends and learn the ropes, you met two colleagues from a neighboring school district and you have to decide to fly or drive with them. When you responded *yes*, *no*, or *depends*, thoughts went through your mind. To respond, what came to mind? What ethical issues did you identify? Was it more important for you to change your plans? If so, Why? Or, why not?

You develop the ethical perimeters for this case study using yourself as the new curriculum director. Be sure to respond in writing to the following questions:

1. What is the size of the school district? What are the academic and student population demographics?
2. What are your specific responsibilities?
3. What are the key ethical issues for you in this scenario?
4. What are your concerns?
5. What steps did you follow to come to your conclusions?

Do you see any patterns that would provide insight into your belief structure or ethical stance?

Summary

This chapter has provided an overview of the role of values and ethics in school leadership. Virtually every profession has a code or belief system that governs behavior. School leaders not only have a code of ethics but other guidelines that can assist in the decision-making process.

When school leaders are confronted with ethical dilemmas, they must strive to make the best possible decision. In doing so, they have to ask themselves: Is it legal? Is it balanced? And how will it make me feel about myself? As educational leaders seek to solve ethical dilemmas, they must use the four benchmarks: truth versus loyalty, self versus community, short-term versus long-term, and justice versus mercy.

School leaders also have a responsibility to ethically address gender and diversity issues within the school. Because women are underrepresented as top-level administrators, schools seem to be saying that women are teachers, but men are leaders. Finally, the chapter presented an opportunity to assess your ethical IQ. This survey provides readers the opportunity to assess their own moral compasses as they respond to ethical dilemmas.

Your Turn

3.1. Take a moment and construct a *KWL* chart regarding gender issues (what you know, what you want to know, and what you have learned). Now jot down a few items in each of the columns. There are things that you already knew about the topic of gender and there are things that you learned from reading this chapter, but what do you still want to know? To learn more about the topic of gender equity, you may find the following references helpful:

AAUW Report: How schools shortchange girls. (1992). Annapolis Junction, MD: American Association of Women.

AAUW Report: Growing smart: What's working for girls in schools. (1995).

Checkley, K. (1996). Reducing gender bias in school. *Association for supervision and curriculum development: Education update. 38,* 1, 1, 6, and 8.

Derman-Sparks, L., & the A.B.C. Task Force. (1989). *Anti-bias curriculum: Tools for empowering your children.* Washington, DC: National Association for the Education of Young Children.

Fenema, E., & Peterson, P. (1987). Effective teaching for girls and boys: The same or different. In D. C. Berliner & B. V. Rosinshine (eds), *Talks to Teachers* (pp. 111–125). New York: Random House.

Gollnick, D., & Chinn, P. (1994). *Multicultural education in pluralistic society.* New York: Merrill.

Grossman, H., & Grossman, S. H. (1994). *Gender issues in education.* Boston: Allyn & Bacon.

Paley, V. (1984). *Boys and girls.* Chicago: University of Chicago Press.

3.2. As campus leaders, what steps can you take to ensure that teachers are informed about issues of bias in their classes? What can you do to enrich the professional lives of teachers as they plan and teach? To assist others means starting with yourself.

  a. What are your attitudes and bias toward diversity? Think about when you were a child; can you remember the first incident that could be called *bias* at home, in school, or with friends? Jot those incidences down and reflect on them. Are there patterns or trends?

  b. For the next few days, think about how you interact with students and teachers and jot these down in your journal.

  c. Over the next several weeks, take a trip to the school library and visit classrooms and assess the types of materials and resources that are available—what literature is provided? What materials for students to use in the centers in classrooms? And assess textbooks and media materials. What traditional and nontraditional role models are presented?

3.3. Your administrative role is changing and after fifteen years as an elementary principal in a once rural school district that is rapidly becoming more urban and extremely diverse, you are now required to complete compliance modules as are your teachers. You decide that having small gatherings with representatives from each grade level is better than having one big session with everyone attending and all members of the same grade level at one time. Your goal is to get collective thinking that is aligned vertically. You decide to use books to get the discussions about stereotyping started. Read the following children's books to prepare for these gatherings:

dePaulo, T. (1979). *Oliver button is a sissy.* New York: Harcourt, Brace, Jovanovich.
Hoffman, M. (1991). *Amazing Grace.* New York: Dial Books for Young Readers.
Zolotow, C. (1972). *William's doll.* New York: HarperCollins.

Now that you have read these books, how can you use them to spark honest dialogue among the teachers? How can you facilitate true reflection about their beliefs and feelings? What questions will you ask to prompt discussion?

References

Adams, D. M., & Maine, E. W. (1998). *Business ethics for the 21st century.* Mountain View, CA: Mayfield Publishing.

Beck, L. G., & Murphy, J. (1994). *Ethics in educational leadership programs: An expanding role.* Thousand Oaks, CA: Corwin Press.

Behr, E. T. (1998). Acting from the center. *Management Review, 87,* 3, 51–60.

Bersoff, D. N. (1996). The virtue of principle ethics. *The Counseling Psychologist, 24,* 1, 86–91.

Blanchard, K., & Peale, N. V. (1988). *The power of ethical management.* New York: William Morrow.

Campbell, E. (1997). Ethical school leadership: Problems of an elusive role. *Journal of School Leadership,* 7, 3, 287–300.

Cardenas, J. (1994 March). A comprehensive approach to gender equity. *IDRA Newsletter, 21,* 3, 3–4.

Carnevale, A. P., & Stone, S. C. (1995). *The American mosaic: An in-depth report on the future of diversity at work.* New York: McGraw-Hill.

Colby, A., & Foote, E. (1995). Creating and maintaining a diverse faculty. ERIC Clearinghouse for Community Colleges, Los Angeles, CA. ERIC Document Number ED 386 261.

Corey, G., Corey, M. S., & Callanan, P. (1998). *Issues and ethics in the helping professions* (5th ed). Pacific Grove, CA: Brooks/Cole Publishing.

Creighton, T. (1999, April 6). Spirituality and the new principalship: Leadership for the new millennium. *International Electronics Journal for Leadership in Learning,* 3, 11 [on-line]. Available http://www.ucalgary.ca/iejll.

Czaja, M., & Lowe, J. (2000). Preparing leaders for ethical decisions. *The AASA Professor, 24,* 1, 7–11.

Flynn, V., & Chambers, R. D. (1994). Promoting gender equity: What you can do. *Learning, 22,* 5, 58–59.

Greenberg, R. A., & Baron, J. (2000). *Behavior in organizations* (7th ed). Upper Saddle River, NJ: Prentice-Hall.

Herlihy, B., & Remley, T. P. (1995). Unified ethical standards: A challenge for professionalism. *Journal of Counseling & Development,* 74, 2, 130–134.

Henderson, V. E. (1992). *What's ethical in business.* New York: McGraw-Hill.

Himelstein, L. (1996, October 28). Shatterproof glass ceiling. *Business Week,* 55.

Kidder, R. M. (1995). *How good people make tough choices.* New York: Simon & Schuster.

Kirkpatrick, D. D. (1996, October 18). Women occupy few top jobs, a study shows. *Wall Street Journal,* p. A7A.

Kitchener, K. S. (1984). Intuition, critical evaluation, and ethical principles: The foundation for ethical decisions in counseling psychology. *The Counseling Psychologist, 12,* 3, 43–55.

Lanning, W. (1997). Ethical codes and responsible decision-making. In J. A. Kottler (ed), *Finding your way as a counselor.* Alexandra, VA: American Counseling Association.

Lockheed, M. (1985). Sex equity in the classroom organization and climate. In S. Klein (ed), *Handbook for achieving sex equity in education.* pp. 189–217. Baltimore, MD: Johns Hopkins University Press.

Love, R. (1993 February). Gender bias: Inequities in the classroom. *IDRA Newsletter, 20,* 2, 8, 11–12.

Lucidi, A. D. (1994 April). Gender equity in education: A review of the literature. ERIC Document Number ED 374 044.

Maxwell, J. C. (1999). *The 21 indispensable qualities of a leader.* Nashville, TN: Thomas Nelson.

McKerrow, K. (1997). Ethical administration: An oxymoron? *Journal of School Leadership,* 7, 2, 210–225.

Meara, N. M., Schmidt, L. D., & Day, J. D. (1996). Principles and virtues: A foundation for ethical decisions, policies, and character. *The Counseling Psychologist, 24,* 1, 4–17.

Nieto, S. (1996). *Affirming diversity.* New York: Longman.

Office of Civil Rights (1990). Women in school administration: Overcoming the barriers to advancement. Washington, DC. ERIC Document Number ED 336 608.

Ornstein, P. (1994). School girls: Young women, self-esteem, and the confidence gap. *WEEA Digest.* Washington, DC: AAUW Educational Foundation.

Osland, J. S., Kolb, D. A., & Rubin, I. M. (2001). *Organizational behavior* (7th ed). Upper Saddle River, NJ: Prentice-Hall.

Razik, T. A., & Swanson, A. D. (2001). *Fundamental concepts of educational leadership* (2nd ed). pp. 366–367. Upper Saddle River, NJ: Merrill Prentice-Hall.

Sadker, M., & Sadker, D. (1994). *Failing at fairness: How America's schools cheat girls.* New York: Macmillan.

Sanders, J. (1999). Teacher education and gender equity. ERIC Clearinghouse on Teaching and Teacher Education. ERIC Document Number ED 408 277.

Skrla, L. (September 9, 2001). Textbook example of a gender gap. *Fort Worth Star Telegram:* Fort Worth, 1F, 6F.

Smith, R., Moallem, M., & Sherrill, D. (1997). How preservice teachers think about cultural diversity: A closer look at factors which influence their beliefs towards equality. *Educational Foundations, 11*, 2, 41–61.

Smither, R. D. (1998). *The psychology of work and human performance.* New York: Longman.

White, L. P., & Wooten, K. C. (1986). *Professional ethics and practice in organizational development: A systematic analysis of issues, alternatives, and approaches.* New York: Praeger.

Yates, A. C. (2000). Good leaders must first be good people. In L. Orozco (ed), *Educational leadership,* pp. 56–57. Bellevue, WA: Coursewise.

4

Legal Issues and School Leadership

ISLLC Standards

Standard 1: A school administrator is an educational leader who promotes the success of all students by facilitating the development, articulation, implementation, and stewardship of a vision of learning that is shared and supported by the school community.

Standard 3: A school administrator is an educational leader who promotes the success of all students by ensuring management of the organization, operations, and resources for a safe, effective, and efficient learning environment.

Standard 5: A school administrator is an educational leader who promotes the success of all students by acting with integrity, fairness, and in an ethical manner.

Standard 6: A school administrator is an educational leader who promotes the success of all students by understanding, responding to, and influencing the larger political, social, economic, legal, and cultural context.

Chapter Objectives

The objectives of this chapter are:

- Discuss the legal requirements that impact the curriculum.
- Identify and discuss the legal aspects of religion as part of the curriculum.
- Discuss the legal issues associated with school reform and higher academic standards.
- Identify and apply federal laws and policies that pertain to personnel decisions including employment and dismissal.
- Identify and apply federal laws and policies that relate to decisions regarding students including privacy, school safety, and sexual harassment.
- Discuss the legal implications related to school operations and programs including student supervision, transportation, and extracurricular activities.

With the passage of the *No Child Left Behind Act*, it has become clear that knowledge of federal legislation as well as state statutes is important for school leaders. A basic knowledge of the legal framework of the educational milieu is necessary because the law impacts every facet of school operations, from curricular activities to extracurricular activities. Formal legal training, though certainly beneficial, is not expected of educators, but given the increasingly litigious nature of our society, a strong foundation in legal issues affecting schools is helpful to today's school leaders. For example, a review of the current state of special education illustrates how pervasive the law is on teaching and learning schools (Redfield, 2001). Several sources of law can inform and guide the actions of school leaders. While constitutional law is the primary source of law in the United States, no provision exists in the United States Constitution requiring the federal government to provide public education. The tenth amendment to the U.S. Constitution provides that powers not delegated to the federal government nor prohibited by the constitution become reserved powers of the states. Rothstein (2000) notes that "All states have, by virtue of that authority, provided for public education, either by state constitution or by state statute or both" (p. 1).

Statutory law is another source and consists of the legislation passed by the lawmaking bodies at the federal and state levels. For example, federal statutes that directly affect public education include the *Individuals with Disabilities Education Act* and *Improving America's Schools Act.* However, because provisions for public education reside with the states, state legislatures have the greatest impact on public education. Although considerable consistency exists across the states, each state enacts statutes (or laws) unique to that state (Yell, 1998).

Another source is case law, which is developed through the court systems. Because case law is often the most visible aspect of the legal system, it is the type of law most people envision when discussing the American legal system. By their actions relating to public education, federal and state courts have had a major impact on schools. For example, the 1954 Supreme Court decision in *Brown v. Board of Education of Topeka* resulted in the desegregation of our public schools and a greater integration of American society.

Laws passed by legislative bodies often provide only a "general framework of policy relating to a particular issue" (Rothstein, 2000, p. 2). Members of the legislative bodies rarely have expertise in the areas covered by the laws passed, so they delegate administrative bodies to refine the policy through regulations. Therefore, regulatory law is also a source, and as it is developed, it must be consistent with the enabling statutory law. Regulatory law results in specific policy implementation guidelines (Yell, 1998). For example, a state legislative body may pass a law requiring that all students pass an examination before they can graduate, but the legislature delegates to the state educational commission the authority to develop the test and the guidelines for administering and passing the test.

Although entire books and courses are devoted to school law, this chapter provides an overview of the major educational issues that have legal implications. The discussion of legal issues is not exhaustive and serves only as a general framework for school leaders to use as they sort through legal questions regarding personnel, test security and administration, and Title IX, to name a few. This chapter focuses primarily on constitutional statutory and case law. It begins with a discussion of curriculum issues that school leaders encounter on a regular basis. It also presents student and school personnel issues that often propel school leaders into the courts. Special attention is given to concerns related to school violence because of the increase of violent acts in the schools. Finally, the chapter addresses school operations and programs, specifically, the supervision of students during transportation and off-campus activities.

Legal Requirements and the Curriculum

Other than addressing constitutional freedoms of religion, press, and speech, the courts have had little impact on public school curriculum. Generally, curricular issues have been left to state and local educational entities. Political forces have had a greater effect on curriculum development and implementation than legal forces. Likewise, curriculum conflicts are often in response to conflicts over culture and power (Spring, 1998). As Pullin (1999) notes, "curricular decisions are influenced by the social, cultural, economic, and political forces at work at the time the curriculum is adopted" (p. 18).

Although judges have rendered decisions that have directly impacted the public school curriculum, most justices have been hesitant to engage in curriculum development via the courts. This hands-off attitude is reflected in the case of *School District of Abington Township v. Schempp* (1963), in which Justice Brennan argued that educators should make curricular decisions, not the justices, because educators ". . . are experts in such matters, and we are not . . . , [and] any attempt by this Court to announce curricular standards would be to decree a uniform, rigid and, if we are consistent, an unchanging standard for countless school boards" (p. 303).

Some notable curricular issues, however, directly affect the general public and generate a sense of passion rivaled only by religious fervor. The inclusion of religion, sex, and race into school curricula tends to play on the emotions of various members of the community. Reform efforts that have increased graduation standards and include high-stakes testing have generated the same sense of excitement. In discussing the raising of standards, Monk and Hussain (1998) explain that although there appears to be considerable support for the raising of standards, there are also concerns. Initial concerns center on the cost of the implementation of the standards and the implications for teachers. Other concerns focus on "what will happen to students who for whatever reason find it difficult if not impossible to perform at the expected levels" (p. 245).

Contrary to popular belief, the Supreme Court has not mandated that religion be excluded from public schools, but has provided direction with regard to specific issues. For example, schools may legitimately study about religion (*Florey v. Souix Falls School District*, 1980), but school-led prayers and Bible readings are unconstitutional (*Abington v. Schempp*, 1963). The politically popular act of posting the Ten Commandments has also been found to be unconstitutional (*Stone v. Graham*, 1981).

Federal legislation, however, has been used to craft the public school curriculum, mostly in the areas of special education, bilingual education, and the education of the disadvantaged. Federal involvement is generally persuasive, using federal funds to encourage states and schools to adhere to national policies. Attempts by the federal government to become intricately involved in educational issues by means of coercion have not proven to be successful (Jaffe, 1999), and such action would be in direct conflict with federal law. In U.S.C.S. 1232(a), Congress proclaims that

> No provision of any applicable program shall be construed to authorize any department, agency, officer, or employee of the United States to exercise any direction, supervision, or control over the curriculum, program of instruction, administration, or personnel of any educational institution, school, or school system.

Regardless, federal policy has had a significant impact on public education, and providing parents with alternatives to a traditional public education is a current national trend. Choice options for parents include charter schools and voucher systems. Charter schools are public schools or "another governmental entity" that operates without the "restraints of school district governance" (Perkins-Gough, 2002, p. 90). Recent legislation in many states indicates that state governments support the charter school concept (Dagley, 2001). Because charter schools are governmental institutions and operate as a governmental agent, few federal constitutional claims arise regarding charter schools.

Voucher plans, on the other hand, often deviate from direct governmental oversight. Voucher plans allow public school students to redeem state-provided monies (vouchers) at the public or private schools of their choosing (McCarthy, Cambron-McCabe, & Thomas, 1998). Consequently, federal legislation and litigation regarding vouchers are on the increase.

The *No Child Left Behind Act* of 2001 amended and reauthorized the *Elementary and Secondary Education Act* of 1965 and serves "as the primary federal policy tool to deliver educational services to disadvantaged children and youth" (American Association of Colleges for Teacher Education, 2002, p. 1). Among other policy initiatives, the *No Child Left Behind Act* provides federal resources to support state and local attempts to improve the education of children most at risk, with an emphasis on K–3 reading instruction. The law also calls for "providing alternatives to students in [low performing] schools to enable the students to receive a high quality education" (20 U.S.C. § 6301 [4]). Alternatives to public education have received support from the courts. In *Zelman v. Simmons-Harris, et al.* (2002), the U.S. Supreme Court held that the Ohio Pilot Project Scholarship Program did not violate the Establishment Clause although most of the students participating in the program used public money to attend religiously affiliated schools. The Ohio Pilot Project Scholarship Program is a voucher program enacted to assist low-income students in a public school system identified as one of the nation's worst performing systems. Although to this date, the use of voucher plans has not been extensive, the Zelman case will likely encourage school choice advocates to push for the implementation of voucher programs on a much greater scale.

Research regarding the effectiveness of charter schools and voucher programs is inconclusive (Perkins-Gough, 2002). The federal government appears willing to support both options for school choice, but the state legislature has the plenary power to carry out the education function of the state, and the state courts decide questions of state law. Thus, true power and control over the public school curriculum resides with the states.

State Control of Curriculum

Every state has statutory prescriptions concerning public school curriculum (Reutter, 1994), and every state relies on its legislature to specify the curriculum in its public schools (Imber & van Geel, 2000). Since the publication of *A Nation at Risk* in 1983, states have honed the curriculum as a mechanism for improving student performance (Kemerer & Walsh, 2000). In fact, Imber and van Geel (2000) persuasively argue that "the state legislature may, if it wishes prescribe the basic course of study down to the last detail . . ." (p. 60). Yet, state legislatures rarely are so definitive. Apart from establishing minimum standards and certain basic content, states, to differing degrees, delegate curriculum matters to state administrative agencies or local boards (Reutter, 1994). While states such as New York encourage districts to raise standards to be in compliance with rigorous state examinations (Monk & Hussain, 1998), other states provide wide authority to state officials to develop a mandatory statewide curriculum. Local boards then adopt reasonable rules and standards for students within each school district (Alexander & Alexander, 1984, p. 30).

Because of dissatisfaction with the achievement results in public schools, states have implemented numerous reforms in an attempt to improve student performance, and school leaders have been thrust into the forefront of such efforts. Although the ultimate benefits of these reforms are still in question, since 1980 at least forty-five states have raised requirements for earning a high school diploma (Rebell & Hughes, 1996). Raising academic standards is often an emotional issue, and parents and advocacy groups have challenged the authority of state and local policymakers on many of the reform policies. Given the general understanding that local factors dictate the level of policy implementation (Spillane, 1998), the courts have generally recognized the authority of the local policymakers, as the ultimate responsibility for establishing courses and course content (Reutter, 1994).

It should be noted that some exceptions exist to the establishment of local policy. For example, religious celebrations have no place in public schools. Such events present a dilemma to educators on how to address community demands that these activities be incorporated into the school curriculum (Fischer, Schimmel, & Kelly, 1999, p. 211). School leaders should work with faculty in emphasizing the secular nature of the celebrations, which often accompany the religious celebrations. For example, teaching the virtues of giving and posting the likeness of Santa Claus is easier to defend in a court of law than displaying nativity scenes or telling stories of Hanukkah.

Sex-education curriculum is another area that often creates local controversy. It should be noted that controversies about sex education are often religiously motivated and arise over conflicts with differing ideologies (Wirt & Kirst, 1997). However, states often take a more directive posture with the sex education curriculum than they do with infusing religion into the curriculum. For example, a Louisiana statute explicitly defines sex education as "the dissemination of factual biological or pathological information," and further directs how the topic will be taught (Imber & van Geel, 2000, p. 64).

Another curriculum *hot topic* with legal implications is the collision of conflicting theories of creation science and evolution science in the schools. Possibly the most notable conflict occurred in the case known as the Scopes Monkey Trial (*Scopes v. State*, 1926). In this case, a Tennessee statute made the teaching of the theory of evolution a criminal offense and it was not overturned. Scopes was convicted in the trial, but little enforcement of the state subsequently occurred (Alexander & Alexander, 2001). Based partly on the Establishment Clause, other state laws that require the teaching of the creationist theory of evolution have been held unconstitutional (see *Epperson v. Arkansas*, 1968; *Freiler v. Tangipahoa Parish Board of Education*, 1999). In an attempt to present a balanced teaching approach, states have tried alternative approaches with limited success. In the case of *Edwards v. Aguillard* (1985), a Louisiana statute that required the equal treatment of creation science and evolution science was overturned. Two other states avoided the courts by using political strategies to address the creation science–evolution science issue. In 1999, the State Board of Education in Kansas voted to remove evolution from the state's curriculum and Kentucky's State Board of Education "voted to discontinue the use of the word 'evolution' from course materials in the state's high schools" (Alexander & Alexander, 2001, p. 316). These political moves will likely be challenged in the near future. An additional issue involves "the arguments that teaching a materialist version of human origins advances secular-humanism," a form of religion that has not been supported by the courts (Valente & Valente, 2001, p. 66).

Yes	No	Questions	Notes
		Is the curriculum free of promoting any single religion over others?	
		Is the curriculum aligned with state or national standards and with test objectives that would allow students to be successful?	
		Does the curriculum address emotion-laden issues such as sex and the origin of humans in a manner that is politically acceptable at the local and state levels?	
		Do classroom and school-wide celebrations reflect sensitivity to students from all cultures and students with varying religious beliefs?	

FIGURE 4.1 *Legal Checklist for Curriculum Issues.* When reviewing your curriculum and curricular practices, check for potential legal and political problems. During review, ask yourself the questions and respond using the chart.

School leaders at the local level have considerable discretion in determining what is to be taught in the schools. Often, state regulatory bodies provide guidance for a local education with a general curriculum. More importantly, however, school leaders must be cognizant of the local politics, which often determine the local curriculum. A wise school leader remains current on the legal and political ramifications of curricular decisions, especially as these decisions relate to the emotionally volatile subjects of sex and religion. Figure 4.1 provides a quick checklist of questions that school leaders can use in making decisions regarding the legality of curricular issues.

To illustrate how legal issues can affect the curriculum, the principal in the View from the Field is having to deal with a parent complaint about the teaching of evolution in the biology curriculum.

View from the Field

Recently, Opal Washington, principal of a large urban high school, received a complaint from a parent about the subject matter being taught in a biology class. Mr. Hernandez teaches the theory of evolution in his biology class. When she questioned him, Ms. Washington discovered that he begins the unit by "announcing that there are competing theories about how humans developed, but I am going to present to you the only theory that is supported by the scientific community." The parent of one of his biology students and a community leader objected and demanded that the biology curriculum include a discussion on the creationism as presented in the Christian *Bible*. Ms. Washington is aware of the political implications associated with this curriculum decision, but now she says, "I have to consider the legal implications while addressing this parent's concern. I'll begin by reviewing the state's curriculum framework as well as the rulings by the State Board of Education and legislation regarding the Education Code."

Technology and the Law

Technology is advancing at an overwhelming rate. At the same time, school leaders are required to address the many challenges that accompany the technological advancement. On one hand, school leaders must address legislation that reflects the efforts of state policy makers to implement technology in the schools. On the other hand, school leaders must address legislation and litigation related to the use of technology in the schools.

Technology such as the use of videotapes and videotaped television broadcasts has been common in schools for quite some time. However, the use of computers, computer software, and the Internet are relatively new technological developments. Policy makers and the courts are struggling with related issues such as providing technological infrastructure, copyright guidelines, and acceptable use policies.

At the same time, school administrators must be aware of the "huge potential for litigation against educational institutions under the American with Disabilities Act for not having accessible web sites" (Issues faced by schools, 2002, p. 2). The *Americans with Diabilities Act* is similar to Section 504 of the *Rehabilitation Act of 1973*, which prohibits discrimination against individuals with disabilities. In their enthusiasm to provide information to district patrons via the Internet, school leaders may inadvertently overlook accessibility issues related to disabled patrons and students. For example, audio clips without accompanying words or graphs may be inaccessible to the hearing impaired. The extent to which districts must provide accessibility for individuals with disabilities is still unclear. However, school leaders would be wise to consider accessibility when designing web sites.

Instructional Initiatives

State legislatures have passed legislation to encourage or require schools to infuse technology into the curriculum. Many states including California, Hawaii, Illinois, Oklahoma, Ohio, and Texas provide grants or other financial assistance to schools to integrate technology into their instructional programs (Dagley, 2001). As a result, teachers are "integrating these resources into original works providing greater flexibility for instruction and learning" (Lane, Van Berkum, & Richardson, 2000, p. 341). Although teachers and other school officials need a greater understanding of copyright laws as a result of the infusion of technology, it is unlikely that necessary additional training is provided. An obvious preventative measure is to provide the necessary training in relevant copyright laws. Regardless, Lane, Van Berkum, and Richardson suggest that school officials try to obtain permission when using copyrighted works, maintain caution when downloading material from the Internet because much of the work is copyright protected, and "exercise integrity when altering another's works and advise your audience to the alternations" (p. 348).

Along with the increased access to technology and information, school leaders will be forced into the conflict generated between students' right to information and schools' (i.e., school boards, parents, school officials) authority to control access to information.

Under the *Children's Internet Protection Act*, the federal government requires agencies that receive federal funds to install filters on computers connected to the Internet. Many school districts have followed the example set by the federal government and implemented policies requiring software to filter access to unsuitable Internet sites. Although case law regarding filtering software in school systems is scant, a federal district court in Pennsylvania held that the federal government cannot require libraries receiving federal funds to install the software filters (Library filtering law, 2002). Regardless, censorship battles regarding the Internet and other forms of technology are likely to increase, just as the censorship issues relating to instructional materials increased in the 1980s and 1990s (McCarthy, Cambron-McCabe, & Thomas, 1998).

School Personnel

School personnel who deliver the curriculum and the students who receive it constitute the very heart of public schools. When making decisions regarding school personnel and students, school leaders must use knowledge of local, state, and federal laws and policies. Entire courses are devoted to personnel and resource management, and the intent here is to highlight major issues leaders should consider concerning school personnel decisions.

Because student performance has been directly linked to the quality of teaching, one of the most important tasks of any school leader is hiring a competent and qualified staff (Darling-Hammond, 2000). With the recent debate about the impact of a pending teacher shortage, a consensus exists that millions of teachers will need to be hired to fill classrooms in the next few years (Wayne, 2000; Fetler, 1997). Locating qualified teachers generally means locating teachers with a state-issued teaching credential (Imber & van Geel, 2000). A teaching credential from one state does not ensure employment, as states and local districts may impose additional requirements (Reutter, 1994). For example, states or districts may require the applicant to (1) live within the boundaries of the district, (2) pledge loyalty to the state or federal constitution, (3) pass a state or national examination, or (4) subject himself or herself to an examination of criminal records (Alexander & Alexander, 1998).

In addition to hiring competent teachers, school leaders are also responsible for removing marginal or inept teachers. Dismissing an incompetent teacher is a time-consuming and often difficult process that requires significant documentation. As a result, astute school leaders do their best to locate the best possible teachers for the positions. The extra care taken to locate and hire competent teachers can lessen the need to make adverse personnel decisions at a later date. In the selection process, school leaders must be diligent, fair, consistent, and use job-related criteria because as Greenberg (1997) notes, "employee selection results in more job discrimination problems than any other personnel practices" (p. 37).

To avoid possible future litigation, school leaders should be knowledgeable of civil rights statutes as they relate to hiring practices. Title VII of the *Civil Rights Act of 1964* requires that employers not discriminate on the basis of an "individual's race, color, religion, sex, or national origin." The following are legally defensible hiring guidelines:

- Employment practices must be applied uniformly, because altering the selection process from applicant to applicant can lead to discriminatory practices (Aquila & Petzke, 1994).
- Employment standards or job criteria must be job-related (Greenberg, 1997; see also *Griggs v. Duke Power Company*, 1971).
- Hiring decisions must be neutral to race, religion, sex, national origin (Title VII of the *Civil Rights Act of 1964*), disability (*Americans with Disabilities Act of 1990*), or age (*Age Discrimination in Employment Act of 1967*).

While hiring decisions are often the primary responsibility of personnel offices or directors, in many schools, especially small schools, the campus leader is responsible for recommending the hiring of all personnel to the board of trustees. To assist school leaders in hiring employees, Rebore (1995) provides a ten-step process:

1. Write a job description that includes a summary of the job responsibilities, job tasks, minimal job qualifications, and the relationship of the job to others in the organization.
2. Establish the selection criteria that defines the characteristics of the individual that will ensure success on the job. Use the selection criteria to develop interview questions.
3. Write the job announcement, advertise the position, and establish a closing date.
4. Receive and review applications.
5. Select the candidates to be interviewed; the number of candidates to be interviewed depends on the number of applicants and the nature of the job (i.e., for teaching positions, it is common to interview three to five people).
6. Interview candidates.
7. Check references and credentials; evaluating references can be a difficult task that is expensive and time consuming, especially when conducting criminal background checks required or allowed by many states. Failure to conduct background checks may lead to considerable liability on the part of the district.
8. Select the best candidate; the best candidate will usually be the one who scored highest on the selection criteria.
9. Issue a job offer and receive letter of acceptance.
10. Notify unsuccessful candidates that the position has been filled.

Because schools are becoming more inclusive in the decision-making process, interviews conducted by groups of teaches are becoming common. To prevent a member of the interview team from asking a legally inappropriate question, it is best to have the questions prepared in advance and ask the same questions of all applicants. Each member of the team rates the candidate's response to the question on a predetermined scoring rubric. Throughout the interview process, the interviewers must evaluate the candidate's responses in light of the selection criteria (Rebore, 1995). To examine the hiring

Yes	No	Questions	Notes
		Does the hiring process discriminate against any individual because of his or her placement in a legally protected category (i.e., sex, age, race, ethnicity, religious belief, disability, national origin)?	
		Are the interviewers trained to focus on objective, job-related characteristics consistent with the advertised position?	
		Does the hiring process ensure the best available candidate will be selected?	

FIGURE 4.2 *Legal Checklist for Hiring Practices.* Public school hiring practices are coming under greater legal scrutiny. Review your hiring practices, ask yourself the questions and respond using the chart.

practices that are used in their school districts, principals may find the checklist in Figure 4.2 helpful.

In the following View from the Field, the principal has involved teachers in school personnel decisions, but has been presented with a legal issue involving interview questions in the process.

In the unfortunate event that a teacher needs to be dismissed, school leaders must follow established procedures diligently. School leaders have the task of determining the professional competence of teachers, and the dismissal of a teacher cannot be arbitrary. Typically, state law determines the acceptable reasons for teacher dismissal as well as the procedure for such dismissals (LaMorte, 1999). Many of the reasons for dismissal are unrelated to the performance of the individuals as a teacher in the

View from the Field

Recently, a number of teachers have left the MacArthur Academy for the Sciences, a prestigious magnet school, which has resulted in a number of vacancies. As Mr. Ngyun, the Principal, describes the process: "I believe in including school personnel in the hiring process, so I decided to include teachers in the interview process for prospective teachers." To maintain consistency and fairness, Mr. Ngyun says, "I held a meeting with the teachers and at that meeting we (1) developed a list of questions that would be asked of the candidates for the positions;

(2) developed a rating scale for each question so that responses could be scored fairly; and (3) discussed the types of incidental (ice breaker) questions that should not be asked." However, during the interview process, one of the teachers inadvertently asked the candidate about the church she was attending. This has created a potential legal issue for Mr. Ngyun, and he called the interview committee together to remind them of inappropriate questions during the inteview process.

classroom (Trebilcock, 2000). As a general rule, state laws generally provide for dismissal for insubordination, incompetency, immoral conduct, neglect of duty, violation of contract or regulations, revocation of a teaching certificate, and/or a reduction in force (Alexander &Alexander, 2001; LaMorte, 1999; Elizalde, 1998; Brown & Scheider-Vogel, 1996; Aquila & Petzke, 1994). State laws also provide for fairness in the dismissal process by requiring procedural due process rights. According to Aquila and Petzke (1994), due process protections commonly include notification of intent to dismiss, reasons given for the dismissal, as well as provisions for a hearing. Teachers also have the opportunity to review the evidence, confront the accuser(s), be represented by counsel, and provide witnesses and evidence in their own behalf.

The pending teacher shortage combined with increasing accountability require-ments highlight the importance of recruiting and selecting qualified and competent school personnel. Consequently, it is more important than ever for school leaders to become familiar with local, state, and federal guidelines for hiring and dismissing school personnel. Failure to remain current on legally supportable hiring and dismissal practices may leave school leaders with a less than able staff and a poor learning environment for students, not to mention the possibilities for law suits.

School Safety

School tragedies such as the shootings at Columbine High School in Littleton, Colo-rado, have placed greater emphasis on student safety (Kemerer & Walsh, 2000, p. 61). A Phi Delta Kappa/Gallup Poll indicates that among other things parents are concerned about lack of discipline, fighting/violence/gangs, and use of drugs (Rose & Gallup, 2000), despite the fact that in 1994 Congress passed the *Safe Schools Act* so that "every school in America will be free of drugs and violence and will offer a disciplined environment conducive to learning, by ensuring that all schools are safe and free of violence" (20 U.S.C.S. § 5961 [a]).

Student Violence

Policymakers have struggled with how to address the increases in student violence (Chamberlin, 1999). Rose and Gallup (2002) note that the concern about school safety has led to greater parental support for *zero tolerance* policies. States such as Massachusetts and Michigan have stringent zero tolerance laws that have led to a radical increase in student expulsions (Pullin, 1999, p. 14). Other states have taken equally strong stands against student violence, but have also made it quite clear that attempts should be made to keep students in school (Kemerer & Walsh, 2000, p. 272).

In addition to these efforts by state and federal authorities to control drugs, guns, and violence (Chamberlin, 1999), local boards are empowered with the authority to establish safe school guidelines and rules for student conduct and disciplinary proce-dures. Imber and van Geel (2000) note that "the law will support school officials when they act reasonably to promote safety and order, but care must be taken not to punish unpopular behavior when there is no legitimate reason to do so" (p. 140).

To promote student safety, school officials should establish reasonable rules of conduct, place the rules in writing, and communicate the rules to the students and parents. The rules should be clearly written in enough detail so that the student understands acceptable and unacceptable behavior. Welsh (2000) suggests "school-based programs that attempt to increase children's school effort, encourage positive associations, and demonstrate that obeying the rules will result in valued rewards may also provide critical foundations for reducing school disorder" (p. 103). Care should be taken not to establish rules that unreasonably limit the students' constitutionally protected freedoms, such as freedom to assemble, freedom of speech, and freedom to practice religious beliefs (see *Tinker v. Des Moines*, 1969, and *New Jersey v. TLO*, 1985).

Corporal Punishment

Frequently, schools use corporal punishment as a disciplinary technique to address school violence and other inappropriate acts. No universally accepted definition of corporal punishment exists, but it is generally considered to be the use of force to correct or control a child's behavior (Imbrogno, 2000). Most people associate corporal punishment with paddling, but corporal punishment may also include having students hold heavy objects for extended periods of time, run a measured distance, or pinching them on the ear or arm.

The U.S. Supreme Court has held that corporal punishment is not a violation of the Eighth Amendment to the U.S. Constitution (*Ingraham v. Wright*, 1977), but it continues to be a highly controversial disciplinary technique. Although many states prohibit the use of corporal punishment in the schools, twenty-four states currently allow corporal punishment as a behavior management technique (Essex, 1999), which results in its use over one million times each year (Adams, 2000).

Those who support corporal punishment argue that it instills respect, teaches students to obey authority, and builds character. Prevention of violence in schools legitimizes the use of violence (corporal punishment) as a socially acceptable means of responding to aggressive behavior. Imbrogno (2000) points out that opponents see corporal punishment as "ineffective, and can have harmful effects on children" (p. 141). These arguments have been persuasive enough to convince prestigious groups such as the American Academy of Pediatrics (2000) to call for the abolishment of corporal punishment in all states. In spite of these recommendations and provided that it has not been prohibited by the state, corporal punishment may be used as a disciplinary technique regardless of the parents' wishes (*Baker v. Owen*, 1975). However, before using corporal punishment, school officials should consider "the nature of the infraction; the student's past record, age, sex, and mental and physical condition; and the suitability of the instrument and the force employed" (Valente & Valente, 2001, p. 103). From a legal standpoint, it is generally agreed that school officials should avoid the use of corporal punishment as a means of behavior management.

Sexual Harassment

Imber and van Geel (2000) note that sexual harassment as impermissible conduct had its origins in employment law. Harassment on the basis of sex is a violation of Title VII of the *Civil Rights Act of 1964*, and federal law deems it an unlawful practice for any employer "to discriminate against any individual . . . because of such individual's race, color, religion, sex, or national origin" (42 U.S.C.A. 2000-e [a][1]). The Code of Federal Regulations defines sexual harassment as "conduct that has the purpose or effect of unreasonably interfering with an individual's work performance or creating an intimidating, hostile, or offensive work environment" (29 Code of Federal Regulations, 1604.11). This definition sets up the first form of harassment—hostile environment sexual harassment. For behavior to be considered sexual harassment it must be severe or pervasive, unwelcome, and based on the victim's sex (Grover, 2000, p. 229). An example of hostile environment sexual harassment is persistent, sexually suggestive comments or inappropriate touching that is unwelcome ("Sexual harassment guidance," 1997). When an individual is asked to exchange sexual favors for a desired benefit, it is called *quid pro quo* sexual harassment. For example, explicitly or implicitly conditioning a student's participation in a school program or activity on the basis of a student's submission to unwelcome sexual favors is considered quid pro quo sexual harassment ("Sexual harassment guidance," 1997).

The best way to avoid sexual harassment claims is to establish good policies and guidelines and then enforce them (Hairston, 1998). Schools are required to have grievance procedures so that students can file sexual harassment complaints (34 Code of Federal Regulations 106.8[b]). The *Brigham Young University Education and Law Journal* ("Responding to public school," 2000) suggests that the policies should (1) provide a definition of harassment; (2) state commitment to protect students; (3) explain the importance of harassment and require staff and students to report incidents; (4) describe what actions the school will take to prevent harassment; (5) prohibit retaliation; and (6) ensure that staff and students understand their individual rights.

Students look to the courts for relief from sexual harassment in the schools. Peer sexual harassment can have a significantly negative impact on the life of a student ("Responding to public school," 2000). In *Davis v. Monroe* (1996), a female student complained that she was being sexually harassed by a fellow male student. Furthermore, the female student claimed that school officials did not take appropriate actions to address the harassment. The court agreed, and school officials were held liable for their indifference. U.S. Department of Education (1997) guidelines state that:

> once a school has notice of possible sexual harassment of students . . . it should take immediate and appropriate steps to investigate or otherwise determine what occurred and take steps reasonably calculated to end any harassment, eliminate a hostile environment if one has been created, and prevent harassment from occurring again. ("Sexual harassment guidance," 1997, p. 1528)

Because of the sensitive nature of sexual harassment, the U.S. Department of Education guidelines also note that steps should be taken to provide confidentiality for the complainant if at all possible. At the same time, school officials should be truthful about actions that may include voiding confidentiality. Additionally, if the information involves an educational record as defined by the *Family Educational Rights and Privacy*

Act (FERPA), then school officials must determine if FERPA guidelines prevent the disclosure of the information provided by the complainant.

Educational and Privacy Rights

School leaders also must be aware of legal issues involved with privacy rights. In 1974 Congress passed FERPA to regulate the release of student records. FERPA provides parents virtually unlimited access to an education record while at the same time limiting access by others to the records. An education record is defined as "those records, files, documents and other materials which contain information directly related to a student; and are maintained by an educational agency or institution or by a person acting for such agency or institution" (20 U.S.C.A. § 1232g[4][A]). Personal notes are not, however, considered an education record.

Alexander and Alexander (1998) note that FERPA requires school leaders to

- Publish the student records policy and notify parents annually
- Obtain written consent before releasing any personally identifiable information in an education record
- Provide parents access to all school records concerning the student
- Provide parents an opportunity to appeal anything in the record that is incorrect
- Allow the parents to provide a written statement to the education record challenging the correctness of the material
- Define directory information and the circumstances under which that information may be released without parental consent (pp. 556–557)

Once a student becomes eighteen years of age, the student becomes an *eligible student* and authority to access and control of the records is transferred from the parent to the student. Schools are allowed to disclose information to school officials who have a legitimate educational interest, to another school system in which a student seeks to enroll, and to state and local education authorities.

A court case originating in Oklahoma provided an interesting interpretation of FERPA. According to the 10th Circuit Court of Appeals, the practice of allowing students to grade each others' papers is a violation of FERPA. The Circuit Court ruled that peer grading violated FERPA's prohibition against the nonconsensual release of an educational record. However, the U.S. Supreme Court reversed the lower court's ruling and held that the peer-graded items were not an educational record under FERPA guidelines. The court reasoned that "even assuming a teacher's grade book is an education record . . . the grades on the students' papers would not be covered under FERPA at least until the teacher has collected them and recorded them in his or her grade book" (*Owasso Independent School District v. Falvo*, 2002, p. 940). Figure 4.3 on page 82 provides a checklist for school administrators to consult in ensuring school safety.

When parents send their children to school, they expect their children to be free from physical, emotional, and psychological harm. Yet, the recent media reports of violent acts and sexual harassment have caused concern among parents and other school patrons. It is incumbent on school leaders to ensure the safety of the students under their watch. Federal reports and numerous commissions provide guidance for school leaders on how to prevent violent acts and how to properly act if violent acts do occur.

School Operations and Programs

Providing leadership to all aspects of a school is, arguably, one of the most difficult and sophisticated jobs in our society. Effective leadership in our schools requires the constant juggling of a complex set of relationships and programs (Hughes & Hooper, 2000; Ubben & Hughes, 1997). Although the ultimate goal should be student learning, student safety must be a major consideration when supervising all operations of the school. The most common form of educational litigation occurs because students are injured while at school (Imber & van Geel, 2000, p. 450). Programs and activities that provide possibilities for safety concerns include student supervision while at school, student transportation, and administering and supervising off-campus activities.

Supervision of Students

A reasonable expectation exists that school officials will supervise students while they are on campus (Alexander & Alexander, 1998). Failure to do so may result in an injury to a student, and school officials may then be held liable for negligence. Negligence occurs when a student is injured and a school official failed to reasonably act to prevent the injury (Fischer, Schimmel, & Kelly, 1999, p. 74). To be considered negligent, four prerequisites must exist. First, the school official must have the duty (responsibility) to protect others. Second, the school official must have failed to exercise a reasonable standard of care. The amount of care is dependent on several factors, such as the age of the student, the risk involved in the activity being supervised, and the circumstances of the situation. For example, a higher standard of care exists when a school official is supervising a shop class than when supervising an activity in the library. Third, there must be a causal relationship between the school official's lack of supervision and the resulting injury. Fourth, an actual damage or loss must exist (Alexander & Alexander, 1998).

Because our society has evolved to a stage where there are ever-increasing interactions between people and institutions, the possibility of one individual causing injury to another has greatly increased (Alexander & Alexander, 1998). School leaders often have protection from civil suits involving negligence because of the doctrine of civil immunity. Many state legislatures have supported the doctrine by enacting supportive legislation, whereas other states have specifically denied educators that protection (Reutter, 1994, p. 354). To avoid litigation, school leaders are advised to:

1. Repair school facilities or grounds where the disrepair may lead to a student injury;
2. Prevent student access to school facilities or grounds under repair;
3. Provide supervision for all student activities, particularly those activities in which there is some risk of injury; and
4. Stop any student behavior that may reasonably lead to injury.

Most schools and educational organizations are cognizant of risk management issues. Every effort must be made to reduce the risk of injury to students, whether a slide on the playground or open and accessible chemical agents.

Student Transportation

Transporting students is an expensive venture and often subjects school districts and employees to liability. Consequently, it is common for states to enact definitive legislation that limits student transportation (Valente & Valente, 1998). Laws governing student transportation vary from state to state, and the courts generally allow school districts the authority to limit transportation services unless state law provides direction otherwise (Valente & Valente, 1998). Indeed, safety factors may justify the denial of transportation services to students (*Rose v. Nashua Board of Education*, 1982; *State of Washington v. Grand Coulee Dam School District*, 1975). For example, students may be denied transportation services when their behavior on the bus is so severe that it may distract the driver and cause safety concerns. Reutter (1994) notes that parents have the basic responsibility to get their children to and from school. Districts must provide transportation for disabled students if the transportation is necessary for students to benefit from an education (*Alamo Heights Independent School District v. State Board of Education*, 1986). Like any related service, transportation requirements will be listed in the student's individual education program.

Off-Campus Activities

Although transporting students to and from school is a costly and time-consuming activity, student transportation issues frequently center on off-campus activities. Off-campus activities include field trips and extracurricular activities and contests. When transporting students to off-campus activities, school leaders have the same responsibility to ensure student safety and control student behavior as they do during the school day (Feld, 2000). Before transporting students on these events, school leaders would be wise to obtain written permission from the parents or guardians for the student to attend the activity. Written permission provides confirmation from the parents that their child will be off of the school campus and informs the parents of the exact nature and location of the activity (LaMorte, 1999). Additionally, school officials should obtain a written release for emergency medical treatment for the student, and special medical needs (e.g., allergies and medical sensitivities) should be noted on the release form.

Participation in some off-campus activities, such as athletic contests, increases the risk to student health and safety. Students assume the elements of risk when they choose to participate in the activity. However, "assumption of risk does not relieve school personnel of executing their duty to instruct, supervise, and provide for the safety of students under their supervision" (Essex, 1999, p. 110).

School is much more than a building in which learning occurs. School encompasses myriad activities on and off the school campus and ranges from before dawn until after dusk. These activities have grown substantially, and the transportation of students to and from these activities has increased the risk of injury to students. School leaders have an increased responsibility to ensure the safety of students as they participate in

Yes	No	Questions	Notes
		Are the students properly supervised at all times?	
		Are district guidelines followed when students are transported to and from the school?	
		Are there guidelines for visitors to your building?	
		Is there written policy governing student conduct that is distributed to students and parents?	
		Is there a crisis management plan for your campus and is it practiced periodically?	
		Is there a sexual harassment policy that ensures that all students and teachers are treated with respect and dignity?	
		Do the guidelines for off-campus activities ensure that parents are notified of the activities, and that students can receive the appropriate medical treatment in the event of a medical emergency?	
		Are there guidelines for corporal punishment, if permissible in your district?	
		Are there steps to follow regarding privacy rights (FERPA)?	

FIGURE 4.3 *Legal Checklist for Student Safety.* Schools are sophisticated and complex communities where learning is the primary goal. However, learning occurs best in a safe and orderly environment. As you review the operation of your school, ask yourself these questions.

these extended learning adventures. Legal checklists are provided in Figures 4.3 and 4.4 to guide school leaders as they make decisions related to student safety and school operations and can serve as risk management overviews.

To illustrate the need for concern for student safety and the possibility of legal liability, the following View from the Field describes the issues confronting Ms. Albrect, a campus leader.

This chapter provides administrators with an overview of the legal implications of several areas of the educational process. These areas include curriculum, school personnel, school safety, and school operations and programs. School leaders may find the Legal Guidelines in Figure 4.5 helpful as a quick and easy reference of things to do and things not to do.

Case Study

Abraham Martin is the principal at a suburban middle school that has an average daily attendance of approximately 1000 students. He shares leadership responsibilities with

Yes	No	Questions	Notes
		Are the students properly supervised at all times?	
		Are district guidelines followed when students are transported to and from the school?	
		Is there a crisis management plan for your campus, and is it practiced periodically?	
		Does your campus have a clearly written student code of conduct that is distributed and taught to all students?	
		Do teachers and students know the appropriate procedures for carrying out the day-to-day activities of the school?	
		Is there a sexual harassment policy that ensures that all students and teachers are treated with respect and dignity?	
		Do the guidelines for off-campus activities ensure that parents are notified of the activities, and that students can receive the appropriate medical treatment in the event of a medical emergency?	

FIGURE 4.4 *Legal Checklist for School Operations.* Schools are sophisticated and complex communities where learning is the primary goal. However, learning occurs best in a safe and orderly environment. As you review the operation of your school, ask yourself these questions.

two assistant principals. Abraham's workdays are always quite busy. Most of his time is spent on instructional support, but time not spent working with instructional activities is devoted to parent conferences, student management, and administrative duties. The school's executive secretary gave Abraham an update on two activities that will demand his attention as the day begins:

1. 8:30 AM: Meeting with Sara McGill, a concerned parent. Ms. McGill's son, Jason, told her that a naked lady was shown during a film that Ms. Jimenez used in class. Ms. McGill is a community leader in a socially conservative movement that advocates a strict review of all instructional material, primarily textbooks. When told that Ms. McGill questioned the instructional film, Ms. Jimenez told the executive secretary that Jason's reference was to a silhouette outline of the human body. The silhouette was generic and gave no indication of a sexual identity.

2. 9:30 AM: Meeting with Dr. Daniels, the district's sexual harassment coordinator. A written report was submitted to Dr. Daniels from a parent alleging that "lewd, inappropriate remarks" were made by a sixth grade boy to a female classmate. The report further alleges that Mr. Roosevelt, a teacher, "knows of the continuing harassment" yet fails to "do anything about it." In fact, the parent alleges that when the girl reported that vulgar comments were made about her, Mr. Roosevelt handled the

View from the Field

Pepperidge Elementary School is one of two elementary schools located in a rural community. Pepperidge has an average daily attendance of 557 students in grades K–6, and the school follows a self-contained curricular structure. Recently during recess, an accident occurred. Ms. Albrect has interviewed the parties involved and has constructed the following account.

During the morning break from academic activities (recess), three 3rd grade classes (sixty-three students) and two 2nd grade classes (forty-four students) were on the school's playground. The playground consists of four acres of land spotted with oak and ash trees and considerable playground equipment. Much of the playground equipment is old and, consequently, the classroom teachers closely supervise student play on the equipment to discourage dangerous behavior. A customary practice is for one classroom teacher to take care of paperwork or other chores while the other teachers supervise the playground activities. On this particular day, Ms. Jones remained in her classroom to prepare for the coming math lesson while the other four teachers supervised the playground. Of the four teachers supervising the playground, one was a novice substitute teacher, Mr. Smith. Toward the end of the fifteen-minute break, Tommy, a 3rd grade student in Ms. Jones's class, fell approximately ten feet from a limb of an oak tree.

The fall resulted in a couple of cracked ribs and a broken arm. Medical attention was sought, and the student is recovering.

Ms. Albrect is assessing the situation to make a report to the superintendent. As a school leader, she has generated the following questions to determine the school's possible legal liability.

- Were the students properly supervised? [Note to self: Develop a written policy for the supervision of students during the break.]
- What emergency procedures should be in place to address a situation of this nature? [Note to self: Review emergency treatment procedures with faculty and staff.]
- Should there be behavioral guidelines in place for students who go to the playground for a break? What should those guidelines be, and how should they be developed?
- Is Ms. Jones liable for Tommy's injuries? Am I liable for Tommy's injuries?
- Was there adequate supervision on the playground? Should there be training for substitute teachers such as Mr. Smith? What kind of training would be needed?

situation by making the two students sit next to each other and "be nice to each other." When confronted by the parent, Mr. Roosevelt explained that he (the teacher) was trying to teach the students to be nice to each other, respect one another, and that the teacher believed the young male's actions would soon pass because "boys will be boys."

Questions to consider: If you were Abraham Martin,

1. How should you begin the conversation with Ms. McGill? What provides the basis of Ms. McGill's concerns? What are the potential legal issues in this situation? Should the instructional materials be censored for children of parents who may find them offensive?

	Do's	Don't's
Curriculum	• Align curriculum with state and national standards and test objectives • Work with the local community to define politically acceptable curriculum related to sex education • Conduct school-wide celebrations that reflect sensitivity to students from all cultures • Encourage activities that are sensitive to varying religious beliefs • Follow state and federal guidelines for curricular programs	• Ignore curriculum topics that may lead to student failure on high-stakes tests • Teach sex education without the involvement of parents, and leaders from the school and community • Use the school's curriculum as a forum for promoting any particular religious belief over other • Ignore federal guidelines for special programs such as special education, bilingual education, and Title I programs
School Personnel	• Hire the most qualified person • Establish hiring practices that are objective, job-related, and consistent with the advertised position • Conduct reference checks • Train staff involved in the interviewing process • Follow district and state guidelines for dismissing personnel	• Vary from district policies and procedures for advertising, interviewing, and selecting personnel • Discriminate on the basis of an individual's race, color, religion, sex, national origin, age, or disability • Violate individuals' due process rights during the dismissal process
School Safety	• Establish a crisis management plan • Have a clearly written student code of conduct • Create and distribute a sexual harassment policy • Follow state and local guidelines for the use of corporal punishment • Use corporal punishment only as a last resort • Release student records as permitted by the Family Educational Rights and Privacy Act (FERPA) • Allow students the opportunity to request the district to withhold directory information	• Fail to periodically practice your crisis management plan • Forget to distribute and teach the student code of conduct to all school personnel and students • Refuse or fail to act on any reported incidents of sexual harassment • Use corporal punishment as an initial intervention strategy • Release student records to individuals or agencies who do not have a legitimate educational interest
School Operations and Programs	• Supervise students at all times • Follow district guidelines when transporting students to and from the school • Obtain written permission from parents for emergency medical treatment that may be necessary at an off-campus activity	• Fail to notify parents of off-campus school activities • Forget to provide adequate supervision and instruction in high-risk school activities

FIGURE 4.5 *Legal Guidelines for School Leaders*

2. After some investigation, you find the allegations made to Dr. Daniels to be true and correct. What are your legal responsibilities? What should you do to address the claim of sexual harassment? What are the possible political repercussions? What, if anything, should be said to Mr. Roosevelt?

Summary

This chapter has focused on areas in which school leaders encounter possible legal issues. Providing leadership in the public schools is fraught with legislative requirements and legal challenges. The first section described how school curriculum is affected by federal and state legislative and court actions. Because state legislatures have plenary power over public education, they may prescribe the school curriculum. Following the reform efforts of the 1980s, states have wrested control over curriculum from local schools. The courts have been supportive of the legislative acts and have upheld many of the controversial reform efforts such as high-stakes student testing and increased graduation requirements.

The second section of this chapter discussed school personnel and students. The vast majority of case law is developed not in curriculum matters, but in employee and student matters. School leaders must remain current regarding legal issues affecting employment. Balancing the right of the district to know about a prospective employee against his or her privacy rights requires a delicate touch. Leaders must be extremely cautious when making employee decisions and must implement practices that are fair, consistent, and job related.

Education is about student learning and student safety. In an age of increased student violence, school leaders are being called on to ensure the safety of students while at school or at school-related activities, on or off campus. Although discipline policies are not new to public schools, school leaders are being asked to review those policies and revise them to address the pervasive issues of drugs, guns, and sexual harassment. Possibly due to the recent high-profile incidents of student violence, the federal courts are allowing schools considerable leeway in controlling students at school. Schools must develop risk-management plans to limit their potential liability.

The last section of this chapter addressed the complex task of providing leadership over school operations. Although it is not feasible to address every aspect of leading a school, this section focused on the duty of school personnel to supervise students at school, during transport, and at off-campus activities. School leaders should ensure that students are properly supervised, with greater degrees of supervision provided for activities that lead to greater risks of injury. Students on school busses, in shop class, physical education class, or engaged in athletic contests require closer supervision than do students in structured, nonlaboratory, classrooms.

By constitutional decree, legislation, court challenges, or administrative regulation, the law impacts every aspect of the operation of a school. School leaders must take an active role in legislative policy development issues but leave the legal altercations in the courts to school attorneys and legal scholars. Those altercations are minimized when sound decisions are guided by current legal information.

Your Turn

4.1. A quick review of the teacher selection process on your campus reveals that many of the interview questions would not be legally defensible. Develop at least five questions that are job related and do not discriminate on the basis of race, religion, sex, national origin, disability, or age. What is meant by the uniform application of an employment practice?

4.2. The state where you reside has recently completed the development of a statewide curriculum in English/language arts and mathematics. The state will use a written performance assessment to hold campuses accountable for teaching the curriculum. What curricular issues are likely to be the most controversial (and litigated) as you lead the alignment of your school's curriculum with that of the state's curriculum? Must public schools abandon any thought of teaching religious concepts?

4.3. Janet, a 17-year-old female student, complains to you that an older boy at the school is always touching her. She claims that he continually makes sexually suggestive comments to her. Furthermore, he shows her sexually explicit photographs and makes inappropriate sexual gestures toward her. As the leader of the school campus, what are your obligations to Janet? Is Janet's complaint a *quid pro quo* complaint or a *hostile environment* complaint?

4.4. The mother of a student at your school complains to you that students are grading each other's papers in English class. The mother is particularly upset because many of the students in the class tease her son because of his inability to perform the work. The mother tells you that she thinks the grades should be confidential and that the grading practice violates FERPA. Does the mother have legal precedent for her claim? How does FERPA define an *educational record*?

4.5. Last week a novice teacher left a classroom unattended to secure a box of chalk to use for the afternoon's lessons. While she was out of the room, two boys got into an argument, which resulted in a fistfight. One of the boys was severely injured when he was knocked against the sharp corner of the teacher's desk. Today you received notice that the teacher, you (the campus leader), and the school district are being sued for negligence. What prerequisites must exist before showing that negligence exists? Do you think that it is likely that any of the parties will be found negligent? Why?

4.6. On a recent field trip to a local wildlife preserve, a poisonous snake bit one of the students. Quick thinking on the part of the teacher and the staff at the preserve prevented the snakebite from seriously injuring the student. On the way to the emergency room of a nearby hospital, the teacher located the permission form required by the school. What purposes does the permission form serve?

References

Abington School District v. Schempp, 374 U.S. 203 (1963).

Adams, A. T. (2000). The status of school discipline and violence. *Annuals of the American Academy of Political & Social Science, 567,* 140–157.

Age Discrimination in Employment Act of 1967, 29 U.S.C. 623a.

Alamo Heights Independent School District v. State Board of Education, 790 F.2d 1153 (5th Circuit, 1986).

Alexander, K., & Alexander, M. D. (2001). *American public school law* (5th ed). Boston: West/Wadsworth.

Alexander, K., & Alexander, M. D. (1998). *American public school law* (4th ed). Belmont, CA: Wadsworth Publisher.

Alexander, K., & Alexander, M. D. (1984). *The law of schools, students and teachers: In a nutshell.* St. Paul, MN: West.

American Academy of Pediatrics. (2000). Corporal punishment in schools. *Pediatrics, 106,* 343.

American Association of Colleges for Teacher Education (AACTE). (2002 February). *Governmental relations update.* Washington, DC: AACTE.

Americans with Disabilities Act of 1990, 42 U.S.C.A. 12101.

Aquila, F. D., & Petzke, J. J. (1994). *Education law: Course outline* (1st ed). Santa Monica, CA: Casenotes Publishing Company.

Baker v. Owen. 395 Supp. 294 (M.D. N.C., 1975).

Brown v. Board of Education of Topeka, 347 U.S. 483 (1954).

Brown, L., & Schneider-Vogel, M. (1996). The first amendment and school employees. In K. Frels, J. Horner, & V. L. Robinson (eds), *Texas school law: A practical guide.* pp. 117–136. Topeka, KS: National Organization of Legal Problems in Education.

Chamberlin, C. W. (1999). Johnny can't read 'cause Jane's got a gun: The effects of guns in schools, and options after Lopez. *Cornell Journal of Law and Public Policy, 8,* 281–346.

Dagley, D. L. (2001). Federal and state legislation. In C. J. Russo (ed), *The yearbook of education law 2001.* pp. 275–319. Dayton, OH: Education Law Association.

Darling-Hammond, L. (January 1, 2000). Teacher quality and student achievement: A review of state policy evidence. *Education Policy Analysis Archives* (Online), *8*, http://olam.ed.asu.edu/epaa/v8n1.html.

Davis v. Monroe County Board of Education, 74 F.3d 1186 (11th Circuit, 1996).

Doe v. Taylor Independent School District, 15 F.3d 443 (5th Circuit, 1994).

Edwards v. Aquilard. 482 U.S. 578 (1987).

Elizalde, C. (1998). Reduction in force: How to successfully eliminate one or more positions with a RIF. *Texas School Administrators' Legal Digest, 14,* 10, 1–6.

Epperson v. State of Arkansas, 393 U.S. 97 (1968).

Essex, N. L. (1999). Handling gang violence in schools: Some costly legal errors and how to avoid them. *ERS Spectrum, 17,* 4, 21–24.

Falvo v. Owasso Independent School District, 220 F.3d 1200 (10th Circuit, 2000).

Family Educational Rights and Privacy Act, 20 U.S.C.A. 1232g.

Feld, D. E. (2000). Right to discipline pupil for conduct away from school grounds or not immediately connected with school activities. *American Law Reports, 53,* 1124.

Fetler, M. (January 8, 1997). Where have all the teachers gone? *Education Policy Analysis Archives* (Online), *5*. http://olam.ed.asu.edu/epaa/v5n2.html.

Fischer, L., Schimmel, D., & Kelly, C. (1999). *Teachers and the law* (5th ed). New York: Longman.

Florey v. Sioux Falls School District, 619 F.2d 1311 (8th Circuit, 1980).

Freiler v. Tangipahoa Parish Board of Education, 185 F.3d 337 (5th Circuit, 1999).

Greenberg, H. (1997). Making sure your hiring practices are keeping you out of legal hot water. *Forum, 179,* 37–38.

Griggs v. Duke Power Company, 401 U.S. 424 (1971).

Grover, S. Sexual harassment. (2000). In S. Refield (ed), *School as boss, school as parent.* Concord, NH: Franklin Pierce Law Center.

Guidelines on discrimination because of sex (29 Code of Federal Regulations 1604).

Hairston, J. B. (1998). Sexual harassment in the workplace: New guidance from the federal courts. *Texas School Administrator's Legal Digest, 14,* 1–7, 20.

Hughes, L. W., & Hooper, D. W. (2000). *Public relations for school leaders.* Boston: Allyn & Bacon.

Imber, M., & van Geel, T. (2000). *Education law* (2nd ed). London: Lawrence Erlbaum and Associates.

Imbrogno, A. R. (2000). Corporal punishment in America's Public Schools and the U.N. convention on the rights of the child: A case for nonratification. *Journal of Law and Education, 29,* 2, 125–147.

Improving America's Schools Act, PL 103-382; 20 U.S.C. § 6301 et seq. (1994).

Individuals with Disabilities Education Act, PL 105-17; 20 U.S.C. § 1400 et seq. (1997).

Ingraham v. Wright, 430 U.S. 651 (1977).

Jaffe, E. (1999). A federally mandated national school curriculum: Can Congress act? *Seton Hall Legislative Journal, 24,* 207–254.

Kemerer, F., & Walsh, J. (2000). *The educator's guide to Texas school law* (5th ed). Austin, TX: The University of Texas Press.

LaMorte, M. W. (1999). *School law: Cases and concepts* (6th ed). Boston: Allyn & Bacon.

Lane, K., Van Berkum, D., & Richardson, M. (2000). Copyright issues in the electronic classroom. In W. Camp, M. Connelly, K. Lane, & J. Mead (eds), *The principal's legal handbook.* pp. 341–357. Dayton, OH: Education Law Association.

Issues faced by schools in the digital age: Part III. (2002, March). *Legal Notes for Education, 15,* No. 11, p. 1. Retrieved July 28, 2002, from Lexis-Nexis Academic Universe database, www.web.lexis-nexis.com.

Lemon v. Kurtzman, 403 U.S. 602 (1971).

Library filtering law violates First Amendment, court rules. (2002, June 18). *Telecommunications Industry Litigation Reporter, 5,* No. 24. Retrieved July 28, 2002, from Lexis-Nexis Academic Universe database.

McCarthy, M. M., Cambron-McCabe, N. H., & Thomas, S. B. (1998). *Public school law: Teachers' and students' rights* (4th ed). Boston: Allyn & Bacon.

Monk, D. H., & Hussain, S. (1998). Policy implications of increased high school graduation expectations. *Annual Survey of American Law,* pp. 245–266.

New Jersey v. TLO, 469 U.S. 325 (1985).

No Child Left Behind Act, PL 107-110; 20 U.S.C. 6301 (2002).

Nondiscrimination on the basis of sex in education programs and activities receiving or benefiting from federal financial assistance, 34 Code of Federal Regulations 106.8(b).

Owasso Independent School District v. Falvo, 534 U.S. 426 (2002).

Perkins-Gough, D. (2002). Special report: RAND report on charter schools and vouchers. *Educational Leadership, 59,* 90–91.

Prohibition against federal control of education. 20 U.S.C.A. § 1232(a) (2000).

Pullin, D. (1999). Whose schools are these and what are they for? The role of the rule of law in defining educational opportunity in American public education. In G. J. Cizek (ed), *Handbook of educational policy.* San Diego: Academic Press.

Rebell, M. A., & Hughes, R. L. (1996). Schools, communities, and the courts: A dialogic approach to education reform. *Yale Law and Policy Review, 14,* 99–168.

Rebore, R. W. (1995). *Personnel administration in education: A management approach* (4th ed). Boston: Allyn & Bacon.

Redfield, S. E. (2001). *Thinking like a lawyer: An educator's guide to legal analysis and research.* Concord, NH: Franklin Pierce Law Center.

Responding to public school peer sexual harassment in the face of Davis v. Monroe County Board of Education. *Brigham Young University Education and Law Journal, 2000,* 287–305.

Rose v. Nashua Board of Education, 679 F.2d 279 (1st Circuit, 1982).

Rose, L. C., & Gallup, A. M. (2000). The 32nd annual Phi Delta Kappa/Gallup poll of the public's attitudes toward the public schools. *Phi Delta Kappan, 82,* 41–58.

Rothstein, L. F. (2000). *Special education law* (3rd ed). New York: Longman.

Reutter, E. E., Jr. (1994). *The law of public education* (4th ed). Westbury, NY: The Foundation Press.

Safe Schools Act, PL 103-227; 20 U.S.C. § 5961 (1994).

School District of Abington Township v. Schempp, 374 U.S. 203 (1963).

Scopes v. State, 289 S. W. 363 (1926).

Sexual harassment guidance: Harassment of students, school employees, other students, or third parties: Notice, 62 Federal Register 12033 (1997). U.S. Department of Education.

Spillane, J. P. (1998). State policy and the non-monolithic nature of the local school district: Organizational and professional considerations. *American Educational Research Journal, 35,* 33–63.

Spring, J. H. (1998). *Conflict of interests: The politics of American education.* New York: McGraw-Hill.

State of Washington v. Grand Coulee Dam School District, 536 P.2d 614 (Washington, 1975).

Stone v. Graham, 449 U.S. 39 (1981).

The Equal Employment Opportunities Act, 42 U.S.C.A. 2000e.

Tinker v. Des Moines Independent Community School District, 393 U.S. 503 (1969).

Title VII of Civil Rights Act of 1964, 42, U.S.C.A. § 2000e-2(a).

Trebilcock, J. (2000). Off campus: School board control over teacher conduct. *Tulsa Law Journal, 35*, 445–465.

Ubben, G. C., & Hughes, L. W. (1997). *The principal: Creative leadership for effective schools* (3rd ed). Boston: Allyn & Bacon.

Valente, W. D., & Valente, C. M. (2001). *Law in the schools* (5th ed). Columbus, OH: Merrill.

Valente, W. D., & Valente, C. M. (1998). *Law in the schools* (4th ed). Upper Saddle River, NJ: Merrill.

Wayne, A. J. (September 18, 2000). Teacher supply and demand: Surprises from primary research. *Education Policy Analysis Archives* (Online), *8*. http://olam.ed.asu.edu/epaa/v8n47.html.

Welsh, W. N. (2000). The effects of school climate on school disorder. *The Annals of the American Academy of Political and Social Science, 567*, 88–107.

Wirt, F. M., & Kirst, M. W. (1997). *The political dynamics of American education*. Berkeley, CA: McCutchan Publishing.

Yell, M. L. (1998). *The law and special education*. Columbus, OH: Merrill.

Zelman v. Simmons-Harris, et al., 122 S. Ct. 2460 (2002).

5

Action Research for School Leaders

ISLLC Standards

Standard 1: A school administrator is an educational leader who promotes the success of all students by facilitating the development, articulation, implementation, and stewardship of a vision of learning that is shared and supported by the school community.

Standard 2: A school administrator is an educational leader who promotes the success of all students by advocating, nurturing, and sustaining a school culture and instructional program conducive to student learning and staff professional growth.

Standard 3: A school administrator is an educational leader who promotes the success of all students by advocating, nurturing, and sustaining a school culture and instructional program conducive to student learning and staff professional growth.

Chapter Objectives _____

The objectives of this chapter are:

- Discuss the role of research in bringing about school reform.
- Explain the importance of the action research movement.
- Describe what action research is and its relationship to quantitative and qualitative research.
- Describe the role of school leaders in conducting research in schools.
- Identify and describe the steps in action research.
- Discuss how action research can support school improvement and professional development.
- Identify action research methodologies, including surveys, case studies, interviews, and classroom observations and discuss their applications to school improvement through action research.
- Identify possible ways that action research contributes to improved practices.

Leaders in today's schools are faced with the pressure to improve professional practice (Stringer, 1999). Finding answers to puzzling problems is a continuous and challenging process, and action research can provide school leaders with a powerful tool for fostering school improvement and renewal. For Calhoun (2002), action research is continual professional development that provides the most "direct route to improving teaching and learning" (p. 18). Mills (2000) views action research as an agent of educational change that promotes a democratic approach to decision making, while at the same time empowering school leaders and teachers as they engage in collaborative research activities. Action research can enhance the role of the campus leader in creating and sustaining a campus-culture that is focused on learning and ensures that learning occurs for all.

The pressures to improve student academic success represent both challenges and opportunities as school leaders deal with occupational, institutional, and community problems that range from violence, poverty, conflict, discrimination, and low achievement to teacher recruitment and retention. Frequently, an expectation occurs on the part of policymakers that school leaders should have the answers to these and many other complex problems that confront teachers and students on a daily basis.

Although school leaders do not have all the answers, they do have access to educational research that can help. An essential attribute of educational research is its systematic approach to finding answers that can contribute to school improvement (Kennedy, 1997). This search for answers is not new; over fifteen years ago, Gable and Rogers (1987) recognized that "professionals" needed to have the ". . . desire and ability to seek answers to puzzling questions—i.e., the desire and ability to do research . . ." (p. 695). Schmoker (1999) says, ". . . for every item of research we adopt, we must conduct on-site action research" (p. 70). He continues by noting, "The [action] research we do at the local level . . . is what makes formal outside research work. Outside research cannot be installed like a spare part—it has to be fitted, adjusted, and refined for the school contexts . . ." (p. 70).

Although research is the theme of this chapter, action research, more specifically, is its focus. The chapter provides suggestions to engage faculty in school-wide systematic inquiry. Such inquiry leads administrators and faculty to research-based explanations and possible solutions that address such problems as how to get ". . . students [to] develop deep understandings of subject matter, situate students' learning in meaningful contexts, and create learning communities in which teachers and students engage in rich discourse about important ideas (Putnam & Borko, 2000, p. 4). Through action research, educators at all levels can find and make better choices about the way students and teachers participate more meaningfully in the teaching–learning process.

This chapter explains the role of research in education, with special attention given to the ways that school leaders can address student improvement and school renewal through systematic inquiry. Although books and entire courses are devoted to research, and specifically educational research, the purpose of this chapter is to provide an overview of the process as a tool that school leaders can use for generating data to guide decision making that promotes success for all students. A brief overview of educational research is presented, along with a brief description of three forms of action research. Four types of methodologies for action research are provided, including surveys, classroom observations, case studies, and interviews. A general discussion of quantitative and qualitative approaches is included, along with a description of the methods for each approach. The chapter also discusses the role that school leaders play in the process of action research and describes how this inquiry process can bridge the gap between theory and practice (Pine, 1992). Finally, action research is highlighted as a useful tool for school leaders to use as they gather information regarding better ways to bring about renewal and improvement at the campus level.

Educational Research

When one hears the word *research*, the notion of tedious and rigorous data collection, number crunching, and statistical procedures often come to mind; some may even equate educational research with quantum physics or brain surgery. For Glesne (1999), research simply involves " a careful and diligent search, and educators have been engaged in a variety of careful and diligent searches without necessarily labeling the process" (p. 3). Even though educators have been conducting research, perhaps unknowingly, the term can still connote fear and intimidation and may cause many educators to shy away from it (Gable & Rogers, 1987; Glanz, 1998). Furthermore, Srouge (1997) and Kaestle (1993) confirm that educational research has an "awful" reputation, and Gable and Rogers (1987) describe this research mystique as "beyond the ken of ordinary people" (p. 691). According to Wiersma (2000), the situation is more complex because, "Expertise and experience for conducting research are limited . . . [and] when it comes to matters of research, the situation of the average elementary or high school . . . administrator is not much different . . ." (p. 1).

Although educators have often found the term *research* uncomfortable, research, specifically action research, is a disciplined inquiry that can uncover new information, and its interpretations can provide insights into the real underlying issues of problems and dilemmas that confront schools. For Wiersma (2000), ". . . research is done for the purpose of explaining and predicting phenomena, and in . . . educational research, those that impact upon teaching and learning and the operation of the schools" (p. 1).

Research can be classified according to one of two major categories, basic or applied, based on the goals or purposes. *Basic research* involves an objective, experimental model that is most often used in the sciences to confirm or document natural phenomena. Its purpose is to examine cause and effect relationships and provide theories or generalizations that help to explain certain phenomena based on the data gathered. Basic research adds ". . . to the existing body of knowledge in a discipline . . . [and] does not always provide results that are of immediate practical use . . ." (Wiersma, 2000, p. 10). *Applied research* seeks to examine social and psychological events or phenomena. It is designed to provide solutions to problems that lead to greater understanding and improved practice.

Applied research uses two major methods to collect and analyze data. One method is *quantitative research*, which involves descriptive, correlational, and group comparisons and is generally ". . . supported by the positivist paradigm, which characterizes the world as made up of observable, measurable facts" (Glesne, 1999, pp. 4–5). *Qualitative research* uses ethnography and historical methods, especially naturalistic observations and case studies, and is ". . . generally supported by the interpretivist/constructivist paradigm, which portrays a world in which reality is socially constructed, complex, and ever changing" (Glesne, 1999, p. 5). As Krathwohl (1993) sums up the two methods, "Qualitative research . . . describes phenomena in words instead of numbers or measures. . . . Quantitative research describes phenomena in numbers and measures instead of words" (p. 740).

Figure 5.1 represents an overview of the research methodologies. As seen in the figure, action research is considered to be a form of applied research that employs different approaches.

In designing applied studies, both quantitative and qualitative methods can be employed. Quantitative approaches include descriptive, correlational, and group comparisons. *Descriptive research* can be either based on survey or observational data and involves tallies or frequencies, numbers, or measurements such as Likert scales or ratings. A study, for example, using observational data could target the classroom in an attempt to learn more about the complexities of classroom life. The researcher may be interested in the number and kinds of classroom interactions between the students and the teacher during a mathematics lesson. Collecting data and describing the events that take place on a day-to-day basis provide a window into the instructional culture of that classroom.

Correlational research uses statistical models to explain or interpret relationships between variables. Correlations describe the degree to which a relationship exists

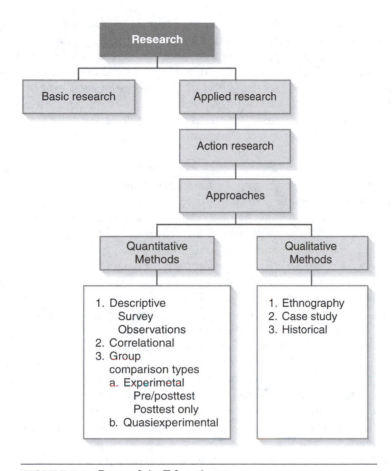

FIGURE 5.1   *Research in Education*

between two variables. For example, a correlational design might seek to answer the following question: Is there a relationship between writing and the tools that students use in the writing process? For example, one group of students would use the rough draft, revise, and rewrite strategy, whereas another group at the same grade level would use the computer in the initial writing, revision, and rewrite stages. Using the computer, the researcher hypothesizes, will motivate the students to write higher quality and longer reports. When analyzing the data, the researcher attempts to determine if there is a relationship between using the computer and generating longer, quality writing pieces.

Group comparison methods are divided into experimental and quasiexperimental studies. Experimental studies are conducted using a different treatment that is compared with a control group. In experimental research educators seek to know not only the degree to which variables relate, but also how much one variable impacts the other(s). For example, a research question for an experimental study might be: To what degree does using hands-on strategies in science produce greater results on the criterion-referenced test at the state level? There would be at least two groups—one group experiencing the treatment (hands-on strategies) and one group (the control) that did not. At the end of the study, the scores on the criterion-referenced test at the state level would be compared. The researcher attempts to answer the question from the results of a group comparison of scores. This study is a randomized experiment with a manipulated independent variable (teaching strategies) to determine the effect on test performance (dependent variable). Quasiexperimental designs involve single measurements, one group with pretest and posttest scores, interrupted time series, or a single subject.

Unlike quantitative research, which begins with a specific research question, qualitative research ". . . begins with the muddle of daily work, with the moments that stand out from the general flow and unless we record those moments they vanish—unavailable as data for reflection, for discerning some larger pattern of experience" (Newman, 1998, p. 3). For Wiersma (2000), "Qualitative research has its origins in descriptive analysis and is essentially an inductive process" (p. 12).

Inquiry is presented as a reflective approach for making sound decisions about an event or situation. "Qualitative researchers might call their work ethnography, case study, phenomenology, educational criticism, hermeneutics, or a number of other terms" (Glesne, 1999, p. 8). Therefore, gaining a holistic perspective is significant to achieving a deeper understanding of a problem or concern.

Qualitative research seeks to understand the problem or situation by looking at the whole, ethnographically. In qualitative research, data are gathered through naturalistic observations or case studies and include extensive notes from interviews that contribute to the context in which the research is being conducted. Teacher journals and other written artifacts can contribute to better understanding the whole picture. These written data sources are analyzed for trends and patterns that can be clustered and interpreted.

Naturalistic observations then, involve observing people within a school or classroom context, and case studies rely on descriptive accounts of events and records of people's insights, thoughts, and reactions to those events. For example, when observing a teaching episode that focuses on the types or levels of questions being asked and then reviewing the teacher's lesson plan and journal entries, the action researcher is in a better position to compare what is actually taking place in this classroom and what the teacher intended and perceives took place. However, it should be noted that "meaning, for a quantitative researcher, is . . . always an incomplete picture [because the] . . . picture is 'rich,' 'deep,' 'thick,' 'textured,' 'insightful,' and best of all, 'illuminative'" and most importantly not supported by empirical data (Shank, 2000, p. 7). Qualitative research is driven less by empirical evidence and more by the information gathered by observing in classrooms and noting the behavior of students in their natural setting of the classroom. The qualitative research method preserves the natural qualities of the situation being studied (Greenberg & Baron, 2000).

To strengthen the conclusions drawn from qualitative research, the action researcher can implement quantitative methods as well by using control groups, student pretest and posttest scores, and results from surveys. Using multiple research sources and procedures, referred to as *triangulation*, increases the credibility of the research findings. "Triangulation refers to the use of multiple independent data sources to corroborate findings" (Sagor, 2000, p. 19). By bringing more than one data source to the reality of the issue, triangulation can be used to ". . . greatly strengthen the study's usefulness for other settings" (Marshall & Rossman, 1994, p. 146).

Action Research Movement

Schools are confronted daily with challenges and opportunities as they seek to meet the needs of an increasingly diverse and mobile student population. To help to address these issues of diversity and mobility, the school reform movement of the 1980s emphasized practitioner research, which focused on issues related to institutional change (van Manen, 1984; Stenhouse, 1985; Smith, 1989; Kincheloe, 1991; Altrichter, Posch, & Somekh, 1993; Cochran-Smith & Lytle, 1993, 1999; LeCompte & Schensul, 1999). Although practitioner research gained popularity as a result of the interest in reforms of the last two decades of the twentieth century, its roots can be traced back to the 1940s when it was first introduced by Kurt Lewin (Lewin, 1946a, 1946b; Christiansen, Goulet, Krentz, & Maeers, 1997; McTaggart, 1997; Boyarsky & Murphy, 1998; Brown & Dowling, 1998; Krulfeld, MacDonald, & MacDonald, 1998; Mills, 2000).

Cochran-Smith and Lytle (1999) note that renewed interest in teacher research as well as other "forms of practitioner inquiry" is a little over a decade old. This *teacher research movement*, as it is called, is going through a critical stage and at the heart of this evolving movement is ". . . the underlying and sometimes competing epistemologies, politics, paradigms and theories of social change . . ." (p. 19). According to Gore and Zeichner (1995), action research focuses on ". . . reflections both inwardly at [one's] own practices and outwardly [to] the social conditions which influence those practices" and contributes to both personal renewal and social reconstructionism (p. 205). Wiersma (2000) says that "action research is usually conducted by teachers, administrators, or other educational professionals for solving a specific problem or for providing information for decision making at the local level" (p. 11). Clearly, action research is done within the context of the school or classroom setting and directly involves educational professionals in the process. Simply stated, action research is initiated by educators who want to improve their situation (Sagor, 2000).

For school leaders, action research can be used as a tool for addressing renewal at the campus level and jointly identifying targets for change, studying the problem, analyzing the data, and taking appropriate action. Action research provides the local level with solutions to day-to-day problems, and there is ". . . little concern about generalizing the results . . . to other educational settings" (Wiersma, 2000, p. 11).

The concept of practitioner research is a valid process to use for school inquiry because of the intellectual traditions that support it (Schön, 1983; Cochran-Smith & Lytle, 1999). Supporters of practitioner inquiry have called it an epistemology of teaching practice that has roots in progressive education and the work of John Dewey (Noffke, 1995). Greene (1978) views it as an opportunity to find the inner voice within teachers as they plan and implement curriculum at the classroom level. According to Mills (2000), action research ". . . helps to develop . . . professional attitudes that embrace action, progress, and reform rather than stability and mediocrity" (p. v). For Sagor (1992), the focus of action research has often been on three related stages of action:

1. Initiating action such as, adopting a text or choosing an alternative assessment strategy.
2. Monitoring and adjusting action, such as seeing how a pilot project is proceeding, assessing the early progress of a new program, and improving current practice.
3. Evaluating action, such as preparing a final report on a completed project. (p. 8)

Research conducted by practitioners, however, is not without its critics. Some of the critiques come from not only a disciplinary perspective, but from social and economic theory and pedagogy as *praxis* perspective (Cochran-Smith & Lytle, 1999). Fundamentally, for practitioner research to generate knowledge about students and schooling, it must be born of the systematic inquiry process "analogous to the science that yields formal knowledge" (Fenstermacher, 1994, p. 48). For Fenstermacher, the knowledge generated by action research is fundamentally flawed because the researcher serves both as the investigator and the interpreter of data collected. Having one person serving in both roles can contaminate or bias the results. A tendency may exist to try to make the results match the hypothesis. Huberman (1996) has also critiqued the methods used and notes that if teachers are to function as the researchers, they must be bound by the rules that include the "provision of evidence, consistency, freedom from obvious bias, and perceptions of the people involved" (p. 128).

Despite these criticisms, practitioner research has gained a foothold in the attempts to breathe new life into school renewal and improvement. Kemmis and McTaggart (1988) point out that practitioner research is an important form of ". . . collective self-reflective enquiry undertaken . . . in social situations . . . to improve the rationality and justice of . . . social or educational practices as well as . . . understanding . . . these practices and the situations in which these practices are carried out" (p. 1). Supporters of this type of applied research view it as having the potential to genuinely transform the school culture. "The current form of action research is grounded in the interpretivist/[constructivist] paradigm with researchers working with others as agents of change" (Glesne, 1999, p. 13).

Such transformative possibilities occur when questions arise regarding (1) who conducts the research; (2) what topics are to be investigated; and (3) what are the implications when one is both a researcher and participant? Answers to these key questions affect the kinds of transformation that will take place within the school culture. Mahlio (2001) notes that there has been a change in academic thinking as action research becomes more and more common as a means of enhancing ". . . a teacher's expertise as a practitioner in the classroom" (p. 71). Teachers who engage in research experience "personal and professional satisfaction, a reduction in isolation, a sense of instrumentality, and new learnings—all of which spill over into their teaching" (Barth, 2001, p. 443). According to Sagor (1992), "Until teachers become involved in generating the knowledge that informs their practice, they will remain cast as subordinate workers rather than dynamic professionals" (p. 4). School leaders can facilitate these experiences that encourage teachers to become professionals rather than mere tenants, as well as owners and investors in their school (Barth, 2001). As researchers too, school leaders become ". . . equal and full participants in the research process" (Stringer, 1999, p. 9).

Examining educational practices and issues using research methodologies follows a pattern established by other disciplines. As Sagor (1992) notes, "all professions are informed by a knowledge base, and teaching is no exception" (p. 3). The assumption is that investigators use methodologies to approach problems and dilemmas in a way that will yield information upon which to base instructional, managerial, and personnel decisions. Such data-driven decision making contributes to teaching effectiveness and student learning which can be ". . . a model for changing the workplace" (Calhoun, 1994, p. 1).

In the following View from the Field, a 7th grade teacher visits with her principal about collecting data on student motivation.

Action Research: Perspective and Practices

Freire (1985) says that all educational practices are rooted in a theoretical stance; a theory becomes the rudder for conducting studies. "This stance in turn implies—sometimes more, sometimes less explicitly—an interpretation . . ." (Freire, p. 43). Without a theory, systematic inquiry does not have clear focus. A theory is simply a way of describing the relationship between concepts, events, or phenomena and thus theories help our understanding of practical situations (Greenberg & Baron, 2000).

View from the Field

Ms. Ling is concerned about her 7th grade students' lack of motivation. She visits with her principal, Mr. Crowder, about collecting classroom data. As Mr. Crowder describes the process he says, "Together we decided that in order for Ms. Ling to find out what motivates her students, she would need to collect some classroom data. Brainstorming together, we decided she could do one or more of the following activities:

1. Develop an interest inventory that asks what students do in their free time and if they have ever visited museums or science places;
2. Pose open-ended questions about their favorite things to do;
3. Conduct informal focus interviews that would identify movies and music they liked; and
4. Have students record in their journal stories about what they did out of school.

We decided that the responses to these activities could provide information that could prove helpful in lesson planning as well as learning activities for the class. Ms. Ling offered to share her findings with the other 7th grade teachers because we both felt that such student input could provide valuable data to improve the teaching–learning process."

As previously indicated, theoretical support for school leaders and practitioners as investigators is provided by the work of Michael Polanyi (1958) and Maxine Greene (1978). Their views guide action researchers in formulating principles that serve to organize the disciplined inquiry carried out in schools and classrooms. These conceptual underpinnings are presented briefly in the following section.

Polanyi (1958), in *Personal Knowledge*, contends that those working in psychology and sociology are the only professionals who are in support of "scientific detachment"; while those working in the hard sciences are aware of the human element and embrace it. For him, "into every act of knowing there enters a passionate contribution of the person knowing what is being known" (pp. vii–viii). Complete objectivity is a myth, and Polanyi replaces it with the concept of *personal knowledge*. He supports school research in two ways; he emphasizes that (1) personal knowledge does not undermine the results of the research, but enhances it, and (2) practitioners *see* school and classroom events that outsiders would miss.

Maxine Greene, in *Landscapes of Learning* (1978), explores the state of *wide-awakeness*, and its importance to levels of consciousness. For her, practitioner researchers are wide-awake and have a sense of consciousness that includes social *praxis*, "a type of . . . participant knowing oriented to transforming the world" (p. 13). As practitioner researchers make sense of their world, they become more autonomous and less power-less and impervious to change. Such inquiry is supported by Greene's philosophical stance when she says that practitioners can reach beyond their immediate situations and their own levels of consciousness through reflection and an examination of the school and classroom environments.

Berthoff (1990) has initiated a dialogue regarding research and educational issues and suggests that teachers as investigators need inquiry skills for examining the data they have. For Berthoff (1990), "re-search," begins with formulating the question and procedures that use dialectic and dialogic language as a tool for finding meaning in the classroom. This tool employs language to recognize events in the teaching–learning process and then language becomes part of the discussion about these experiences.

What Is Action Research?

Action research is an enterprise of inquiry in which school leaders working in collabo-ration with their faculty participate in a cycle of planning, researching, analyzing, self-reflection, and action. Action research then can be categorized as both basic, fundamental research and applied research. According to Pine (1992), action research is "somewhere between 'big-R' university research on the one hand and teachers' daily intuition on the other" (p. 657). The knowledge generated serves to inform practice regarding school and curriculum development, classroom instruction, parent involve-ment, and campus-based management; the knowledge generated becomes the catalyst for subsequent action, change, and improvement. Over the past several years, action research has been defined and described in a number of ways. The following list provides a sampling of the definitions:

- Systematic inquiry conducted by teachers, principals, or other stakeholders that furthers the efforts of effecting positive changes (Mills, 2000)

- A collective process of defining and redefining understanding on which the organizational life is built (Stringer, 1999)
- A disciplined process of inquiry conducted by and for those taking the action (Sagor, 2000)
- Process of systemic study by teachers for the purpose of improving classroom instruction (Miller & Pine, 1990; Loucks-Horsley, et al., 1987; Loucks-Horsley, et al., 1998)
- Practice-based professional inquiry and practical classroom problem solving in the natural language of teachers (Duckworth, 1986)
- A professional development strategy, which is central to restructuring schools (Carr & Kemmis, 1986)

For us, action research serves as a type of investigation that school leaders can implement in their schools to provide data for decision making at the campus level to transform the school culture. This investigative approach also serves to promote equity and an awareness of teaching and learning that can result in increased student achievement and a greater sense of teacher professionalism. Action research can also serve as a pathway to "reinforce and cement the belief that together [teachers and administrators] can make a difference" (Glanz, 1998, xi).

The emphasis is on action, which addresses local practices. Action research takes a local focus, ". . . even as [it] pertain[s] to the more universal concerns that guide our political and pedagogical work" (Gore & Zeichner, 1995, p. 211). It should be noted, however, that ". . . schoolwide action research is no panacea; it does not offer a magic potion to . . . automatic, painless school improvement" (Calhoun, 1994, p. 3). It does offer an alternative for moving schools beyond the status quo to potential solutions for identified educational issues and promoting success for all students.

Site-based research puts practitioners at the epicenter of the investigative process and emphasizes their voices in restructuring and renewing schools and classrooms. For Stenhouse (1985), such a voice is essential if school leaders are to understand and change the world of schools and classrooms. First and most important, action research takes place in naturalistic settings of schools and classrooms. Second, the researchers are practitioners—school leaders and teachers who are integrally involved in planning and implementing the study. These investigators address classroom, school, and district issues in a systematic way that can yield insights from information gathered. "These insights into classroom life help us understand situations much better than we ever did . . ." (Kennedy, 1997, p. 6).

As a form of applied research, action research is inquiry that is on-going, situation-based, and process-oriented and leads to explanations that enable school leaders and teachers to better understand the nature of a situation or event, and then identify possible solutions. Three commonly used forms of action research exist: (1) individual, undertaken by practitioners; (2) collaborative, involving several members within the school community; and (3) schoolwide, investigating broader issues and involving members of the larger educational community (Glanz, 1998). Although the distinction between collaborative and schoolwide research is subtle, these forms of action research are important to the type of projects conducted. School leaders can be instrumental in promoting and supporting all forms of action research in their schools.

In the daily world of schools, there are small problems to solve, such as "How can I introduce this lesson?" "How do I complete my lesson plan book?" and there are more serious, complex, and pervasive problems, such as "How can we reduce the large numbers of dropouts in our high school?" It is the more serious problems that impinge on the professional lives of school leaders. Conducting studies helps to generate plausible explanations that increase the amount of information school leaders have with which to make decisions and pose solutions. School leaders working at the school and district levels can apply action research paradigms to investigate the interactional complexities of school life.

Steps in Action Research

The common thread running through the definitions of action research is a people orientation that emphasizes looking, thinking, and taking action. For Kemmis and McTaggart (1988), action research steps are not linear, but spiral in nature. Calhoun (1994) and Sagor (2000) suggest the following steps that leaders can use in conducting schoolwide action research: (1) select area of study or focus; (2) collect data; (3) organize data; (4) analyze and interpret; (5) report data; and (6) develop a plan of action. One step may lead to another, but many times the path may take different directions throughout the research process. Figure 5.2 provides a composite series of steps that school leaders can use in planning and implementing action research in their schools to promote school improvement and student success.

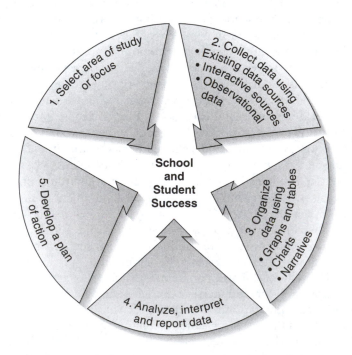

FIGURE 5.2   *Steps in Action Research*

For example, if a school leader is interested in promoting parental involvement as a means of curbing the dropout rate in his school, following the steps to conducting an action research in Figure 5.2 will prove helpful. It is critical for parents to stay connected to the school. The principal believes that if more parents were involved in the *school business*, the dropout rate would be lower. A research question for this principal might be: What are the barriers that prevent parents from coming to PTA/PTO meetings and/or volunteering during the school day? Conducting a telephone survey or interviewing parents may be the first place to begin to collect data that can be analyzed for patterns to identify barriers and ways to respond to the research question. If the data are not conclusive, other methods can be implemented. From data generated, an action plan can be written and strategies implemented to involve more parents in school activities.

Action Research: Suggestions for School Leaders

For school leaders, fads and quick fixes have often characterized the answers offered for instructional and managerial problems. But as educators know, these fads are frequently short-lived. Action research, on the other hand, provides a unique opportunity for involving school leaders in a collaborative endeavor with faculty and others to address specific school-related issues. School leaders can use the research inquiry process as a catalyst for school change by involving teachers in improving the working conditions and learning climate at their campuses (Gore & Zeichner, 1995). Through the multiple step process of action research, teachers (1) explore ideas, (2) compare what is found with current practice, (3) participate in training sessions to support needed changes, and (4) study the impact of these changes on themselves, their students, and their colleagues (Calhoun, 2002). One way that leaders can attain individual and collective school goals is by establishing a research agenda in their schools. It is through action research that social systems in schools can change and support continual professional growth and development for teachers.

With attention focused on improved student achievement, action research can provide a way to generate research-based ideas that can lead to improved learning (Darling-Hammond & Berry, 1998; Cochran-Smith & Lytle, 1990, 1998, 1999; Lytle & Cochran-Smith, 1990; Rearick & Feldman, 1999). By implementing action research, school leaders can help to conceptualize concerns, design studies, observe outcomes, and analyze results to promote student learning. For Lewin (1946b), the benefit of action research is that it can transform ". . . a multitude of unrelated individuals frequently opposed in their outlook and their interests, into cooperative teams, not on the basis of sweetness but on the basis of readiness to face difficulties realistically, to apply honest fact-finding, and to work together to overcome them" (p. 211).

The merits of action research as a means for creating professional learning communities were identified nearly sixty years ago. School leaders can use action research to build an organization that supports inquiry that leads to school improvement.

According to McLean (1995), action research requires a long-term commitment from all involved and helps school leaders to ". . . begin examining . . . current and future practices in a systematic way" (p. ix). Implementing a research agenda requires a commitment of time to conduct studies and involves collecting data by observing, interviewing, and surveying participants in the study, engaging in self-reflection, and then drawing conclusions and generating recommendations (McLean, 1995). School-wide action research may be the most complex and difficult undertaking because it requires members of the school organization to *buy in* and be willing to participate in the inquiry process. For Calhoun (1994), the purpose of schoolwide action is school improvement, in three senses: ". . . improvement of the organization as a problem solving entity . . . [the] improvement in equity for students . . . [and] the breadth and content of the inquiries themselves" (p. 11).

School leaders who value the research process see it as a way to advance teaching and learning practices. To value research means to make it an integral part of a school's mission so that members of the educational community view reflective inquiry as routine and valuable to their growth as individuals and to the improvement of their campus culture. Therefore, campus leaders must build research into their vision for capitalizing on the potential of both teachers and students. For many school leaders, the challenge is getting members of the school community to value and appreciate research as a viable approach for informing and reforming schools. Action research involves a commitment to keeping written accounts of daily events, implementing a problem-solving approach, and engaging in self-reflection. A first step in identifying issues and reflecting on concerns begins with teachers keeping journals. Over time, these journal entries go beyond descriptive comments and move to recording feelings, perceptions, and concerns. As teachers think about the teaching–learning process, different connections emerge that lead to constructive dialogue and a greater understanding of classroom life.

An important first step in gaining the support of the entire faculty is a small core group of teachers forming study groups that use the results generated from research. In addition, the small group structure chips away at teacher isolation (Arnold, 1998). Having members of the faculty develop a positive attitude toward research is essential. Providing teachers with information is key to change, and school leaders can begin by copying articles that discuss the benefits of conducting research and its impact on learning and distribute these to the faculty. Some of the questions that teachers have may be answered in these articles, whereas other questions can be answered during grade or departmental meetings.

Building a Research Agenda

To integrate a research agenda into the school's culture, there needs to be time during the school day for faculty and staff to engage in action research activities. One way to do this is to arrange teaching schedules so that teams of teachers have common planning times. Arnold (1998) identified a lack of a common planning time as a major barrier to an action research project that focused on integrating art, physics, and geometry at Galax High School in Virginia. Another essential step is to provide necessary resources, including information sessions on action research as a regular feature at school faculty meetings.

Other resources may include laptop computers, software packages, and a budget to copy relevant materials for specific research projects. Financial support may be required to pay substitutes for members of research teams who need to have free time

View from the Field

Mrs. Mesa recently became the new principal at Elmore Intermediate School. She says, "When I assumed the principalship role in September, the students were performing below district expectations on standardized achievement tests. The campus goals reflected a need to improve student performance by developing critical thinking skills that were aligned to the achievement test. In the first few months there, I began making informal *walk throughs* in each teacher's class. In November, on one of my routine walk throughs I noted that teachers were asking mostly low-level questions consistently across all subjects areas. Regardless of the content, teachers were asking primarily knowledge, comprehension, and convergent questions. Such questioning strategies seemed to run counter to the school's mission of 'nurturing students to think and make choices based on information.'"

Mrs. Mesa realized that to accomplish the mission and vision of the school, changes were needed in the types of questions that teachers asked. As a way of building support for this aspect of the school's mission and vision, Mrs. Mesa says, "I decided to initiate an action research plan to foster instructional changes, and I implemented the following steps to address this research program:

1. Created research teams of teachers who shared common interests;

2. Had each teacher keep a daily log (or tape) of his or her lessons;

3. Had teachers review and reflect on the information collected;

4. Asked teachers to identify in their journals the patterns and trends in the kinds of questions they asked;

5. Encouraged teachers to share and discuss their findings within their research teams;

6. Had teachers analyze their findings and make recommendations collaboratively; and

7. Had research teams decide on a plan of action to change the types of questions asked."

Over the course of the next three months, as teachers at Elmore Intermediate School engaged in this cycle of inquiry, Mrs. Mesa began to see changes in the types of questions students were asked. The changes in student responses were predicated on the questions asked. As Mrs. Mesa notes, "Students were being challenged to think beyond the obvious. In addition, faculty meetings became a time for celebrations when teacher research teams began to share what they had observed about what they were doing now compared to what they had been doing three months earlier. They saw the differences in their students and were so excited."

to observe classroom instruction, interview colleagues and parents, or to travel to other schools or districts to investigate a specific instructional program. In taking these steps, members of the faculty and staff will have opportunities to ". . . look for connections when none seem evident" as Lieutenant Leaphorn says in the *Sacred Clowns* (Hillerman, 1993, p. 36), or as Wheatley (1999) says, look for information or data that disconfirms what we believe to be true. The goal is to make decisions based on findings. In the next View from the Field, Mrs. Mesa uses data collected to make decisions about ways to improve the questioning strategies implemented.

In this View from the Field, Mrs. Mesa, as the school's leader, demonstrated an ability to promote on-going professional growth of the faculty and staff, which in turn had an impact on student achievement. By involving faculty in the research process, an infrastructure was provided that proved to be a potent tool for school improvement (Arnold, 1998). Sagor (2000) suggests that school leaders help to put the *action* in action research by focusing on the data collected. Leaders can use four basic strategies for engaging in action. First, they may simply present the data and let it speak for itself. As Sagor (1992) says, "Sometimes unembellished data alone can convince people of the need to change" (p. 70). A second strategy is to establish a pilot program based on promising practices identified by the original research. Next, the pilot program can be expanded to include competing programs. There may be two trends that show promise and each group could seek to determine the best way. Finally, a fourth strategy is to use initial results from the classroom or grade level and expand it to include the total school as a work group to analyze the data and determine recommendations for change.

Three Sources of Data Collection

A critical aspect of action research is the collection of data. While the data collected are generally for the benefit of the researcher or action research team, Sagor (1992) notes that "The guiding principle behind the data collection process is that the information collected should be compelling enough to convince any skeptic . . . [for] skeptics or cynics usually need overwhelming data to convince them of anything" (p. 28). Wierisma (2000) also cautions that data should not be collected in a "haphazard or ad hoc manner . . . [because] the process . . . requires proper organization and control so that the data will enable valid decisions to be made . . ." (p. 3).

Data available to action researchers generally come from three main sources. The first source includes historical or existing data in the form of student records, student work, and other specimens of student archival work. The next source of data comes through an interactive process that solicits input in the form of surveys, questionnaires, and interviews. A third source of data can be considered observational data and includes journals, videos, photographs, and shadowing.

Existing Data Sources

Action researchers can collect and review existing documents or select specimen records as a way of obtaining data. "Schools are naturally data rich environments, and simply opening our eyes to some of the most . . . easily obtainable sources of data can make . . . the data collection process much easier" (Sagor, 1992, p. 31). For example, if researchers are concerned about the effect of grading patterns on achievement test performance they can review school recorders such as grade books and report cards as existing sources of data. In schools where students keep portfolios, examples of student work could be selected for the database. School files are rich sources of data and include information regarding family background and income (especially low socioeconomic status), discipline referrals, grades, attendance, and performance data on any standardized achievement test. Teacher grade books and lesson plan books that have been filed from previous years can yield valuable information.

Interactive Sources

Data from students, teachers, parents, and administrators provide a second form of information for action research. Interviews, surveys, and questionnaires can offer valuable data about what people know and believe, and how they feel. When using the interview process, questions should be written in advance. Guidelines for constructing questions include (1) keep the number of questions to four to six; (2) limit the number of follow-up questions—for example, What do students like most about science class? Follow-up of question—Why do you think so?; (3) use simple sentence construction because those being interviewed are asked questions orally and must remember the question before developing a response; and (4) integrate key points into more than one question to validate responses given.

Before starting an interview, develop a system for recording the responses so that the responses can be analyzed and interpreted. Using a tape recorder requires prior permission from all parties. Accurate and complete notes are critical to the analysis and recommendation steps in the action research process. Surveys and questionnaires also provide a way for school researchers to obtain data. "A good bit of the efforts of a questionnaire . . . are directed toward constructing good items and getting respondents to complete the questionnaire" (Wiersma, 2000, p. 167). Surveys and questionnaires are especially effective for assessing "emotional, cognitive, and attitudinal issues" (Sagor, 1992, p. 38). General rules of thumb in constructing surveys and questionnaires include (1) be short and sweet—clarity and brevity are essential; (2) avoid leading questions or suggesting a response; (3) make confidentiality a central element to the process; and (4) provide an opportunity for respondents to make additional comments.

Interviewing provides a face-to-face opportunity to find out what people are thinking. A 9th grade social studies teacher, for example was concerned about the 10 percent failure rate in geography over the past two years. She and her principal thought there might be a connection with the dropout rate among high school students. She set out to find some answers. She decided to talk to her colleagues in the social studies department, during and after the school day. Although talking to colleagues appears informal, she did ask them the same questions and asked follow-up questions to clarify points and to expand on ideas shared. What she found was that a disproportionate number of students who failed geography and dropped out of school at the end of the 9th grade were Hispanic students. Her findings were shared with her principal and central office administrators. While the teacher did not discover a cause-and-effect relationship between failing geography and dropping out of school, she did uncover data that proved helpful as intervention strategies were implemented and a specific student population was targeted.

Observational Data

Observations are also useful when conducting action research. Observing in classrooms provides an extra pair of eyes for examining teaching–learning behaviors. Observations conducted as part of action research are *not* meant to be assessments. The primary goal of observation as a study tool is to collect classroom data. To accomplish this goal and create a nonthreatening environment, action researchers must talk to and build trust with the teacher(s) so that being observed becomes more comfortable for them and they are more confident in their teaching (Sahakian & Stockton, 1996). A clearly articulated purpose and agenda for the observation is important to the data-collection process.

Some guidelines for classroom observations may prove helpful. The observer should (1) focus on a limited number of student or teacher behaviors during one observation and focus on an interest of the teacher; (2) maintain an element of normalcy by not disturbing the natural setting of the classroom; (3) keep a detailed written record with notations that are clear and accurate; and (4) reflect on and analyze the data collected to inform teachers about their practice (Beach & Reinhartz, 2000). These guidelines provide a greater degree of objectivity and help the researcher be more effective when conducting classroom observations.

Echevarria, Vogt, and Short (2000) have developed the Sheltered Instruction Observation Protocol, which has been used with teachers to promote reflective teaching and self-evaluation. This observation during instruction addresses content objectives, language objectives, content concepts, supplementary materials, adaptation of content, and meaningful activities and builds background by providing comprehensible input, strategies, interactions, practice/application, and lesson delivery. Sheltered Instruction Observation Protocol was used in a study involving teachers who worked with English language learners at all levels. This observation protocol proved helpful to these teachers who became better planners, instructors, and evaluators because of the feedback provided by peer coaches (Echevarria & Short, 2001). Observation data are powerful in getting teachers to talk about their teaching with the added benefit of getting feedback.

By using a variety of data-collection procedures for classroom observation, the researcher can focus on specific events of interest to the teacher being observed as well as the researcher. Procedures such as timelines, topical data capture chart, on-task and off-task behavior checklists, lesson transitions and pacing sheets, and mapping teacher mobility, classroom management, and teacher–student and student-to-student interactions using sociograms can provide opportunities for closely examining questioning strategies, student and teacher responses, use of teacher time, effectiveness of instruction, and the amount of time teachers spend with specific students. According to Goldhammer, Anderson, and Krajewski (1993), as the data are analyzed one begins ". . . to formulate some initial impressions of the kinds of patterns characterizing a teacher's work. . . . Think back to what [was] observed . . . to see whether certain ways of dealing with problems or talking or reacting to the students or moving around represents a persistent pattern" (p. 113).

In addition to observations, researchers can also use journals, videotapes, or shadowing techniques to obtain classroom data. Journals provide a *snapshot* of teacher thinking and can be collected to provide a picture of the action research issue. Video-tapes used in observing classrooms can allow several pairs of eyes to review practices. Shadowing helps researchers to see people and circumstances in context or as they really are. Researchers can collect a picture in the typical day in a naturalistic setting.

Existing data, interactive data, and observations can be used by action researchers as they investigate issues at the classroom, school, and district levels. Through the use of action research school leaders and teachers become professional problem solvers who are committed to improving school practice and student outcomes (Mills, 2000).

Case Study

In the case that follows, Jim tells his story of the second grade math team. With the support and encouragement from you (their principal), the team members decide to investigate student perception of intelligence. This is a topic that has intrigued the team members for some time and has often been a topic of discussion. You recognize that Jim and his team members are sincere, and you have agreed to provide an all-day substitute once a month during the school year so Jim can collect and analyze the data as well as chair the Howard Elementary School Research Committee.

Jim is a second grade teacher who has been interested in knowing how his students perceive their own capabilities or levels of intelligence. His research question is, "How do children define their own intelligence?" To answer this question, he turned to his second graders at Howard Elementary. Working closely with his second grade level colleagues, they frame questions that will provide the information that Jim is seeking. Jim began this quest by having all of the second grade students complete the following questions:

1. What does it mean to be smart?
2. Do you think you are smart?
3. How do people get smart?

As Jim reviewed and organized their responses, he began to identify some trends. Some of the second graders perceived their ability to be fixed—"I've never been very smart"—meaning they believed that they were not smart. Others perceived their intelligence as being unlimited—"The harder I try, the smarter I get."

Guided by the voices of these second graders, Jim worked with the other second grade teachers to attempt to build a bridge between theory and teaching practice. Using what they learned from these students, they changed their thinking about the classroom environment. The second grade teachers began to establish a culture that addressed the responses from the students. The second grade team began to teach their students to set clear and measurable goals and then helped them to link effort and persistence with success and learning.

Jim and the second grade team learned a lot about teaching and learning. In sessions with members of the Howard Elementary Research Committee, he posed questions and listened as others shared ideas and discussed various issues. Through such dialoging and reflection Jim and the second grade team made changes in their class-rooms.

As the campus leader/administrator, how would you respond to the following questions:

1. In what ways is Jim's story about action research?
2. How could you, the campus leader, have supported other efforts of the team?

3. How has action research used a *change agent* in this case study?
4. What other research could these second grade teachers conduct in their classrooms as a follow-up?
5. What next steps should you, the leader, take to build on the work of these action researchers?

Summary

Action research studies are inquiry driven and demonstrate a questioning, reflective posture toward teaching and learning and have the potential to change schools by providing for renewal. Action research demonstrates the virtue of bringing theory and practice closer together.

School leaders can help to demystify the research process by supporting efforts to investigate issues of concerns; they can invite teams of teachers to develop a research agenda and rely on each other and pool their collective professional needs and interest. Studying teaching and learning leads to improvement because it supports best practices. What results from engaging in research is information that is personally owned and based on qualitative, practice-oriented inquiry that can be shared with others. For school leaders, the outcome expectancies for conducting action research in elementary and secondary classrooms are high—improving teaching practices so that all students learn. Conducting research in school has been described by Britton (1987) as a "quiet revolution." What results is the way school leaders and their teachers do business. As change occurs from within, leaders and teachers become learners who discover their own learning as an ongoing process.

The chapter described three ways that data can be collected—case studies, interviews, and observations. Data collection procedures provide school leaders and teachers with rich insightful descriptions of how students, for example, perceive the culture of the classroom. Decisions regarding what to teach, when to teach it, and what order, for example, are made based on the data.

Knowledge gleaned from research can guide both school leaders and teachers toward systems thinking strategies for accommodating all learners in a classroom. And as school leaders look toward the future, the goal is to have experiences for their faculty that are ". . . participatory, dialogic, transformative, and educative" in nature (Janesick, 1998, pp. 6–7). Such a climate improves the way a school operates, how individuals behave, and how students learn.

Your Turn

5.1. A mandate from the central school administration office requires use of the same lesson plan template. At your campus, several teachers have asked questions regarding its origin, purpose, and the research base supporting this template. Questions also were raised about the level of involvement of teachers in implementing this plan. As the campus leader, your role is to work with campus faculty in implementing this format.

More specifically, your role will be to chair the campus Research Committee. What steps will you take to find answers to the questions posed by members of your faculty? How will you go about initiating an action research study that investigates this problem at your campus? As you begin, think about and make notes to yourself regarding how you will:

- Determine the need for an action research study
- Identify the question to focus the research study
- Identify a common time to meet
- Select the ways data will be collected
- Determine the length of the study and when the final report will be presented
- Identify how the data will be analyzed

5.2. There has been a movement to teach character education in the school district. Character education is an emotional topic among faculty and parents. In the last three forums to discuss this topic, tempers flared and the meetings ended with nothing resolved. You recognize the need for data. Design an action research study to *inform the dialogue* on the topic of character education. Follow the steps presented in the text and outline a timeline for investigating character education. Use the Internet to identify studies that have investigated this topic. Individually or in teams, answer the following questions to help you prepare:

- What areas need to be investigated to frame the research question?
- How will the information be collected?
- How will the data be analyzed?
- What conclusions can be drawn from the information that you have collected?

References

Altrichter, H., Posch, P., & Somekh, B. (1993). *Teachers investigate their work: An introduction to the methods of action research.* New York: Routledge.

Arnold, D. E. (1998). Action research in action: Curricular articulation and integrated instruction. *NASSP Bulletin, 82,* 596, 74–78.

Barth, R. S. (2001). Teacher leader. *Phi Delta Kappan, 82,* 6, 443–449.

Beach, D. M., & Reinhartz, J. (2000). *Supervisory leadership: Focus on instruction.* Boston: Allyn & Bacon.

Berthoff, A. (1990). *The sense of learning.* Portsmouth, NH: Boynton/Cook.

Boyarsky, N., & Murphy, N. (1998). *Action research* (Black dog series, Vol. I). NP: Art Books International.

Britton, J. (1987). *A quiet form of research. Reclaiming the classroom: Teacher research as an agency for change,* pp. 13–19. In S. Goswami & P. R. Still. Upper Montclair, NJ: Boynton/Cook Publishers.

Brown, A., & Dowling, P. (1998). *Doing research/reading research: A mode of interrogation for education.* London: Falmer.

Calhoun, E. F. (2002). Action research for school improvement. *Educational Leadership, 59,* 6, 18–24.

Calhoun, E. F. (1994). *How to use action research in the self-renewing school.* Alexandria, VA: Association for Supervision and Curriculum Development.

Carr, W., & Kemmis, S. (1986). *Becoming critical: Education, knowledge, and action research.* Geelong, Victoria: Deakin University Press.

Christiansen, H., Goulet, L., Krentz, C., & Maeers, M. (eds). (1997). *Recreating relationships: Collaboration and educational reform.* Albany: State University of New York Press.

Cochran-Smith, M., & Lytle, S. L. (1999). The teacher researcher movement: A decade later. *Educational Researcher,* 15–25.

Cochran-Smith, M., & Lytle, S. L. (1998). Teacher research: The question that persists. *Leadership in Education, 1,* 1, 19–36.

Cochran-Smith, M., & Lytle, S. L. (1993). *Inside/outside: Teacher research and knowledge.* New York: Teachers College Press.

Cochran-Smith, M., & Lytle, S. L. (1990). Research on teaching and teacher research: The issues that divide. *Educational Researcher, 19,* 2, 2–11.

Darling-Hammond, L., & Berry, B. (1998, May 27). Investing in teaching: The dividend is student achievement. *Education Week, 17,* 37, 48–49.

Duckworth, E. (1986). Teaching as research. *Harvard Educational Review, 56,* 4, 481–495.

Echevarria, J., & Short, D. J. (2001). The sheltered instruction observation protocol (SIOP) and the achievement of English language learners. Presentation at American Educational Research Association, Seattle, WA, April 12, 2001.

Echevarria, J., Vogt, M. E., & Short, D. (2000). *Making content comprehensible for English language learners: The SIOP model.* Boston: Allyn & Bacon.

Fenstermacher, G. (1994). The knower and the known. The nature of knowledge in research on teaching. In L. Darling-Hammond (ed), *Review of research in education.* Washington, DC: American Education Research Association.

Freire, P. (1985). *The politics of education.* South Hadley, MA: Begin & Garvey.

Gable, R., & Rogers, V. (1987). Taking the terror out of research. *Phi Delta Kappan, 68,* 9, 690–695.

Glanz, J. (1998). *Action research: An educational leader's guide to school improvement.* Norwood, MA: Christopher-Gordon Publishers.

Glesne, C. (1999). *Becoming qualitative researchers: An introduction* (2nd ed). New York: Longman.

Goldhammer, R., Anderson, R. H., & Krajewski, R. J. (1993). *Clinical supervision: Special methods for the clinical supervision of teachers* (3rd ed). Fort Worth, TX: Harcourt Brace Jovanovich.

Gore, J. M., & Zeichner, K. M. (1995). Connecting action research to genuine teacher development. In J. Smyth (ed), *Critical discourses on teacher development.* New York: Cassell.

Greenberg, J., & Baron, R. A. (2000). *Behavior in organizations: Understanding and managing the human side of work* (7th ed). Upper Saddle River, NJ: Prentice-Hall.

Greene, M. (1978). *Landscapes of learning.* New York: Teachers College Press.

Hillerman, T. (1993). *Sacred clowns.* Toronto: HarperCollins.

Huberman, M. (1996). Focus on research moving mainstream: Taking a closer look at teacher research. *Language Arts, 73,* 2, 124–140.

Janesick, V. J. (1998). *Stretching exercises for qualitative researchers.* Thousand Oaks, CA: Sage.

Kaestle, C. (1993). The awful reputation of education research. *Educational Researcher, 22,* 1, 23–31.

Kemmis, S., & McTaggart, R. (1988). *The action research planner.* Geelong, Victoria, Australia: Deakin University Press.

Kennedy, M. M. (1997). The connections between research and practice. *Educational Researcher, 26,* 7, 4–12.

Kincheloe, J. (1991). *Teachers as researchers: Qualitative inquiry as a path to empowerment.* New York: The Falmer Press.

Krathwohl, D. R. (1993). *Methods of educational and social science research: An integrated approach.* New York: Longman.

Krulfeld, R., MacDonald, J. R., & MacDonald, J. L. (eds). (1998). *Power, ethics and human rights: Anthropological studies of refugee research and action.* Savage, MD: Rowman & Littlefield.

LeCompte, M. D., & Schensul, J. J. (1999). *Designing and conducting ethnographic research.* Walnut Creek, CA: AltaMira.

Lewin, K. (1946a). Action research and minority problems. *Journal of Social Issues, 2,* 34–46.

Lewin, K. (1946b). Action research and minority problems. In K. Lewin (ed), *Resolving social conflicts: Selected papers on group dynamics* (compiled in 1948). New York: Harper & Row.

Loucks-Horsley, S., Harding, C. K., Arbuckle, M. A., Murray, L. B., Dubea, C., & Williams, M. K. (1987). *Continuing to learn: A guidebook for teacher development.* Andover, MA: The Regional

Laboratory for Educational Improvement of the Northeast and Islands and Oxford, OH: The National Staff Development Council.

Loucks-Horsley, S., Hewson, P. W., Love, N., & Stiles, K. E. (1998). *Designing professional development for teachers of science and mathematics*. Thousand Oaks, CA: Corwin Press.

Lytle, S. L., & Cochran-Smith, M. (1990). Learning from teacher research: A working typology. *Teachers College Record, 92*, 1, 83–103.

Mahlio, M. C. (2001). The effects of participation in action research: Overview and framework. In J. D. Rainer & E. M. Guyton (eds), *Research on the effects of teacher education on teacher performance*. Dubuque, IA: Kendall/Hunt Publishing Company.

Marshall, C., & Rossman, G. B. (1994). *Designing qualitative research*. Thousand Oaks, CA: Sage.

McLean, J. E. (1995). *Improving education through action research*. Thousand Oaks, CA: Corwin Press.

McTaggart, R. (ed.) (1997). *Participatory action research: International contexts and consequences*. Albany: State University of New York Press.

Miller, D. M., & Pine, G. J. (1990). Advancing professional inquiry for educational improvement through action research. *Journal of Staff Development, 11*, 3, 56–61.

Mills, G. (2000). *Action research: A guide for teacher researcher*. Columbus, OH: Merrill/Prentice-Hall.

Newman, J. M. (1998). *Action research: Exploring the tension of teaching*. New York: Teachers College.

Noffke, S. (1995). A conversation about action research and democratic schooling. *Action in Teacher Education, 16*, 4, 82–86.

Pine, N. (1992). Three personal theories that suggest models for teacher research. *Teachers College Record, 93*, 4, 456–472.

Polanyi, M. (1958). *Personal knowledge: Towards a post-critical philosophy*. Chicago: University of Chicago Press.

Putnam, R. T., & Borko, H. (2000). What do new views of knowledge and thinking have to say about research on teacher learning? *Educational Researcher, 29*, 1, 4–15.

Rearick, M. L., & Feldman, A. (1999). Orientations, purposes and reflection: A framework for understanding action research. *Teaching and Teacher Education, 15*, 4, 33–34.

Sagor, R. (2000). *Guiding school improvement with action research*. Alexandria, VA: Association for Supervision and Curriculum Development.

Sagor, R. (1992). *How to conduct collaborative action research*. Alexandria, VA: Association for Supervision and Curriculum Development.

Sahakian, P., & Stockton, J. (1996). Opening doors: Teacher-guided observations. *Educational Leadership, 53*, 50–53.

Schmoker, M. (1999). *Results: The key to continuous school improvement* (2nd ed). Alexandria, VA: Association for Supervision and Curriculum Development.

Schön, D. (1983). *The reflective practitioner*. San Francisco: Jossey-Bass.

Shank, R. C. (2000). A vision of education for the twenty-first century. *T. H. E. Journal, 27*, 6, 42–45.

Shulman, J., & Kepner, D. (1994). The editorial imperative: Responding to productive tensions between case writing and individual development. Unpublished paper. San Francisco: Far West Laboratory.

Smith, D. L. (1989). *Becoming your own researcher*. Wentworth Falls, N. S. Wales: Social Science Press.

Srouge, G. E. (1997). Improving the "awful reputation" of educational research. *Educational Researcher, 26*, 7, 26–28.

Stenhouse, L. (1985). In J. Rudduck & D. Hopkins (eds), *Research as a basis for teaching: Readings from the work of Lawrence Stenhouse*. London: Heinemann Educational Books.

Stringer, E. T. (1999). *Action research* (2nd ed). Thousand Oaks, CA: Sage.

van Manen, M. (1984). Action research as a theory of the unique: From pedagogic thoughtfulness to pedagogic tactfulness. Paper presented at the American Educational Research Association, New Orleans, Louisiana.

Wiersma, W. (2000). *Research methods in education* (7th ed). Boston: Allyn & Bacon.

Wheatley, M. J. (1999). *Leadership and the new science: Discovering order in a chaotic world* (2nd ed). San Francisco: Berrett-Koehler Publishers.

6

Organizational Leadership: Decision Making and Communication

Standard 2: A school administrator is an educational leader who promotes the success of all students by advocating, nurturing, and sustaining a school culture and instructional program conducive to student learning and staff professional growth.

Standard 3: A school administrator is an educational leader who promotes the success of all students by ensuring management of the organization, operations, and resources for a safe, effective, and efficient learning environment.

Chapter Objectives

The objectives of this chapter are:

- Describe group processes in school organizations.
- Identify basic group processes including cohesiveness, conformity, cooperation, and competition.
- Explain roles and norms of learning groups and communities.
- Describe decision-making processes and models.
- Explain the role of effective communication in a school setting.

Leading a productive organization means knowing and understanding human behavior in the workplace and applying this information specifically to schools. A major role of school leaders is getting members to work together toward fostering the growth and development of all students so they are academically successful. Finding the best match between the needs of the school organization and the talents and interests of its members is becoming more challenging for school leaders. People are, indeed, any organization's most important asset and, further, people define a school's character by ". . . [their] capacity to perform and represent the knowledge-base of the organization" (U.S. General Accounting Office, 2002, p. 4).

School leaders, in their ever changing roles, are attempting to transform the culture of schools so that they ". . . become less hierarchical, . . . stovepiped, and inwardly focused and more flat, results-oriented, integrated, and externally focused" (U.S. General Accounting Office, 2002, p. 4). For example, teacher shortages continue to plague school leaders in many urban and rural schools, as does teacher retention. According to a recent study, the number leaving the teaching profession has accelerated in recent years. Up to 30% of all beginning teachers leave in the first three years, which costs districts as much as $46,000 to replace them (Texas Higher Education Coordinating Board, 2002). Recruiting and keeping faculty is directly related to the leader's ability to match, marshal, manage, and maintain faculty in order to maximize the school's ability to foster student achievement. School leaders must engage in human capital recruitment and retention in order to ensure accountability within a results-oriented school culture.

Principles that guide school leaders in continuous school improvement are embedded in the scientist–practitioner model, which comes from the research in the field of industrial and organizational psychology (Riggio, 2000; Muchinsky, 2000). Drawing on the field of organizational behavior, leadership in organizations includes insights from economics, sociology, psychology, and political science, as well as organizational communication, fiscal management, and human relations. For Beach and Reinhartz (2000), "the workplace of the school is shaped by both the sociocultural system and the school's desired outcomes. As institutions of society, schools can be viewed as multifaceted organizations that are both similar to and different from other workplaces in form and function" (p. 47).

Based on the long history of the study of organizations, four major trends have applications for schools. These trends include (1) the nature of the school workplace is changing, with an ever increasing emphasis on technology, (2) the availability of human resources (teacher recruitment and retention) follows economic conditions, (3) schools, like society, are becoming more diverse, and (4) the globalization of teaching and learning has made the world a classroom (Craigor, 1997; May, 1998; Vandaveer, 1998; Harrison, Price, & Bell, 1998; Adler, 1991).

School leaders also need to find ways to tap into the talent of their school organizations to facilitate the types of decisions that lead to school improvement. Successful organizations have been shown to have groups that work collectively and cooperatively toward solutions related to school issues such as (1) finding better ways to teach, (2) improving student attitudes toward learning, (3) identifying better ways to assess learning, and (4) providing greater accountability to parents. Within the organizational structure, appropriate scaffolding should be provided for mentoring new and experienced teachers and for collaborative interactions that foster life-long learning.

This chapter provides the backdrop for school leaders to understand their roles in creating and sustaining the workplace of faculties as groups. Knowledge of group processes is critical when linked to making decisions and impacting the social behavior of group members. As school leaders build a foundation for creating learning communities (described in Chapter 2), they must apply their knowledge of how groups work and function, but also their understanding of effective communication.

This chapter presents the school organization as the context in which leaders work and implement key organizational processes such as developing teams and work groups at school, making effective decisions, and communicating effectively. The study of organizational behavior associated with group dynamics and group processes is crucial to managing human resources and enhancing skills, knowledge, and performance. A knowledge and understanding of how organizations work helps to explain how groups function within and external to the school.

Organizational Membership

To fully understand and appreciate the behavior that occurs in educational organizations called schools, leaders cannot focus on individual teachers working alone, but must also be mindful of how teachers work in groups as well as within the larger context of the school or campus. "To comprehend fully, the complex dynamics of behavior in organizations," leaders must focus "on three distinct levels: individual, groups, and organizations" (Greenberg & Baron, 2000, p. 5).

Like other organizations, schools too have organizational citizenship behaviors (OCBs), which have been defined as those that benefit the organization (Penner, Midili, & Kegelmeyer, 1997; Graham, 1991; Schnake, 1991; Organ, 1988). These behaviors, such as teacher morale and the feelings that one makes a difference in the classroom, are essential for achieving a school's mission. For Van Dyne, Graham, and Dienesch (1994), OCBs have three major characteristics that are (1) personal, (2) situational, and (3) positional. If educators have a positive attitude, value their jobs, are motivated, and have job security, they contribute to the overall effectiveness of the school because the OCBs are high. At the central office level, job classification, workplace values, and job security are considered important in setting the course for an effective school system. Cynicism or poor teacher morale, on the other hand, negatively impacts OCBs and results in limiting the attainment of school goals.

Organizational effectiveness, according to Podsakoff and Mac Kenzie (1997), is linked to OCBs in the following ways: If teachers go the extra mile, such as coming early and staying late, they are more likely to: (1) mentor new members of the organization, which assimilates them into their roles quicker; (2) be satisfied with their positions; (3) help recruit new teachers; and (4) assume new and different roles and responsibilities without having them as a part of the original job description.

In such an environment, teacher recruitment and retention are more easily achieved, which benefits the school. What makes such a school environment possible? School leaders can provide teachers with a variety of incentives, especially those that decrease the competition among colleagues. Although some competition is a natural behavior, it can contribute to an escalation of conflict and lower the overall effectiveness of the educational program. If incentives are a part of the overall strategy that school leaders employ, the guidelines for their use should be developed by a diverse group of teachers, so that the processes for obtaining these incentives are clearly articulated and understood by everyone. Such involvement helps teachers to feel like they are a part of the group, but more importantly, they feel empowered. Conger and Kanungo (1988) define empowerment as "a process of enhancing feelings of self-efficacy among organizational members through identification of conditions that foster powerlessness and through their removal by both formal organizational practices and informal techniques of providing efficacy information" (p. 3). Lambert (2002) summarizes the situation by saying that schools ". . . need to develop leadership capacity among all members of the school community" (p. 37).

Developing teacher leadership within the school organization provides the construct for penetrating the isolation that often exists among and between teachers and administrators. For Lambert (2002), "Our lesson is clear; instructional leadership must be a shared community understanding. Leadership is the professional work of everyone in the school" (p. 37). School leaders need to provide a school environment in which teachers work in collaborative teams to establish learning communities that are built on the principles of trust, cooperation, research, and technology. Training in the use of ActiveInk (2001) technology platform, for example, creates virtual meetings for team members, which complements the face-to-face meetings. By linking all members of a group who may or may not be in the same school location electronically via ActiveInk, opportunities are created for immediate input, access to resources, and ongoing dialogue. Members of the work teams become active participants in an online learning community.

Building School Work Groups and Teams

The work of teachers, staff, parents, and students is key to the success of the school organization. These groups interact, both in formal and informal work teams, and these teams are often reconfigured over the course of the school year as tasks, priorities, and timelines change. Some work teams may be extremely informal, such as colleagues socializing at lunch and after school hours or casually discussing teaching activities they have seen or heard about. During these informal settings, group members take the opportunity to discuss and resolve school business. As Uchiyama and Wolf (2002) note, "The implementation and learning teams made deliberate and considerate decisions with the rest of the faculty because they well understood that commitment to new ideas is more certain when teachers are a part of the decision-making process" (p. 80). Other teams function more formally when investigating a specific school problem or issue. Within informal and formal work groups, participants play different roles and gravitate toward other specific members of the group forming subgroups. The way groups function and how relationships are established is called *group dynamics* (Riggio, 2000). School leaders can ensure that groups work together effectively by carefully determining the best procedure for the composition of the work groups to produce the best results.

For example, work teams may conduct a schoolwide action research study to investigate ways to improve mathematics computation skills and numeracy literacy. Figure 6.1 illustrates how the three work teams have been structured to align the K–7 mathematics curriculum and improve math achievement for their district.

As seen in the figure, team members represent both elementary and middle schools. Team I focuses on the students; members of this team are to gather student data, especially scores on the 3rd, 5th, and 7th grade mandated mathematics tests, along with district benchmark test scores in mathematics. Other data to be collected include qualitative data from student, teacher, and parent interviews and mathematics attitude surveys. Work Team II is investigating the classroom learning environment; this study includes the resources that are available to teachers, namely manipulatives that support developmentally appropriate instructional strategies. This group is also collecting data through classroom observations on the *climate* of the classroom and the use of technology when teaching math concepts and skills. The last team, Work Team III, is concentrating on the school and district mathematics curriculum and the degree of congruency with the National Council of Teachers of Mathematics (NCTM) National Standards. This work team is reviewing local curriculum documents and textbooks to ensure that there is alignment. These data will help to determine if students are prepared to take advanced math courses when they move to high school. The work of all three teams seeks to identify ways to align the mathematics curriculum as well as ways to increase student learning in mathematics.

In building and sustaining work groups or teams on the campus the role of the school leader is to promote collaboration and cooperation among and between group leaders and members. When working in formal and informal groups, teachers assume

Work Teams	Major Focus	Location of Information	Roles/ Responsibilities of Team Members
Work Team I: students	Student information including: • Scores on mandate state tests for last three years beginning with 3rd graders who are now 8th graders • Scores on district benchmark tests for last three years • Overall student grades in math for past five years		
Work Team II: classroom environment and resources	• District textbook series, date and last adoption • Manipulatives used in each grade level • Types of professional development provided, types and kinds • Educational technology available and used daily • Types of library resources for teachers • Support staff available • Degree to which parent/community volunteer program is developed		
Work Team III: mathematics curriculum	• Examination of textbook series; district curriculum standards; campus curriculum standards; NCTM Standards; strategies used to introduce, practice, and master concepts; external data NAEP		

FIGURE 6.1 *Work Teams to Align and Improve Mathematics Curriculum.* Objective: To align and improve the mathematics curriculum in grades K–8. Goal of Action Research Study: To prepare students to take advanced mathematics classes.

different roles, follow rules and norms, and have different responsibilities as they seek to accomplish a task. Within a dynamic group configuration, a teacher or two may emerge as the *group leaders*. Often, these colleagues take a major role in moving the goal of the group forward and implementing the campus vision.

Conflict may develop if competition exists between and among group members relative to their specific roles or ideas. The group leader, who may be appointed or who may emerge from the group, becomes the rudder that serves to keep the group focused and maintains a commitment to the agenda or task. Before deliberations begin, the group leader helps to set the ground rules from which the group operates. For example, the leader might use a consensus building strategy such as "Please consider or can you support the proposed suggestion or decision with at least a number 3, on a scale of 1 to

5, and if you can, then the suggestion holds." By having these guidelines for deliberations, conflicts can be minimized and group goals are fostered.

As teachers work in groups or teams, they also engage in basic group social processes including cohesiveness, conformity, cooperation, and competition. These social processes ". . . regulate group behavior, coordinate group activities and stimulate action by group members" (Riggio, 2000, p. 310). Adhering to group norms through the process of conformity and consensus building contributes to the group's identity by putting pressure on group members to follow these norms. School norms are powerful shapers of behavior, especially at the campus and grade level group meetings. School leaders must be able to use school norms in constructive ways to help the school achieve academic success for all students.

Secondly, group cohesiveness is the degree to which teachers work together because they know each other and want to work together; cohesiveness is linked to member satisfaction. For Steers (1984) group cohesiveness is the degree to which teachers are attracted to the group, are willing to assume personal responsibility for its tasks, and work collaboratively to achieve the campus goals. To foster or promote group cohesiveness, campus leaders can make teachers feel that they are valued members of a team or group. One way of developing group cohesiveness among faculty is to develop book study groups that encourage teachers to share in informal settings. In such a setting, they begin to develop a sense of belonging and become more committed to group processes. It is particularly important for school leaders to develop cohesiveness in newly formed groups or teams as they begin their work or task. Cohesiveness is also important when principals open new schools and faculty members are new to the campus. School leaders need to work at building a culture that is committed to working toward a common goal.

Campus administrators must develop strategies that move team members toward understanding and sharing the campus or the committee goals. School leaders can see evidence of group cohesiveness when teachers are willing to work beyond school hours with their colleagues on committee activities or as they assume leadership roles to ensure that the goals and objectives identified in the site-based improvement plan are implemented. School leaders may need to monitor or structure group size because smaller groups tend to have greater cohesiveness. Consideration should also be given to the nature of the composition of the group. For example, when the status of the group members is similar or equivalent, the titles and roles are alike, and when group membership is stable, then group cohesiveness tends to be stronger (Cartwright, 1968; Riggio, 2000). In the View from the Field, Ms. Lavone describes the work of teams that are a part of her campus culture.

Collaboration and cooperation are fostered when the task is well defined and the group has a sense of working toward a common vision, as presented earlier in the example in Figure 6.1. The activities listed help to promote the attainment of professional, personal, and school organizational goals. In school organizations, small work groups or teams help to break the cycle of isolation that is often commonplace, particularly in middle and secondary schools. Within traditional school settings, teachers have few opportunities to interact with each other or to contribute significantly to policies and practices that impact best practices. School leaders can create ways to build common planning periods into the schedule in order to foster dialogue and discussion

View from the Field

Two years ago, Ms. Lavone became the principal at Heritage Middle School. It is a campus that is located in a suburban neighborhood and draws students from the new housing development going in. The community itself is located next to a large military base, and so there is a high percentage of both student and teacher turnover each year.

As Ms. Lavone recounts the situation, "The first thing I did as principal was to develop grade level teams. Each team had a science, social studies, math, and language arts teacher, and each team selected a leader to attend grade level departmental meetings. Each grade level developed a theme for the year and then planned activities around that theme. Just this last year, the 7th grade chose "Star Wars: The Twenty-Fifth Anniversary" as its theme. Each grade level team chose a name related to "Star Wars": We had the Light Sabre Team, the Darth Vader Team, the Princess Lea Team, and the R2D2 Team. By organizing themselves into interdisciplinary teams, they took the general theme and developed their own specific activities around the theme. The different teams often tried to out-do each other. We found at our school that this work team approach was especially successful in addressing the issues related to teacher turnover. New teachers were quickly integrated into the teams, which gave them a support group, as well as a focus for their planning. Once I took steps to create collaboration within the faculty, I was ready to have them help me work toward greater student academic success."

about curriculum alignment issues. In addition, they need to be proactive in soliciting information from all members of the school community to gain insight into school issues and problems. Ms. Lavone demonstrated that she valued her faculty as she engaged them in a dialogue with each other while getting their support to address student issues at their school.

Viewing teachers as thinkers and inquirers who possess a vast store of knowledge is key to systematic school improvement. Such a perception of teachers makes them valued members of the educational team within the school organization. According to MacLean and Mohr (1999), viewing teachers as constructors of knowledge makes them objective outside observers who can reflect not only on their own classroom practices, but those implemented schoolwide as well. By participating in work groups and teams, teachers engage in continuous reflection and begin to build their own coherent professional development programs by investigating topics of interest and concern to themselves as well as to their students, parents, and colleagues. As teachers collect and examine ". . . their own data to make informed decisions about instruction, schoolwide improvement can be the result" (Keith, 2001, p. 34).

Working in teams, committees, and groups is not something teachers often seek to do on their own to affect decision making by members of the campus-based committees (Marzano, Pickering, & Pollock, 2001). By providing the organizational structure and incentives, school leaders can encourage teachers to work in teams to investigate concerns and solve problems, such as stemming the tide of students dropping out of school or identifying ways to increase parent involvement. Educational leaders link theory to practice by bringing together the best that is known about group processes in school organizations to ensure that campus improvement goals are met.

Stages of Group Development

Just as individuals go through stages of development and maturation, groups also pass through similar stages. Tuckman and Jensen (1977) have identified a five-stage model of group development that includes forming, storming, norming, performing, and adjourning. In the forming stage, group members get to know one another and establish ground rules regarding the accomplishment of the task as well as interpersonal relations. This stage is complete when members come to think of themselves as a group. School leaders must provide opportunities for not only their school faculties to *form* but for subgroups such as grade levels or content areas to come together as well.

The second stage, storming, is characterized by tension and conflict within the group as members resist control by group leaders. Open hostility may even develop and if conflicts are not resolved they can result in members withdrawing and being uninvolved or at the worst, the disruption and disbanding of the group. School leaders must be aware of the conflict within school groups and monitor those situations carefully. The third stage, norming occurs as cohesiveness builds and the group works together to build close relationships and a sense of camaraderie. A sense of purpose and group identity occurs during the norming stage as members work to accomplish the goal or task. School leaders can help to create group norming through rituals and celebrations in the school. The fourth stage, performing, occurs as group members set about to accomplish their tasks or goals. For a school group it might be curriculum alignment. As members work together they focus on their job in order to be successful. The last stage, adjourning, occurs after the group has accomplished its task or met its goals. Often the group, if temporary or informal, will be disbanded once the goal has been met. Other, more formal groups will adjourn and then reconvene when presented with another task or assignment. For example, site-based decision-making committees or groups meet to review or modify and approve the campus improvement plan. Once that task has been accomplished, they adjourn until reconvened for another specific task or function.

The next View from the Field illustrates how the five-stage model works within an educational setting.

Gersick (1989) has presented a different view of how groups form and function called the *punctuated equilibrium model.* As groups form, their early focus is on the task or goal they have been given, but these initial efforts are often superficial as they overcome inertia. It is not until the deadline for action or results nears that the group gears up for an all-out effort to attain the goal or accomplish the task. This model is more time sensitive and recognizes the impact of deadlines on group function. Figure 6.2 presents the punctuated equilibrium model.

Strategies to Improve Group Effectiveness

Kohm (2002) has suggested four strategies to improve group interactions and discussions. These strategies include brainstorming, dot voting, round robin, and six points of view. Brainstorming involves group members in generating as many ideas or solutions

View from the Field

Jerry Stone, a district instructional specialist, has been asked to chair a group that will examine science curriculum alignment for the district in grades K–12. Jerry describes the process as he observed the group and how it functioned. "The District Science Alignment Task Force met for the first time in early October. My job was to convene the group and make sure the science curriculum achieved vertical alignment. I remember that first meeting well. There were eight elementary (K–6) group members and six secondary (7–12) members. There was some initial concern about the 'unbalanced' numbers and tension was thick as members negotiated relationships and began to work with me, the chair of the task force to establish procedures and protocols for accomplishing our task and keeping the peace. Although there was some conflict in the first two meetings, we were able to move beyond individual personal agendas and focus on the task for the group. By the end of October, after three and four meetings, we had moved beyond forming and storming to the norming and performing stages. The group developed its own identity and as group leader, I looked for ways to recognize and confirm consensus and celebrate successes as we developed a clearly articulated and aligned science curriculum for grades K–12. The group chose to use the National Science Standards and inquiry skills as a framework and as each grade level was completed we celebrated our success. We presented our alignment document to the superintendent and board in April. With our task completed, the group adjourned."

as possible to a given topic or problem. The purpose of this group activity is to create multiple options for consideration, not to determine the validity or quality of ideas. Dot voting is a strategy that can be used to quickly assess the thinking of the group and to begin to establish commonalities or priorities once ideas or solutions have been generated. Each group member has two to three colored dots and places them next to the idea or solution that the member believes is the most important statement or best solution. One variation of dot voting is to give each member a red dot to place beside an idea or solution he or she simply cannot support. This generates areas of agreement as well as areas of disagreement.

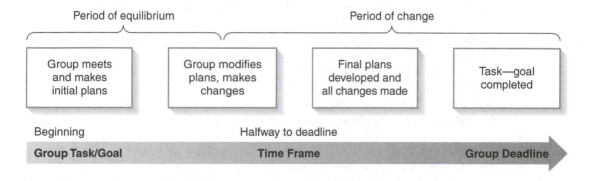

FIGURE 6.2 *Punctuated Equilibrium Model of Group Work*

In the round robin activity, each member gives a short response to an open-ended question such as, "What is the one suggestion discussed that you think will improve student performance in writing?" or "What one idea have you gotten from the conversation today that you can use in your classroom tomorrow?" As group members respond, a great deal of information is generated quickly as teachers share with one another. The six points of view activity asks group members to discuss a problem or issue from six perspectives such as student, parent, teacher, national standards, testing authority, and administrator or leader. This group process helps members to see the many sides and complex nature of an issue.

Decision-Making Process

Making decisions is part of the work of any organization, but it is a daily concern for school leaders. Simply put, decision making is the process of making a choice from among alternatives. Sometimes the different alternatives are not clear, but there are always choices to be made. Both school leaders and teachers make many, perhaps hundreds of decisions each day. The decisions that school leaders make impact students, teachers, and staff members. These decisions impact such areas as what teachers teach, how they teach, and how they manage students. School culture and group effectiveness is enhanced through the quality of the decision-making process, and as noted by Snowden and Gorton (2002), "the ability to make effective decisions is vital to the performance of a school administrator" (p. 3).

Decision making is a primary function of school leaders, and they need to be able to make effective decisions when seeking the success of teachers and all students. For Botvin (2000), decision making is "the act of making up one's mind" (p. 5). In making decisions, the leader should (1) seek information; (2) anticipate consequences; (3) act with integrity or in an ethical manner; and (4) minimize possible negative aspects. Green (2001) says that making good decisions ". . . is contingent on the nature of the situation and the process used by the leader" (p. 132). Decision making then, becomes the process of making a choice based on available information, alternatives presented, values held, and intended outcomes. Decision making is influenced by choices available, the process employed, and the nature of the decision itself. The most common model of the decision-making process is the analytical approach (Wedley & Field, 1984):

1. Identifying the problem
2. Determining the desired outcome
3. Generating possible alternatives
4. Analyzing and evaluating alternatives
5. Making and implementing choice
6. Following up on the outcomes

While these steps are sequential, they are general in nature and may not be followed precisely in all circumstances.

Rowe, Boulgaides, and McGrath (1984) have suggested a decision-making model based on the conceptual styles by which leaders reach a decision. *Directive style* leaders prefer simple, clear solutions and tend to make choices quickly by following exist-ing protocols or rules and use minimal information or alternatives. *Analytical style* leaders tend to carefully analyze alternatives to complex problems and generate or use as much data as possible in seeking to solve the problem or find the best answer. Leaders who use the *conceptual style* are socially oriented and therefore their approach is more artistic and humanistic as they seek broad-based alternatives and creative solu-tions. The *behavioral style* is adopted by leaders who have a deep commitment to people and the organization and a genuine interest in helping others. They are open to suggestions and tend to rely on meetings to solve problems or come to agreement on decisions.

As school leaders make decisions every day, some decisions are considered routine whereas others require careful thought and study. Only in emergency situations do decisions have to be made immediately. Therefore, most situations allow leaders the opportunity to involve others in the decision-making process and the collection of relevant data. For example, a principal was asked by the superintendent to consider adopting block scheduling for the next school year. In order to obtain pertinent data and information, the principal asked members of the Block Schedule Task Force to visit campuses where this schedule had been used. The members of the task force then made a list of pros and cons to present to the total faculty as they discussed options regarding the implementation of block scheduling. Green (2001) suggests that effective decision making requires educational leaders ". . . to understand the values and culture of the school and community they serve, identify and use appropriate decision making models, and act using a professional code of ethics. Their primary objective will . . . be the involvement of all stakeholders in a manner that will generate decisions that reflect the common good" (p. 143).

The processes involved in group decision making include (1) establishing goals; (2) selecting among courses of action; and (3) establishing appropriate group behavior. Job-related decision making takes place in a number of different ways. The most efficient and easiest decision-making strategy is autocratic; group leaders use only the information they have to make the decision. A school leader, for example, might investigate the allegation by some parents and board members, "that center activities in classrooms for 5 and 6 year olds are merely opportunities for play and do not contribute to the academic agenda of the school's mission." To expedite the investigation, the leader simply decides that teachers should eliminate all center work. In this example of autocratic decision making, the chances for carrying out the leader's decision without alienation is marginal at best.

The opposite of autocratic decision making is democratic decision making, in which group members determine a course of action through some process of voting or consensus building. Although the democratic decision-making strategy often takes more time because it relies on all group members to fully participate in the process, members of the school organization can develop a greater commitment to the action plan and therefore tend to be more satisfied with the outcomes. School organizations continue to rely on group decision making because it takes advantage of the varied experiences and broad levels of knowledge that a faculty possesses. Implementation of site-based decision making or shared decision making has as its major goal increased autonomy for teachers and staff. For Holman (1995),

> If embraced in spirit as well as form [and] if supported . . . site-based decision making provides a vehicle whereby each school can adjust curriculum, scheduling, staffing and budget to address needs . . . [T]he resulting empowerment and ownership should result in an improved instructional program and increased student achievement. (p. 65)

It should be noted that one major disadvantage of group decision making, however, is that it can be slow, and perhaps more importantly, conflict may arise among members as time is devoted to each person's point of view or opinion.

Group Decision-Making Models

A model provides a process that can be used to guide groups or individuals as they make a decision. A series of questions can be applied that help determine the effectiveness of the process that is used. These questions are (1) does the process foster the inclusion of all relevant criteria? (2) Does the process foster the consideration of the alternatives? (3) Does the process encourage the use of the most accurate information?

These questions provide school leaders with a starting point for identifying, diagnosing, and making group and individual decisions. They help to overcome disagreements, which often stand in the way of making a decision. A model also is designed to help school leaders to effectively involve their faculty and staff in daily decision making and developing an action plan that produces increased academic learning.

Models of decision making, developed by Vroom and Yetton (1973) and Vroom and Jago (1988), are built on the theory that leaders make the decisions alone or in conjunction with or after consulting a group such as the school's site-based committee. The final decision, however, may be made by the school leader. Morgan and Bowers (1995) have identified a decision-making model that has four components: (1) assessment, (2) metacognition, (3) shared mental models, and (4) resource management. The first component of the decision-making model is assessment, which involves the identification of a problem and the gathering of information. The second component, metacognition requires refining the problem. Through group processing skills, members develop a common understanding of the problem, which is step 3, shared mental models. Finally, with resource management, the last component, members make decisions using the group members' skills, experience, and knowledge to solve the problem under review. For example, a site-based decision-making committee seeks to determine why their reading scores on assessment tests decline as students progress through the elementary grades. They begin to gather data from a five-year period and disaggregate the data to refine their understanding of the problem. As the committee begins to examine the data they see several issues that could be contributing to the problem. They notice that students who were marginal in the early grades seem to fall further behind as they move from grade to grade. The site-based decision-making group decides to target this group and allocate additional campus resources to support these students in reading.

As part of the standards and accountability movements discussed in Chapters 8 and 9, school leaders are confronted with many challenges. Addressing these challenges successfully requires the best from all those involved. By using Morgan and Bowers'

(1995) decision-making model, school leaders can take advantage of each grou ber's experience and expertise. Often principals change schools or districts or are reassigned when changes are needed at specific school sites. When this occurs, the principal may be the only new member of the school team because the teachers have been working together as a group for a long time. The principal, to engender trust and confidence in his or her leadership ability to bring about a change, especially in curriculum matters, should strategically seek input and feedback from all faculty members in defining the problem. Faculty members are the leader's best assets; their perspectives need to be solicited and their points of view need to be integrated into the overall plan for achieving the school's mission of success for all students, especially when it is measured by high-stakes testing. Inclusiveness is key to a school leaders' success in getting the faculty to develop mental models for ways to improve student learning in curricular areas and for identifying the resources that are needed to support the decisions that are made.

In addition to decision-making models that can be used, school leaders may use one of three approaches—cognitive, affective, and evaluative—to make a decision. When adopting a *cognitive approach*, the group uses data to make a decision regarding, for example, hiring a department chair for English. These data may include the candidates' education, past teaching, experiences, and administrative experience, after hour activities, and the degree of collaboration with colleagues and community members. The group members would assimilate and analyze the data and then come to some recommendation regarding hiring one of the candidates. An *affective approach* to decision making involves relying on the emotions that are generated. For example, in hiring an English department chair, the group responds to the nature of the interactions between the interviewers and the candidates and the interpersonal nuances that are generated. Using such informal criteria as eye contact and a positive disposition, the interviewers may decide that this person would work well with other members of the English Department, the students, and parents. If, on the other hand, the candidate during the interview is shy and abrupt, the members of the committee might decide that this is not the type of person who would fit in and reject the application.

The last approach, *evaluative*, relies on specific criteria to make a judgment about an issue. Using the same example of hiring a Department Chair for English, the evaluative approach would be to compile a job description that articulates the skills, knowledge, and experiences that the successful candidate should possess. Each candidate is then judged against these criteria. Often a grid is prepared with the stated criteria; it is completed using the information gleaned from the written material provided as well as the information from the interviews. When the final decision is made, it is perceived as fair based on the stated objective criteria and is more likely to be accepted by other faculty members.

When making decisions, there are three components to each decision that is made: (1) the criteria by which alternatives are evaluated; (2) the alternatives or positions as a course of action to follow; and (3) the cause-and-effect beliefs that link alternatives to the criteria identified. For example, ineffective decision making results when: (1) the criteria are incorrect; (2) the criteria are weighed improperly; or (3) not all of the criteria relevant to the problem are considered.

Regardless of the models used, or whether the decision is made by a group or individual, good decision making requires vigilance in identifying relevant questions, generating pertinent data, and posing viable alternatives. "Decision making then, can be defined as a process in which an individual or group considers information within the context of a value system when proposing various solutions to a problem, a concern, or a need" (Beach & Reinhartz, 2000, p. 298). Huddleston (1996), however, cautions that no decision-making model or process is perfect and will not necessarily guarantee success. Perhaps the key idea is that educational leaders should strive to constantly look for ways to improve the decision-making process in their schools. Osguthorpe and Patterson (1998) challenge school leaders to go beyond the common models and approaches to decision making through what they call shared discernment, the ongoing process of searching for the best decision that eventually emerges from a continuous problem-solving focus.

Communication

The importance of communication is critical to all aspects of organizational operations (Fulk, 1995). Green (2001) says that "In today's schools, the importance of communication cannot be overemphasized. Through effective communication, relationships are built, trust is established, and respect is gained" (p. 95). The literature has referred to communication as the glue that holds the organization together (Roberts, 1984). The ability to communicate clearly and concisely is essential for school leaders. Beach and Reinhartz (2000) note that ". . . the ability to communicate may ultimately determine the degree of success [that leaders] have as they interact with others and seek to improve instruction" (p. 103). In a school context, leaders not only initiate communication, they monitor and respond to the communication of others.

Communication in school settings involves person-to-person and group interactions, telephone conversations, email, and informal notes and comments. Good communication involves not only speaking and writing, but reading and listening as well. Effective communication hinges on other people understanding your message and responding in a way that moves the exchange (spoken or written) forward. For Hamilton and Parker (1993), communication is "the process of people sharing thoughts, ideas, and feelings with each other in commonly understandable ways" (p. 5). Communication then, is a two-way process by which school leaders seek to get things done, pass on and obtain information or data, reach decisions, and develop relationships. In fact, Weisinger (1998) says that, "The basis of any relationship is communication. Without communication—be it sign language, body language, email or face-to-face conversation—there is no connection and hence no relationship" (p. 107).

Good communication also requires the development of skills, and the following skills can enable school leaders to be more effective and productive (Weisinger, 1998):

- Self-disclosure—the ability to tell others what you feel, think, and want
- Assertiveness—the ability to support and stand up for your thoughts, ideas, views, and beliefs while also showing respect for others

- Dynamic listening—active attentive listening that ensures that you truly hear what others are saying
- Criticism—the ability to constructively provide feedback about another person's ideas or performance
- Team communication—the ability to communicate in a group situation

In addition to these skills, Hiller (1998) suggests these additional skills to be an effective communicator:

- Using body language—the ability to monitor physical movement
- Recognizing prejudice and cultural implications—the ability to overcome stereotypical views and being sensitive to cultural differences
- Asking questions—the ability to ask the appropriate type of question (open, closed, fact-finding, follow-up, or feedback) to meet your aims
- Taking notes—the ability to quickly and accurately record or highlight important information
- Giving feedback—the ability to confirm that you have heard or seen accurately
- Using information technology—the ability to use email, fax, or the Internet appropriately

As seen in these lists of skills, effective communication is a complex process that involves more than speaking and listening. More and more school leaders are overwhelmed with written documents, whether they are emails, memos, faxes, or letters. An important skill for school leaders is to be able to prioritize their communication demands. Because schools are busy places, it would not be unusual for a school leader to arrive at work and find a teacher needing to discuss a student problem, the PTA/PTO president needing to discuss the book fair the next day, or the janitor who found broken glass from a break-in. All these examples require that the principal be a good listener and communicator so that each of these concerns is addressed in a way that each person feels that his or her concern has been heard. It takes a skilled leader to make a decision on the spot so more often than not, each concern will need to be addressed when there are opportunities to consider alternatives and to hear all aspects of the concern. The key to a school in which all participants have a voice is communication.

Mr. Morano in the View from the Field has a dilemma that has been compounded by technology as he decides how to respond to one of his teachers who has just emailed him.

Emailing is a great communication tool, but it has become so easy to type a response that can send the wrong message because before thinking, the send button is pressed and off the message goes. Mr. Morano was almost pulled into responding at that moment. But what he decides to do is to have a face-to-face meeting that would provide an opportunity to listen actively and to clarify comments. In doing so, he implemented the skills of a good communicator by not responding online; at the meeting he can offer constructive feedback, ask questions to gather additional data, and confirm what he thinks she is saying.

View from the Field

Mr. Morano, the Vice Principal at Cobbs Inter-mediate School, is just making the final sweep through his emails before going home. He is tired; it has been a long day—he opened the building for those coming in for band practice at 6:45 AM. As he views his inbox, he notices a new email from one of his teachers he has been supervising closely because of some outspoken parents and community members.

"As I read the email, it is obvious that Ms. Rogers is very angry and wants to know if I support her or am I trying to get her fired or to resign." Mr. Morano begins to type, wanting on the one hand to be supportive, while on the other hand to be truthful about areas that need im-provement. He continues to type and before he knows it, he has written a full page of text with-out a paragraph. By now Mr. Morano is very emotional, angry, and frustrated, and he is ready to click the *send* button when he realizes that he has not been a good reader (listener via email), he is not taking the time to consider alternatives, nor has he considered the best way and place to respond. As these ideas flash through his mind, he begins to settle down and consider the best path to take—because he is tired. He does email Ms. Rogers back, but this time he suggests that they meet during her planning period so that they can discuss her concerns.

Case Study

You have just been appointed the principal of a new high school in your district. The district has just adopted a new character education curriculum and your campus has been selected as the first campus to implement the new program. The program is designed to help students make responsible choices regarding not only their personal behavior, but behavior related to social responsibility as well. A very vocal group of parents would like to prevent the character education program from being implemented at your new school. They complained loudly to the school board when the program was first proposed and now they are pressuring you to delay implementation at the new school.

You feel caught in the middle. On one hand, the character education program has been mandated by the school district and your new campus has been designated to be the first to implement this pilot program. On the other hand, you have a vocal group of parents you are going to have to deal with as you open a new school and you want things to go smoothly. As the school leader of this new campus, how will you implement the mandated character education program while also addressing the objections of the parents? What steps will you take to resolve this issue? Review the information presented in this chapter and prepare a presentation outlining these steps as a way to solve this problem.

1. What work groups will you form?
2. Who will you invite to serve on these work groups?
3. What decision-making model will you encourage group members to use?

Principles for Making Decisions	Barriers to Making Decisions	Ways to Overcome Barriers
1. Using data		
2. Taking a risk; thinking out of the box		
3. Analyzing the data relative to decision to be made		
4. Supported by the organization		
5. Respecting organizational chain of command		
6. Acknowledging no solutions are perfect		
7. Considering organizational structure and context		
8. Recognizing role of personal beliefs and bias		
9. Collaborating with others		
10. Ongoing assessment of decisions		

FIGURE 6.3 *Principles for and Barriers to Making Decisions*

4. What communication skills will you need to implement?
5. Use Figure 6.3 as part of the decision-making process and provide a response for each area.

Summary

This chapter has focused on the role of the educational leader in developing schools as productive organizations. A knowledge and understanding of human behavior is essential as administrators seek to promote cooperation among school faculties and a commitment to school goals. Viewing schools as organizations or within the workplace helps leaders to recognize (1) the changing nature of the environment; (2) the impact of technology on leading, teaching, and learning; (3) the availability of resources; (4) the diverse nature of school populations; and (5) the globalization of education.

Chapter 6 describes the role of leaders in developing work groups or teams as a means of sustaining the work of the faculty and staff. The use of group processes is vital in building learning communities, especially when coupled with decision making and the social behavior of teachers in the school. Both formal and informal work teams play important roles in completing tasks. School leaders help to ensure the success of work teams by carefully structuring the composition of the various groups.

As teachers work in group or teams, they engage in important social processes of building cohesiveness, cooperation, and collegiality. These social processes also contribute to organizational citizenship behaviors that include teacher morale and feelings and a willingness to work to accomplish the school's goals and mission. When teachers have a positive attitude, value their work, are motivated, and feel secure, they contribute to the overall success of the school campus.

The role of the school leader in the decision-making process is discussed, especially as it relates to group decisions. Group decision making involves establishing goals, selecting courses of action, and then establishing appropriate group behavior. The use of models can also guide campus leaders in making decisions. Key questions serve to help identify, diagnose, and make effective decisions.

Educational leaders must be able to understand and manage conflict within their school organizations. Disagreements occur between and among the various constituencies of a school, and leaders must have the skills to resolve the conflicts that arise. Leaders must ask themselves the following questions: (1) Does a conflict exist? (2) How can the conflict be framed or understood? (3) How do the people involved feel about the issues? (4) Is there a pattern of behaviors that contributes to the conflict? Answers to these questions provide leaders with information that should inform their behaviors as they work toward the mission and goals of their school organizations.

Finally, school leaders must be effective communicators. This chapter provides several communication skills that school leaders can develop as they work with various constituencies. Effective communication is a complex process that requires not only speaking and listening, but reading and writing, as well as the appropriate use of technology.

Your Turn

6.1. How are decisions made? Gather data firsthand. Ask permission to observe as a group of educators charged with a mission carry out their objective. Develop a strategy for observing group interactions. For example, assign members of the group numbers or letters and in your observation journal enter the following:

- The role each member plays
- The member who emerges as the group leader
- The alternatives generated and by whom
- The underlying beliefs that guide options/courses of action

After observing at least three sessions, prepare a report on "How Groups Make Decisions," summarizing the data you have collected. Basically, this task is to analyze how tasks are carried out and group decisions are made.

6.2. Obtain a copy of *Dispelling the Myth Revisited: Preliminary Findings from a Nationwide Analysis of "High-Flying" Schools* published by the Educational Trust in December

2001, which describes the *myth* as those schools that are high in minority enrollment and poverty do not perform at the level as low minority and poverty schools. Principal Wendy Gudalewicz, Gilroy High School, California, wrote a letter to parents that can be accessed online at www.gilroyhighscool.com.principal/Newsletter4.doc. She explains that her school is part of the database that dispels this myth. Analyze her letter that was sent to Families and Friends on January 2002 for the following organizational elements: (1) engendering a collaborative partnership; (2) delineating the parental role in the success story she describes; (3) identifying the school's accomplishments as a cooperative enterprise; and (4) writing the mission statement for Gilroy High School.

6.3. A key question to ask local, state, and national school policymakers and educators is, "How much data from effective schools is needed to persuade policymakers/educators of the educability of children who are poor? What type of school organization is needed to address the limited expectations for these children? Research at least three effective school organizations across the nation that have a high number of children from poor homes, yet are high performing.

- What group processes and techniques are used to define roles, delegate authority, and determine accountability?
- What campus decision-making strategies and models are used to solve problems?
- How have members of the educational community including teachers, staff members, parents, and students implemented the change processes?

6.4. You have been asked to assemble a team of ten members to investigate the feasibility of building an academy, grades 5 through 8, that would have an environmental education focus. To match group members with this task, ask all potential participants to take the Myers-Briggs learning/leadership instrument online at www.humanmetics .com. After group members complete the instrument, analyze the data in light of the group task and identify each person's suitability to serve on the team. Give each participant an identification number, do not use real names, and, in your journal, write notes for each set of data by participants that can be reviewed.

References

ActiveInk Network. (2001). ActiveInk Corporation. Austin, TX: www.activeink.net.

Alder, N. (1991). *International dimensions of organizational behavior* (2nd ed). Boston: PWS-Kent.

Beach, D. M., & Reinhartz, J. (2000). *Supervisory leadership: Focus on instruction.* Boston: Allyn & Bacon.

Botvin, G. J. (2000). *Lifeskills training: Promoting health and personal development.* Princeton, NJ: Princeton Health Press.

Cartwright, D. (1968). The nature of group cohesiveness. In D. Cartwright & A. Zander (eds), *Group dynamics: Research and theory* (3rd ed). pp. 91–109. New York: Harper & Row.

Conger, J. A., & Kanungo, R. N. (1988). *Charismatic leadership.* San Francisco: Jossey-Bass.

Craigor, J. P. (1997). Technology, organizations, and work in the 20th century. *The Industrial-Organizational Psychologist, 34,* 89–96.

Fulk, J. (1995). Social construction of communication technology. *Academy of Management Journal, 36,* 421–950.

Gersick, C. J. G. (1989). Marking time: Predictable transitions in task groups. *Academy of Management Journal, 32,* 274–309.

Graham, J. W. (1991). An essay on organizational citizenship behavior. *Employee Responsibilities and Rights Journal, 4,* 249–270.

Green, R. L. (2001). *Practicing the art of leadership: A problem-based approach to implementing the ISLLC standards.* Upper Saddle River, NJ: Prentice-Hall.

Greenberg, J., & Baron, R. A. (2000). *Behavior in organizations* (7th ed). Upper Saddle River, NJ: Prentice-Hall.

Hamilton, C., & Parker, C. (1993). *Communicating for results: A guide for business and the professions* (4th ed). Belmont, CA: Wadsworth.

Harrison, D. A., Price, K. H., & Bell, M. P. (1998). Beyond relational demography: Time and the effects of surface- and deep-level diversity on work group cohesion. *Academy of Management Journal, 41,* 96–107.

Hiller, R. (1998). *Communicate clearly.* New York: DK Publishing.

Holman, L. J. (1995). Should site-based committees be involved in the campus staffing process? *NASSP Bulletin, 79,* 65.

Huddleston, M. W. (1996). *The public administration workbook* (3rd ed). White Plains, NY: Longman.

Keith, A. (2001). Action research brings results. *Science and Children, 39,* 3, 32–35.

Kohm, B. (2002). Improving faculty conversations. *Educational Leadership, 59,* 31–33.

Lambert, L. (2002). A framework for shared leadership. *Educational Leadership, 59,* 8, 37–40.

MacLean, M. S., & Mohr, M. M. (1999). *Teacher-researchers at work.* Berkeley, CA: National Writing Project.

Marzano, R. L., Pickering, D. J., & Pollock, J. E. (2001). *Classroom instruction that works: Research-based strategies for increasing student achievement.* Alexandria, VA: Association for Curriculum Development and Supervision.

May, K. (1998). Work in the 21st century: Recruiting in a tight labor market. *The Industrial-Organizational Psychologist, 36,* 39–41.

Morgan, B. B., Jr., & Bowers, C. A. (1995). Teamwork stress: Implications for team decision making. In R. A. Guzzo & E. Salas (eds), *Team effectiveness and decision making in organizations.* pp. 262–290. San Francisco: Jossey-Bass.

Muchinsky, P. M. (2000). *Psychology applied to work: An introduction to industrial and organizational psychology* (6th ed). Belmont, CA: Wadsworth/Thomson Learning.

Organ, D. W. (1988). *Organizational citizenship behavior: The good soldier syndrome.* Lexington, MA: Lexington.

Osguthorpe, R. T., & Patterson, R. S. (1998). *Balancing the tensions of change: Eight keys to collaborative educational renewal.* Thousand Oaks, CA: Corwin Press.

Penner, L. A., Midili, A. R., & Kegelmeyer, J. (1997). Beyond job attitudes: A personality and social psychology perspective on the causes of organizational citizenship behavior. *Human Performance, 10,* 111–131.

Podsakoff, P. M., & Mac Kenzie, S. B. (1997). Kerr and Jermier's substitutes for leadership model: Background empirical assessment and suggestions for future research. *Leadership Quarterly, 8,* 117–125.

Riggio, R. E. (2000). *Introduction to industrial/organizational psychology* (3rd ed). Upper Saddle River, NJ: Prentice-Hall.

Roberts, K. H. (1984). *Communicating in organizations.* Chicago: Science Research Associates.

Rowe, A. J., Boulgaides, J. D., & McGrath, M. R. (1984). *Managerial decision making.* Chicago: Science Research Associates.

Schnake, M. E. (1991). Organizational citizenship: A review, proposed model, and research agenda. *Human Relations, 44,* 735–759.

Snowden, P. E., & Gorton, R. A. (2002). *School leadership and administration* (6th ed). Boston: McGraw-Hill.

Steers, R. M. (1984). *Introduction to organizational behavior.* Glenview, IL: Scott Foreman.

Texas Higher Education Coordinating Board. (2002). *Teacher recruitment and retention.* Austin, TX: Texas Higher Education Coordinating Board.

Tuckman, B. W., & Jensen, M. A. (1977). Stages of small group development revisited. *Group and Organizational Studies, 2,* 419–427.

Uchiyama, K. P., & Wolf, S. A. (2002). The best way to lead them. *Educational Leadership, 59,* 80–83.

United States General Accounting Office. (2002). *A model of strategic human capital management.* Washington, DC: United States General Accounting Office. GAO-02-373SP.

Vandaveer, V. V. (1998). As we enter the twenty-first century. *The Industrial-Organizational Psychologist, 35,* 99–102.

Van Dyne, L., Graham, J. W., & Dienesch, R. M. (1994). Organizational citizenship behavior: Construct redefinition, measurement, and validation. *Academy of Management Journal, 37,* 765–802.

Vroom, V. H., & Jago, A. G. (1988). *The new leadership: Managing participation in organization.* Englewood Cliffs, NJ: Prentice-Hall.

Vroom, V. H., & Yetton, P. W. (1973). *Leadership and decision-making.* Pittsburgh, PA: University of Pittsburgh Press.

Wedley, W. C., & Field, R. H. G. (1984). A predecision support system. *Academy of Management Review, 9,* 696–703.

Weisinger, H. (1998). *Emotional intelligence at work.* San Francisco: Jossey-Bass.

7

School Leadership: Resource Management

Standard 3: A school administrator is an educational leader who promotes the success of all students by ensuring management of the organization, operations, and resources for a safe, effective, and efficient learning environment.

Standard 6: A school administrator is an educational leader who promotes the success of all students by understanding, responding to, and influencing the larger political, social, economic, legal, and cultural context.

Chapter Objectives

The objectives of this chapter are:

- Identify major historical and legal developments in public school finance.
- Discuss sources of school financing.
- Identify and describe public school finance equalization models.
- Explain the principles of public school finance, including federal, state, and local sources of funding and regulations that affect public schools.
- Describe the school budget development process, including major steps in developing a district-level or campus-level budget.
- Discuss building-level fiscal management, including major concepts and terms associated with building-level accounting, budgeting, record keeping, and reporting and appropriate techniques and applications of cost analysis.
- Identify current financial and resource management issues that are affecting public school resources.
- Discuss how budget development relates to student outcomes in meeting school goals, including apportionment of resources and evaluation of the use of resources.

Leadership involves managing human and financial resources to foster school goals and accomplish educational objectives. The management of fiscal and human resources is at a critical juncture in educational history because school leaders are being held to the highest standards of public accountability at a time when resources are scarce; they are expected to be efficient and effective managers of resources so that all students are successful. Administrators are faced daily with critical decisions concerning the allocation of human and fiscal resources to support programs so that all students at their school achieve academically because, in education, student achievement is the ultimate measurement of success. According to Smith (1998), the importance of fiscal and human resources administration has greater importance today for school leaders because "Many of the management functions . . . previously centralized for control and standardization are now being decentralized to the building level where they become the responsibility of the principal and/or the school-based council" (p. 5).

In order for school leaders to make meaningful instructional decisions that promote learning for all students, they must have the necessary authority to commit fiscal and human resources that enable the implementation of instructional or curricular decisions (Guthrie, 1998; Odden & Busch, 1998). As Biddle and Berliner (2002) describe the situation, "Most people believe that students do better in well-funded schools and that public education should provide a level playing field for all children" (p. 48).

Hanushek (1989), however, made the bold claim that research from several decades "provides strong and consistent evidence that expenditures are not systematically related to student achievement" (p. 49). Cameron (2000) also found no direct linkage between funding and student performance but noted that,

> it is clear that money is an important part of the educational process, however it is not clear exactly what part money plays. School districts must determine the needs of their individual [campuses], and then find ways to budget their resources in a way that is both efficient and effective. (p. 91)

Laine, Greenwald, and Hedges (1996) concluded that "school resources are systematically related to student achievement and that those relations are large [and] educationally important" (p. 384). Variables such as class size, school size, teacher ability, and teacher experience do relate to funding and appear to impact achievement.

Clearly fiscal and human resource management are important leadership skills; for as Smith (1998) notes, "School-based leadership is the framework in which the human [and fiscal] resources function . . . [and] it is incumbent upon the principal to develop knowledge, skills, attributes and ability to be effective in this redefined role" (p. 5). Thompson and Wood (1998) warn that in light of recent events school leaders will be faced ". . . with strong competition for resources and an increasingly fragmented society that is in no mood to pour significant new money into education in return for a vague promise that 'things will get better'" (p. 16). Biddle and Berliner (2002) say that because "nearly half of public school funds in the United States come from local property taxes, the system generates large funding differences . . ." (p. 51).

At a time when money and resources for schools are becoming increasingly limited, leaders must be creative as they maximize not only funds and personnel, but instructional resources and facilities as well. It is essential that school leaders know the mechanics of constructing a budget, defending it to policy and key decision makers, and implementing it at the campus level. At a time when every person who is hired is critical to the success of the school program, leaders must recruit, retain, and retrain wisely. Human resource management becomes as important as books, bricks, and budgets.

This chapter addresses the challenges that school leaders face as they examine the diverse components of fiscal management and human resources. It begins by providing an overview of the foundational aspects of financial management, which sets the stage for understanding modern school resource management through a discussion of the major historical and legal funding programs of public schools in the United States, as well as school finance equalization models.

The chapter then discusses the budgeting process, including the steps involved in budget building, the possible sources of revenue, and major categories for budget expenditures. It concludes with a discussion of the use of technology for managing the fiscal resources and addressing the financing of facilities and the current financial issues that are affecting public school resources.

Foundational Aspects of Fiscal Resource Management

To promote the success of all students, school leaders must not only secure adequate resources, but demonstrate prudence in the allocation of funds. Razik and Swanson (2001) note that "Education is big business with more than $350 billion spent annually . . ." education budgets are ". . . the largest single budgetary component of state and local governments. . . . But education is more than a business [for it] deals with matters that relate to the hearts and souls of individual citizens" (p. 417).

Funding for public schools in the United States comes from many sources, including federal, state, and local sources. However, federal revenue may represent a small proportion (10% or less) and is generally in the form of categorical aid. Historically, the responsibility of state government for education is paramount, as provided under the Tenth Amendment, which states, "the powers not delegated to the United States by the Constitution, nor prohibited by it to the States, are reserved to the States respectively, or to the people." For example, Section I, Article VII, in the current Texas Constitution, written in 1876, requires "the legislature . . . to establish and make suitable provision for the support and maintenance of an efficient system of public schools." The state carries the burden for public education, and for Ray, Hack, and Candoli (2001), "Given the principle of states having plenary power in matters of public education, state legislatures have the responsibility for developing funding plans for the financial support of schools" (p. 47).

History and Development of Public School Funding in the United States

Public school finance as a state function is distinguished by five overlapping periods that are not marked by dates, but rather as stages of development. These stages are based primarily on the size of a state, its educational needs, and its educational leadership. Five periods of state and local relations have been identified by Burrup, Brimley, and Garfield (1999). The first period, *local financing*, involves little or no state assistance with local communities or churches providing for education. Due to wide differences in local tax-paying abilities, extreme disparities in educational opportunities often result. *State responsibility*, the second period, identifies education as a state function and supports local districts with the use of flat grants, subventions, and other nonequalizing state allocations. The third period, *foundation programs*, is designed to ensure equalization of educational opportunity by supporting basic state educational programs. A fourth period, *refined foundation programs*, is modification that allows a greater degree of equalization through the use of flat grants. These modifications help to equalize the tax burden and distribute state funds equitably with greater state control. The fifth period, *equalization practices*, involves the state and local districts in sharing educational costs and providing a basic program of education to every child in the state, regardless of the child's place of residence. Thedford and Patrick (2000) have proposed a sixth period, *public school options*, as an evolving trend that allows for school choice vouchers that can be used in charter schools and even private and for profit companies. Recent court rulings (see Chapter 4) allow for the expenditure of state funds in such a way. As school leaders seek to develop instructional programs that promote success for all students, they will have to work with local boards and authorities, as well as with state and federal programs.

Public School Finance Equalization Models

States have long struggled with the equal distribution of resources in support of education. "The mechanisms that states use to distribute state revenue to individual school systems also vary a great deal. . . . Hawaii is the only state organized without local boards of education, local property taxes, and the conventional state-local partnerships" (Ray, Hack, & Candoli, 2001, p. 47). Other states, however, rely on various plans for financing public education. As Biddle and Berliner (2002) note, "The funding of public schools through local property taxes has deep historical roots . . . [yet] . . . funding inequities exist both within and between states, the ideal way to address them would be through changes in federal policies . . ." (p. 56).

As competition for resources increases, schools and school leaders have come under increased pressure to be more equitable in the distribution of resources. For Razik and Swanson (2001), equity involves a sense of fairness, justness, and impartiality, and "horizontal equity refers to the equal treatment of equals . . . [whereas] vertical equity refers to the appropriate unequal treatment of unequals" (p. 417). Litigation over equity issues left the responsibility for solving such dilemmas with state legislatures until the landmark *Serrano v. Priest* decision in 1971 in which the California Supreme Court found the state's school finance program to be unconstitutional based on violation of equal protection for all of its school pupils. The disparity of school funds per pupil due to dependence on local property taxes for school funding was ordered to be corrected, which has resulted in subsequent attempts to correct finance formula inequities in other states as well.

However, in 1973 in *San Antonio Independent School District v. Rodriguez*, the United States Supreme Court found the Texas school funding system to be constitutional and did not require equal funding among school districts. According to Biddle and Berliner (2002), "This decision effectively foreclosed federal court action to remedy inequities in school funding . . ." (p. 56). The 1973 ruling made it clear that education was a matter reserved for state legislatures, not a fundamental right under the U.S. Constitution. Almost all state legislatures began to address equality of educational funding and, at the same time, additional lawsuits were filed in state courts, with two of the most protracted being *Abbott v. Burke* from 1985 through 1994 in New Jersey and *Edgewood I, II, IIa, III, and IV* from 1984 through 1995 in Texas (Kemerer & Walsh, 2000). Over the years, state courts have rendered opposing decisions based on either the *Serrano* or the *Rodriguez* approach; however, several basic principles have emerged regarding school funding. These funding principles include (1) education is a compelling state interest; (2) revenue may be obtained from local property taxation; and (3) school district expenditures do not have to be an equal amount per student (Burrup, Brimley, & Garfield, 1999).

Gold, Smith, and Lawton (1995) have identified the following state aid programs or funding models: (1) flat grants, which allocate state revenues on a per unit basis without regard to district wealth or tax base; (2) foundation programs, which establish a dollar value for each pupil and local support; (3) percent equalization programs, which consider the districts' fiscal efforts coupled with state support; (4) guaranteed tax base/yield programs, which guarantee all school districts a given tax yield; and (5) full state funding in which the state totally fulfills the fiscal responsibility for education. Three of these models address basic equalization finance theories: foundation programs, percent equalization or guaranteed yield programs, and power equalizing. *Foundation programs* are based on the concept that state funds are provided to ensure that districts receive state funds to establish a minimum program. Local districts may increase expenditures above the foundation program. *Percent equalization or guaranteed yield* formulas are based on a local–state partnership approach. A foundation level is established, and the ratio of state to local funds is determined by the wealth of the district. The wealthier the district (in terms of taxable property), the greater the local contribution. *Power equalizing or recapture* combines the principles of equalization and reward for effort. The state provides differing amounts of equalized aid to schools, and there is recapture of local dollars in excess of a certain level (Patrick, 2000; Burrup, Brimley, & Garfield, 1999; Walker & Casey, 1996).

Today, in most states, various aspects of these basic theories determine the school finance plan: district wealth, district needs, district tax effort, district tax yield, and state assistance. With a variety of combinations of state aid estimated at four hundred, states use equalizing grants, foundation programs, power equalization, and categorical funding, among other plans. Worth noting, however, is that "all of the models are mathematically equivalent," . . . but . . . "emphasize different aspects or types of equity" (Clark & England, 1997, p. 4). As court decisions related to school finance have been rendered in recent years, two of these funding plans, full state funding and district power equalization, appear to pass current legal scrutiny.

Full state funding has its proponents and opponents, but few states can function as one district, as does Hawaii. Therefore, three different variations within state participation have emerged: (1) *state operation* of public schools; (2) complete *state support*; and (3) *foundation program*. Proponents argue that full state funding meets the requirement of court decisions that the education of a student should be dependent only on the wealth of the state, and not the district or the parents. This model also equalizes revenue among school districts by providing greater taxpayer equity, reduces interdistrict competition for state funds, and relieves local districts of the problem of obtaining funds. Opponents point out that full state funding results in loss of local control, creates a leveling down process, curtails innovation, puts public schools in more direct competition with other state agencies, makes a minimum program the maximum, and penalizes districts with comparatively high salaries and operational costs (Burrup, Brimley, & Garfield, 1999).

Another school financing plan, district power equalization appears to be a more acceptable alternative to full state funding. Because each local district has the right and the responsibility to determine what the local tax rate should be over and above the mandated foundation program levy, local control is assured and state partnership is mandated. Also known as *equalized percentage matching* or *open-end equalization*, district power equalization means that "each local district mill levy should produce the same number of dollars of total school revenue per mill per weighted student in every district, and the last mill to be levied should produce the same total funds as the first one" (Burrup, Brimley, & Garfield, 1999, p. 99).

Budgeting Process

The budgeting process is a legal requirement in most states and the "plenary power allows the state to mandate that school districts develop budgets and to determine the format, calendar, [and] procedures . . . for the budgeting process" (Ray, Hack, & Candoli, 2001, p. 123). Educational leaders must have the skills that keep schools open and running, including knowledge of the nuts and bolts of budgeting as well as the management of fiscal and other resources; in other words, school leaders must be able to develop and implement a budget. It should be noted, however, that, "the budget is not just a document containing a list of receipts and expenditures but it is a process by which the people in a democracy exercise their . . . right to govern themselves" (Johns & Morphet, 1969, p. 441). However, the term *budget* may mean different things to people in government, business, service organizations, and education.

For Burrup, Brimby, and Garfield (1999), "a *budget* is a financial plan that involves at least four elements: (1) planning, (2) receiving funds, (3) expending funds, and (4) evaluating results—all performed within the limits of a predetermined time . . . usually a year for school districts" (p. 280). Another view of an educational budget suggests that it is "the translation of educational needs into a financial plan which is interpreted to the public in such a way that when formally adopted it expresses [the] kind of educational program the community is willing to support . . ." (Roe, 1961, p. 81). For Thompson and Wood (1998), a budget includes a description of the intended educational program, an estimate of costs and expenditures, and an estimate of probable income or revenues and "leads to one result: budgeting is critical to the success of everything that happens in schools" (p. 108).

Figure 7.1 represents the cyclical nature of the six steps in the budgeting process described by Burrup, Brimley, and Garfield (1999). The budgeting process as seen in Figure 7.1, begins with determining the educational needs of each campus or school district, especially the instructional or programmatic needs of each school. When these needs have been determined, then educational goals are developed which reflect the needs. Once the goals have been stated, they can then be prioritized so that fiscal and other resources can be committed to support the most important needs. The prioritized goals are translated into specific objectives with measurable results or outcomes. Objectives require the selection or creation of educational programs or materials to accomplish the objectives. Once these steps have been accomplished, then schools adopt

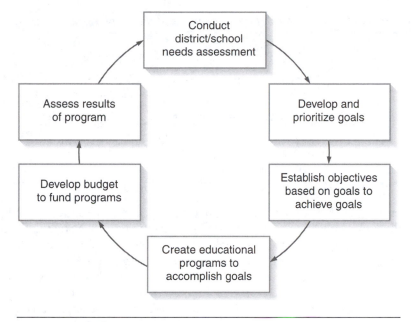

FIGURE 7.1   *The Budgeting Process*

a budget based on anticipated revenues for funding the programs or obtaining the materials. Once programs or materials have been funded, then there is a need to assess results. A fundamental resource allocation question is, "Based on the results, was the money wisely spent?" Depending on the outcomes or results, the process starts again with the assessment of new needs.

Table 7.1 represents how the budgeting process provides the opportunity for school leaders to align fiscal, material, and human resources to support the needs and goals of a campus. Table 7.1 represents how the budgeting process becomes an alignment process.

One of the identified needs of Academy Junior High School is the improvement of instruction for other language learners. In the needs assessment process, the school recognized the need to improve language-based instruction, which resulted in a prioritized goal of additional support for limited English proficiency (LEP) students. In order to meet that goal, a budget item of $100,000 is included to hire additional personnel. The level of accountability comes from increased student performance of LEP students on state-mandated tests. A noninstruction related need that was identified was parental involvement, which is reflected in budget funds to hire a parent volunteer coordinator and to print brochures to publicize the program.

As budgets are developed, schools must anticipate revenue or income from various sources. Figure 7.2 illustrates the possible sources of revenue for school budgets. As Figure 7.2 illustrates, three general categories serve as possible sources of revenue for schools. As discussed earlier, most districts rely on this tripartite system of funding, which includes local, state, and federal revenues (Alexander & Salmon, 1995). Local

TABLE 7.1 *Aligning Fiscal, Material, and Human Resources to Support Campus Needs and Goals*

Needs	Prioritized Goals	Objectives	
Language-based instruction	Additional support for LEP students	Increased student performance in state-mandated tests	
Parental involvement	Additional parental support	More parent aides	
School safety	Installation of security screening stations to prevent contraband items in the school	Ensure student safety	

revenue is generated from taxes, fees, investments, gifts, loans, bonds, and property sales. Revenues also come from the state in a variety of forms including flat matching and equalization grants. Finally, school districts receive revenue from federal sources through flat, matching or equalization grants, or funded projects.

Just as schools must anticipate revenues, they must also track expenditures as a part of the budget development process. Figure 7.3 represents common categories that leaders can use in tracking budget expenditures. Costs are generally accounted for in three major categories: instructional expenditures, capital outlay, and debt service. Instructional costs have the most areas for tracking and include student support services,

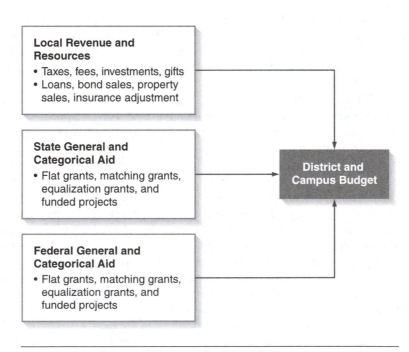

FIGURE 7.2 *Sources of Revenue for School Budgets*

Source: Modified from Fowler, W. J. (1990). *Financial accounting for local and state school systems.* Washington, DC: U.S. Government Printing Office.

Programs/Materials	Budget	Assessment
Special pull-out or supplemental instruction	$100,000 to hire additional teachers/aides	State benchmarks and tests
Recruiting, brochures and parent volunteers/coordinators	$30,000	More parental participation survey
Install metal detectors	$78,000 for security personnel and equipment	Reduce incidents of having dangerous items taken to school

instructional staff, general administration, school administration, operation and maintenance and transportation services. Capital outlay expenditures include major equipment purchases and facility construction. Finally, debt service includes payments on loans or other debt reduction efforts.

Ray, Hack, and Candoli (2001) suggest that planning and budgeting include:

- A plan of action for the future
- An analysis of past activities as they relate to planned activities
- A formulation of work plans
- A coordinated plan throughout the school organization
- The establishment of a system of management controls
- The creation of a public information system

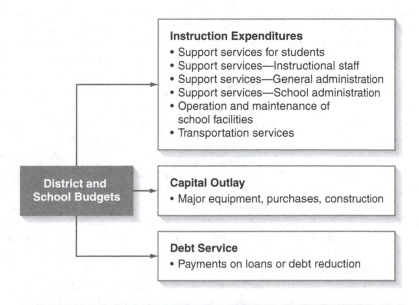

FIGURE 7.3 *School Expenditures by Function*

The budget and budgeting process can take a variety of forms including (1) the mechanical budget, which presents estimated yearly receipts and expenditures; (2) the yearly budget, which elaborates on the mechanical form and attempts to make quick projections about receipts and expenditures without regard to needs or program opportunities; (3) the administration-dominated budget, which is developed strictly as a management function with little or no input regarding needs or programs; and (4) the centralized budget, which treats all schools in the district the same, with little or no attention given to differences among the various constituencies (Ray, Hack, & Candoli, 2001).

Other commonly used approaches to budgeting at the district level include (1) incremental budgeting; (2) line-item budgeting; (3) program budgeting; (4) program, planning, and budgeting; (5) zero-based budgeting; and (6) school-site budgeting. *Incremental budgeting* is a commonly used model that builds on the previous year's expenditures. *Line-item budgeting* is also a widely used model that assigns different amounts to each line of the budget, with increases made to the base of each line. *Program budgeting* internally organizes the various funds in a budget according to the specific purpose of the fund. *Program, planning, and budgeting* systems, later extended to include *evaluation*, represent a shift to link outcomes to fiscal decisions through systematic planning. *Zero-based budgeting* begins the process with nothing budgeted and requires justification for each expenditure each year. *Site-based budgeting* represents the currently popular decentralized approach of site-based management, in which fiscal recommendations are made by a committee at the individual school level (Thompson & Wood, 1998).

The school budget is commonly viewed as comprising the three sides of an equilateral triangle: program, expenditures, and revenues. The program is the base of the triangle and represents the ". . . fiscal expression of the educational philosophy of the district" (Thompson & Wood, 1998, p. 105). Revenues and expenditures represent the sides of the triangle. Although these two budget processes may be common, most lack the ability to address educational program concerns. Site-based budgeting is seen as the most appropriate way to address the need for greater involvement of principals and teachers in instructional decision making and provides for greater fiscal flexibility. Site-base budgeting involves teachers and other professional staff members in requesting program expenditures for the coming school year and "many progressive districts ask teachers to also submit requests for . . . supplies and facilities required for optimum or superior program . . ." (Burrup, Grimby, & Garfield, 1999, p. 284).

School districts have a great deal of latitude when it comes to the flow of money to each individual campus; therefore, each of the nation's 16,000 school districts may approach building a campus budget with a different philosophy (Thompson & Wood, 1998). Each school district typically has a budget calendar that begins soon after the previous year's budget has been approved, and campus leaders are becoming increasingly more involved at most stages of the budget process. With the advent of site-based decision making, the campus budget-building process has become less decentralized. Assigned greater responsibility for the budget, effective school leaders seize this opportunity to incorporate the input of internal and external stakeholders through campus committees with the primary focus being improved student performance. Table 7.2 presents a general timeline for the development of a campus budget.

TABLE 7.2 *Campus Budgeting Process Timeline*

September	Close out previous year's budget and make final entries. Transfer remaining funds to new budget. Verify amount of revenue from all sources (federal, state, and local). Solicit expenditure requests from current school year
October	Track expenditure requests based on approved categories and programs
November	Adjust anticipated revenue and expenditures based on actual budget to date
December	Prepare and present a quarterly budget report to superintendent and site-based committee. Monitor expenditures with regard to budgeted amounts
January	Review revenue and expenditures to date and adjust budget accordingly
February	Collect campus budget requests based on their identified needs for the next school year. Engage in preliminary budget discussions having grade levels or departments submit requests
March	Forecast enrollment for campus for next school year and formalize budget. Engage in review of annual improvement plan and tie budget requests to identified instructional needs
April	Review campus data, needs assessment, and input from campus stakeholders to finalize budget process
May	Submit final campus budget to central administration for approval and recommendation to Board of Trustees
June	Campus budgets are combined with district budgets and submitted to Board of Trustees for final approval
July	Any budget modifications are addressed and discrepancies reconciled. Second formal discussion with Board of Trustees
August	Final input, checking, modifying, and balancing completed and submitted to Board of Trustees for approval and adoption

The View from the Field represents the changes that are occurring at the campus level as school leaders involve teachers in the budget development process. As a new campus leader, the principal is working through a process that solicits greater input from the professional staff.

Using Technology for Effective Fiscal Management

School leaders are given both opportunities and challenges with the technology available, and technology will continue to evolve as an important tool for effective fiscal management in gathering and sorting data. Educational technology can be divided into two general categories: administrative and instructional. Both aspects are critical for effective fiscal management as school leaders seek ". . . to build a learning environment

View from the Field

Mr. Robert Garcia, the newly appointed principal at Shady Valley Elementary, has been asked by the superintendent to develop a campus budget for the next school year. Student performance at Shady Valley has declined over the last three years, and the superintendent has given the new principal a timeline of two years to improve student achievement.

The school's only secretary, who has generally been responsible for preparing the budget the past several years, informed Mr. Garcia that, "The budget development process we used last year to comply with the new state site-based management requirements took a lot of time and didn't work because various special interest groups couldn't agree." She also explained "That committee last year did not consider student performance data to guide their decision-making because it was just too complicated to understand. You should return to the old way of campus budget development where I helped the principal develop the budget. To comply with state mandates, we can just give the completed budget to the site-based committee for their review and approval."

Mr. Garcia thanked his secretary for her input; he realized that cooperation of the school secretary was critical to accomplish the timely preparation of the budget. However, as he confided to a colleague, "I viewed the involvement of the larger school community in the budget development process as a real opportunity to communicate the needs of the school for improvement of student learning."

Because the budget was due at the district office at the beginning of the second semester, Mr. Garcia began with a series of steps that he believed would improve development of the new budget. As he describes the process, "Beginning in early fall, I set up weekly site-based committee budget development meetings. I asked my secretary to take notes at the weekly meetings and to bring the results of the previous week's session to each subsequent meeting for review and modification. The first several meetings were spent analyzing the campus performance reports from the current and previous years. The committee utilized the data to determine the school's strengths and weaknesses and develop goals and objectives. These objectives were prioritized, and the budget was developed according to identified program needs. Some of the committee members were disappointed when their favorite programs were scheduled to be reduced or eliminated, but I continued to remind the committee that all budgeting decisions were to be made according to one rule: Will this decision improve student learning where it is needed the most at this campus?"

that makes the best use of computer technology for the benefit of the leader" (Izat & Mize, 2000, p. 507).

The International Society for Technology in Education (2002) has noted that the use of technology across all aspects of a school or school system involves systemic reform and requires capable leadership to optimize the benefits of technology in learning, teaching, and school operations. The International Society for Technology in Education has developed technology standards for school administrators that serve as indicators of effective leadership for technology in schools. These standards can be found online at www.iste.org and serve as guidelines for school leaders as they seek to be more competent in the use of information and technology tools common to information age professions. As an educational leader seeking to improve the use of technology, the standards can be helpful in making decisions for school operations.

Although technology is used across all aspects of a school's mission and function, the administrative category is the focus of discussion here. In the administrative category, school districts have the opportunity to purchase existing software or to develop their own information management systems as they seek to be effective stewards of school resources. However, the instructional and administration categories are connected. For example, effective use of technology in the performance of administrative tasks such as attendance reporting, inventory control, and fiscal accounting can result in more money for instructional use (Rebore, 2001). "Software is available that enables . . . school districts to disaggregate their financial data" in order to provide for greater accountability and accuracy in decision making (Razik & Swanson, 2001, p. 408). Ray, Hack, and Candoli (2001) define such a management information system ". . . as a computer-based system that provides management [school leaders] with useful information for decision-making within an appropriate time frame" (p. 93). Although a variety of management information systems are available to educators, In$ite is a computer-based information management tool that can be used on a personal computer. This tool allows school leaders to track and analyze fiscal data for different educational functions including instruction, instructional support, operations, leadership, and other fiscal commitments.

In tracking and analyzing the instruction function, school leaders can examine expenditures related to (1) face-to-face teaching and (2) classroom expenses. When tracking instructional support funding, school leaders need to examine categories such as pupil support (i.e., guidance and counseling), teacher support (i.e., staff development activities), and program support (i.e., program evaluators). When examining the operations function, In$ite can track and analyze funding for operations that include noninstructional pupil services (i.e., transportation or food service), facilities (i.e., building maintenance and utilities), and business services (i.e., data processing). In examining leadership functions, school leaders can disaggregate the data according to school management functions (i.e., administrators), program and operations management functions (i.e., supervisors), program and operations management functions (i.e., department heads, special assignments), and district management functions (i.e., superintendent and central office).

Other fiscal commitments that can be tracked and examined using technology include capital expenditures (capital projects requiring major financing), out-of-district obligations (i.e., state equilization directives), budgeted contingencies, and legal obligations. Busch and Odden (1998) note growing trends in states to monitor and track fiscal resources at the school or campus level. Facility planning also requires that classrooms and buildings use technology for building communications, security systems, and energy conservation. Instructional technology is also a concern for school leaders in terms of successful integration and application. Izat and Mize (2000) support a seamless technology integration model, which recommends that administrators not focus on hardware, but (1) be concerned with selecting software packages based on their ability to support existing course content; (2) be willing to devote a significant position of the technology budget to training and developing faculty and staff; and (3) be willing to support technological changes. Examples of technology that impacts classroom learning include distance learning, satellite links, VCRs, personal and laptop computers, the Internet, local area networks, CD-ROMS, laser disks, computer-aided design, and interactive multimedia. The greatest challenge for school leaders and the use of technology is keeping up with the ever changing field. As a result, districts and campus leaders must carefully plan future budgets to accommodate both technology and facilities that support technology-based learning.

Financing School Facilities

The problems of financing public school facilities are much the same as those of financing current operating expenditures. Financing of construction of school buildings has remained almost entirely the responsibility of local school districts. Court decisions rendered in such equalization cases such as *Serrano* and *Rodriguez* in the 1970s focused primarily on financing current expenditures. During the last fifteen years, however, court decisions have emphasized the need to correct inequities in school facilities.

More recent trends indicate a movement toward greater participation for financing facilities at the state level, and in a majority of the states, provisions for state assistance now exist. Variations of state financing of capital outlays to local districts can be summarized in the statement that there is little similarity among the methods. For example, some include capital outlay as part of the foundation program, whereas others use grants, building authority rentals, or a combination of programs (Burrup, Brimley, & Garfield, 1999).

Historically, federal funds for capital outlay have been minimal. In 1950, Public Law 815 provided funds for areas affected by federal installations and defense projects. In 1995 the reauthorization of the *Elementary and Secondary Education Act* included $100 million for the *Education Infrastructure Act* (Title XII) to help urban and rural districts repair, renovate, and construct public elementary and secondary school facilities (Thedford & Patrick, 2000).

Capital outlay finance plans at the local level have been one of three types: pay-as-you-go financing, tax reserve funds, and bonds. Today, the pay-as-you-go plan is not used as commonly as it was when lower construction costs made it a convenient method. Accrual of tax reserve funds to construct facilities is a method used in a few areas, although the accrual of tax funds is illegal in some states.

Bonding is the most commonly used approach by local districts to finance capital outlay. In order for a district to issue long-term school bonds to one or more competing companies on the basis of the lowest interest rate bid, local taxpayer approval is required. Local property taxes are then levied to retire the debt and the accrued interest over a period of years, generally ten to thirty years. Bonds are sold through competitive bidding, with interest rates determined by the current market conditions, and investors consider these municipal bonds attractive because their earnings are exempt from federal and state income taxes. The increasing complexity of issuing school bonds has prompted most local school boards to employ a bond attorney.

Other options for local financing of school facilities have included impact fees to local developers or the donation of land within a new subdivision. Year-round schedules have been also used to increase the capacity of school buildings. As school populations increase in many regions and school buildings age, the need for equalized facilities is increasing.

The wise school leader must keep in mind that a bond election is an ongoing public relations process, regardless of when the election is to be scheduled. For example, citizen review committees may be used in determining future building needs. The next View from the Field describes the role of the Citizens' Budget Review Committee on the outcome of a bond election. Cheryl Jones, the fiscal officer for the districts, discusses the situation.

Issues Affecting Public School Resource Management

No discussion of the management of fiscal and human resources leadership would be complete without addressing current issues that impact resource management. As Thompson and Wood (1998) note, "Schools are changing with profound implications for the future" (p. 306). Although the parameters of the problem may appear to be simple—the provision of equal educational opportunities for all students—the resolution of the problem is troublesome. School leaders will have to obtain agreement on diverse goals, which will require enormous amounts of money in order "to implement

View from the Field

Happy School District is a fast-growing suburban school district located between two major urban metropolitan areas. To provide adequate facilities for its ever increasing student population, the district regularly holds bond authorization elections about every three to five years. As Cheryl Jones describes the situation, "Never had a bond election failed to pass, until the most recent election when the proposal failed by a two to one margin. This left the district to face an uphill battle to cope with all of the demands of growth and providing facilities and programs for students."

"We were surprised when citizens complained that the school board and administration were not listening to their concerns about increased school taxes, and they wanted to increase student performance. To make matters worse, the local media said that the district spent too much money on administration and athletics."

As Cheryl describes the outcome she says, "Our superintendent and the school board appointed a Citizens' Budget Review Committee that represented a broad spectrum of district constituents. The advisory committee began by examining every detail of the previous year's budget, including a comparison of the district to other districts in the state, particularly in the areas of administration and athletics. The facts revealed that the district was well below the state average in each of these areas, as well as several others. After the committee established the budget priorities for the following year, they recommended to the school board that another bond authorization election be scheduled. In the months before the election, the Citizens' Budget Review Committee played a major role informing the community about the need for the bond election and the school district's financial efficiency. This time the bond election won by a two to one margin."

starkly divergent expectations" (Thompson & Wood, 1998, p. 306). Specifically, school leaders must be cognizant of emerging school choice options in which parents and students may choose alternative educational settings, with the per-pupil allocation following the student. The continuum of school choice ranges from choices within public schools such as magnet programs, transfers, open enrollment, or public charter schools, to choices outside public schools such as vouchers for private schools. The number of students participating in one of these options has increased each year, which has introduced an element of competition for public school tax dollars that was virtually nonexistent before 1990. School administrators need to be informed of the various options within their own communities.

Other school-related issues that impact school budgets, although not directly related to instruction, include school safety, high-stakes testing, and systemic change. Schools have had to increase security measures at the district and individual campus levels to ensure student safety. Schools have had to budget for more security officers to patrol individual campuses on a twenty-four-hour, seven-day-a-week basis, as well as screening all individuals entering buildings. Surveillance cameras have been installed in common areas of the schools as well as on school buses. On many high school campuses, student identification badges have been instituted, along with metal detectors at all entrances. These additional security measures, although designed to make schools safe havens, are costly additions to a school budget and siphon off funds that could support instructional efforts.

As more and more states have embraced high-stakes testing as a means of supporting accountability and ensuring student success, more funds are needed to provide tutoring services and materials for these students. Often these students are classified as underserved and have diverse needs. They are tracked as part of the accountability process because they have a history of failing to meet state standards. If schools are to ensure "success for all—whatever it takes," then there must be an additional investment made in personnel, equipment, and other instructional resources.

Finally, as schools seek to sustain educational reform and change, they will have to employ a systemic approach that looks at all factors that impact student learning. Change efforts must be monitored and evaluated, which may require additional support staff who not only track the proposed changes, but also develop ways to assess the impact of the change(s) on student success. Quality change is not cheap, and schools will have to budget more of their resources to sustain the changes that are implemented.

A significant trend in funding focuses on the sources of funding, which have changed over the last four decades. The typical school district receives revenues from the following sources: 7% federal, 45.2% state, 45.1% local, and 2.7% private (U.S. Department of Education, 1996). This revenue mix is ". . . highly varied on a state-by-state basis, with local support ranging from a low of .8% in Hawaii to a high of 86.2% in New Hampshire in the same year" (Thompson & Wood, 1998, p. 61). In the future, these discrepancies will shift, but the local emphasis on school funding will continue to be strong and may increase, despite the heavy dependence on property taxes as the primary source of local revenues. Thompson and Wood (1998) suggest that ". . . progress comes from seeking a balanced tax system" (p. 307). Stakeholders must work to secure a greater share of state revenues for school funding.

Case Study

Central Middle School is in an older neighborhood with a transitional population that includes retirees, new immigrants, and young families. Recently, a charter school obtained a permit to start up next school year. In the last five years the school community has become more diverse, and the school reflects this diversity. Student performance data have consistently ranked among the best in the district, but in the last two years test scores have decreased. The faculty at Central are concerned that several active parents and student leaders may leave the traditional campus in favor of the *bells and whistles* promised at the new charter school. Central will lose funding for each student who transfers to the charter school and that will result in less money for the remaining students.

At the end of a school meeting with parents and community business leaders the following issues were voiced:

- Drugs and violence in public schools in general
- Lack of curricular offerings (i.e., foreign languages and advanced math courses)
- Poorly prepared students for high school and the workforce
- Gradual declines in student achievement scores

The new director of the charter school has visited the Central campus and has asked for assistance in developing courses and in meeting required curriculum content. After visiting the Central campus she called a meeting with the press and talked about how the curriculum offerings at the charter school would be more responsive to student and community needs. She emphasized that foreign language would be an integral part of the charter school curriculum, along with advanced courses in math and science.

You have just accepted the position of principal at Central Middle School. As the new campus leader:

1. What must you do to maintain your school's viability?
2. How is the situation a *budget issue*?
3. What are your options? Where would you begin?
4. In developing an action plan, what must you consider and what steps would you take to address the issues voiced by faculty, parents, and community leaders?

Summary

School leadership and resource management involve complex issues that cannot be adequately described in one chapter of a book. Entire books have been devoted to the topic of financing public education or the study of a particular component, such as human resources administration.

The historical and legal overview provided at the beginning of this chapter provides a context for understanding current practice. As state educational systems have developed, school funding has followed a general pattern in which revenues are generated from three primary sources: local, state, and federal. Today, a variety of funding patterns exist ranging from mostly state funded to a distribution among the various sources.

In recent decades, equalization lawsuits were filed in almost every state, resulting in increased pressure to address equal opportunities for all students, regardless of the school district or the student's place of residence. Various equalization models are described in the chapter, but the U.S. Supreme Court has generally left the matter of school funding in the hands of state legislatures.

The chapter also describes the budgeting process that begins with a campus or district needs assessment. Additional steps include the developing and prioritizing of goals; establishing of objectives; selecting and developing programs and materials; adopting a budget; and assessing results. School leaders must track and monitor school revenues and expenditures as they seek to ensure fiscal responsibility and accountability. Greater community interest in the school district budget has been generated through concerns about taxation increases. By increasing the involvement of external and internal stakeholders in site-based budget building, school leaders have the opportunity to build support for funded programs. The budget should reflect the educational philosophy of the school's mission, with the ultimate goal of improving student performance.

Technology has emerged as both an administrative and instructional tool, and today's school leaders have to employ the effective use of technology in managing the school budget within other information management systems. Facilities remain largely unequalized and largely the responsibility of the local school district. Typically, bonds are sold to finance the construction and renovation of local public schools. The chapter ends with a brief discussion of issues that can impact future resource management including school safety, high-stakes testing, and systemic change.

Your Turn

7.1. Develop a budget field project. The following guidelines will prove helpful in getting started. Use information from your campus performance system report and from an interview with your building principal to write a report discussing the following points.

- Budget autonomy: (1) How much autonomy does the principal have regarding budget development and expenditures? (2) What part of the budget is controlled by the central office and what percent of the total local campus budget is this amount? What part is left to the discretion of the local building principal? (3) What controls are in place to ensure that money is spent according to the budget? (4) If the campus has student and/or teacher activity funds, how much money is generated through each activity fund source?
- Budget development: (1) How and when is input from teachers, parents, and community received to determine goals, apportion resources, and evaluate use of

resources? (2) How is this information compiled and passed along to the central office?

- Budget expenditures: (1) What if money is needed in a different category than it was budgeted? (2) What happens if there is not enough money to cover an expenditure? (3) What happens at the end of the fiscal year if budgeted funds are not spent?
- Campus demographics: (1) How much is the *total* (including personnel salaries) most recent annual campus operating budget, and what is the amount of money allocated for salaries? (2) How many teachers are on this campus? What is the teacher to pupil ratio? (3) How many administrators are on this campus? What is the administrator to pupil ratio? (4) What is the total school population for what grade span, and what special programs are housed on the campus? (5) Describe numbers and percentages in the ethnic and socioeconomic makeup.
- Resource allocation: (1) What is the most recent student performance rating for the campus? (2) How does resource allocation at the campus level relate to school goals and desired student outcomes?

7.2. Investigate the stages of the school finance system in your state. What are these stages of school funding development in your state? Use the information in the chapter to guide your investigation. It may be helpful to conduct telephone interviews with state officials. Keep a journal of all of the information you collect.

7.3. Go online and research federal grant opportunities. What are the major areas of support? What are the trends for grants in the next five years? Select a categorical grant of the federal government and describe how it is allocated and administered at the state, district, and campus levels. Be specific in identifying this grant.

7.4. You have been asked to brief a group of educators who are preparing to be school leaders. They need to know about school finance litigation. As part of your presentation, identify three of the important court cases decided in recent years concerning school finance reform. Use a role-playing strategy; get members of your audience involved and in doing so, become aware of the issues and results from each court case.

7.5. Find out if any school choice options (charter schools, vouchers, private management) exist in your area, and if possible, visit one of these schools to learn more about it. Talk with local traditional school administrators about the impact of this choice on the affected school district. Present the information you collect to the school board to provide the future direction of this option.

References

Alexander, K., & Salmon, R. G. (1995). *Public school finance*. Boston: Allyn & Bacon.

Biddle, B. J., & Berliner, D. C. (2002). Unequal school funding in the United States. *Educational Leadership, 59*, 8, 48–59.

Burrup, P. E., Brimley, V., Jr., & Garfield, R. R. (1999). *Financing education in a climate of change* (7th ed). Boston: Allyn & Bacon.

Busch, C., & Odden, A. (1997). Introduction to the special issue—Improving education policy with school-level data: A synthesis of multiple perspectives. *Journal of Education Finance, 24,* 238.

Cameron, R. M. (2000). An analysis of district per pupil expenditures on selected indicators of the academic excellence indicator system (AEIS) in Texas public schools. Doctoral Dissertation, Texas AM University-Commerce.

Clark, C. P., & England, C. (1997 October). Educational finance. Briefing paper: *Texas public school finance and related issues.* Austin, TX: Texas Center for Educational Research.

Gold, S. D., Smith, D., & Lawton, S. B. (1995). *Public school finance programs of the United States and Canada 1993–94.* Albany: American Education Finance Association, Center for the Study of the States, Nelson A. Rockefeller Institute of Government, State University of New York.

Guthrie, J. W. (1998). Reinventing education finance: Alternatives for allocating resources to individual schools. In W. J. Fowler, Jr. (ed), *Selected papers in school finance.* Washington, DC: U.S. Department of Education.

Hanushek, E. A. (1989). The impact of differential expenditures on school performance. *Educational Researcher, 18,* 4, 45–65.

International Society for Technology in Education. (2002). *National educational technology standards for administrators.* www.iste.org.

Izat, J. G., & Mize, C. D. (2000). Texas schools, technology integration, and the twenty-first century. In J. A. Vornberg (ed), *Texas public school organization and administration: 2000* (7th ed). pp. 505–518. Dubuque, Iowa: Kendall-Hunt Publishing Company.

Johns, R. L., & Morphet, E. L. (1969). *The economics and financing of education.* Englewood Cliffs, NJ: Prentice-Hall.

Kemerer, F., & Walsh, J. (2000). *The educator's guide to Texas school law* (5th ed). Austin, TX: University of Texas Press.

Laine, R., Greenwald, R., & Hedges, L. (1996). Money does matter: A research synthesis of a new universe of education production function studies. In L. Picus & J. Wattenbarger (eds), *Where does the money go?* Thousand Oaks, CA: Corwin Press.

Odden, A., & Busch, C. (1998). *Financing schools for high performance: Strategies for improving the use of educational resources.* San Francisco: Jossey-Bass.

Patrick, D. (2000). Financing schools in Texas. In C. W. Funkhouser (ed), *Education in Texas: Policies, practices, and perspectives* (9th ed). pp. 47–54. Upper Saddle River, NJ: Prentice-Hall.

Ray, J. R., Hack, W. G., & Candoli, I. C. (2001). *School business administration: A planning approach* (7th ed). Boston: Allyn & Bacon.

Razik, T. A., & Swanson, A. D. (2001). *Fundamental concepts of educational leadership* (2nd ed). Upper Saddle River, NJ: Prentice-Hall.

Rebore, R. W. (2001). *Human resources administration in education: A management approach.* Boston: Allyn & Bacon.

Roe, W. H. (1961). *School business management.* New York: McGraw-Hill.

Smith, R. E. (1998). *Human resources administration.* Larchmont, NY: Eye on Education.

Thedford, J., & Patrick, D. (2000). Financing Texas public schools. In J. A. Vornberg (ed), *Texas public school organization and administration: 2000* (7th ed). pp. 297–323. Dubuque, IA: Kendall-Hunt Publishing Company.

Thompson, D. C., & Wood, R. C. (1998). *Money and schools.* Larchmont, NY: Eye on Education.

U.S. Department of Education. (1996). *Digest of education statistics 1996.* Washington, DC: U.S. Government Printing Office.

Walker, B., & Casey, D. T. (1996). *The basics of Texas public school finance* (6th ed). Austin, TX: Texas Association of School Boards.

8

Curriculum Development and Alignment

ISLLC Standards

Standard 1: A school administrator is an educational leader who promotes the success of all students by facilitating the development, articulation, implementation, and stewardship of a vision of learning that is shared and supported by the school community.

Standard 2: A school administrator is an educational leader who promotes the success of all students by advocating, nurturing, and sustaining a school culture and instructional program conducive to student learning and staff professional growth.

Chapter Objectives

The objectives of this chapter are:

- Identify and describe the components of the curriculum development and alignment processes.
- Explain how school leaders can support continuous school improvement through curriculum development and alignment.
- Discuss the role of the principal as an instructional leader.
- Explain what is meant by learner-centered curriculum.
- Describe the process of implementing campus curriculum planning and alignment.
- Discuss best practices related to curriculum standards.

As school leaders seek to promote the success of all students, they must advocate, nurture, and sustain instructional programs that emphasize student learning. The national dialogue has primarily been about the measurement of student learning through the use of achievement tests. Not since the Sputnik era have educators and noneducators alike been so interested in achievement scores (Reinhartz & Beach, 1992). With such an increased emphasis on student-achievement and high-stakes testing, many states have revamped their curriculum as a part of an accountability and standards system (see Chapter 9). The focus on student performance also has created a renewed interest in the role of curriculum in teaching and learning and instruction is once again at center stage in schools.

With the adoption of *Goals 2000: Educate America Act* (Public Law 103-227), Congress established for the first time a national mission statement for the public schools in America (Weiss, 1994). These national goals included the following eight priorities:

1. All children in America will start school ready to learn.
2. High school graduation rates will increase to at least 90%.
3. All students leaving grades 4, 8, and 12 will demonstrate mastery over all subject matter and will demonstrate responsible citizenship, continued learning, and be capable of productive employment.
4. All teachers will have access to and engage in programs for their continued professional improvement.
5. The United States students will rank first in the world in tests of mathematics and science.
6. All adult Americans will be literate.

7. All schools in America will be drug and violence free and will have a disciplined environment conducive to learning.
8. All schools will engage in home partnerships in order to increase parental involvement and participation in promoting the social, emotional, and academic growth of children (National Education Goals Panel, 1994).

As Reinhartz and Beach (1997) note, Goals 2000 was a noble attempt to shine a national spotlight on education and their purpose was ". . . to set national standards for student achievement in the core curriculum (mathematics, science, history, geography, and language arts), [but] . . . much of the work has to be done at the state and local levels" (p. 33).

More recently, educational leaders have begun to examine the impact of curriculum on what occurs in classrooms because "people on a grade level, in a subject area, or teaching a course at a high school are [feeling] a responsibility to have the same destination" (Liebowitz, 2001, p. 2). Having the curriculum drive teaching and learning can make a difference in helping to ensure that every student succeeds. "Today . . . a rich base of research and exemplary practice . . . points the way to school renewal through curriculum reform" (Zemelman, Daniels, & Hyde, 1998, p. 6). The curriculum must be kept at the center of the conversation in schools, for as Berliner (1996) notes, curriculum is undergirded by a belief system or ideology that provides a context for teaching and learning. Conversations about curricular issues help to break down the feelings of isolation that often exist between administrators and teachers and between teachers at all levels by providing a *systems* view of teaching and learning. Such conversations also help to establish performance expectations for all students to attain. "Having a professional belief system guides the development of a personal vision for teaching; this vision embodies both the means and ends of curriculum development" (Reinhartz & Beach, 1997, p. 101). When conversations occur in schools about personal visions of teaching and learning, along with the content, process, and context, then schools are well on their way to becoming successful in promoting academic success for all.

National, state, and district standards for areas of study are a part of the curriculum conversation and are embedded within the process of curriculum development. Views of curriculum must also be inclusive and sensitive to the needs of all students without regard to students' ethnic backgrounds or their socioeconomic status. Making connections between and among what is planned, implemented, and assessed is central to a comprehensive approach to curriculum development.

For many schools, local and state standards guide development of instructional plans for course or grade levels while also establishing performance objectives. When the curriculum is aligned, it can be viewed as an educational photo album that tells the whole instructional story rather than as isolated snapshots. Instead of seeing teaching and learning occurring as discrete moments in time, the moments become connected as students move through the subjects and grades of the educational system. Most parents (55%) in a poll on the Public's Attitudes toward the Public Schools agree that "all students have the ability to reach a high level of learning (Rose & Gallup, 2000). The public's perception of learning, as well as recent national legislation, suggests that no child should be left behind, and Lezotte (1997) says effective schools emphasize "learning for all—whatever it takes" (p. 2).

The responsibilities of school leaders are changing, just as the contexts for schools are changing, yet one of the most important duties for a campus leader is to ensure that every student is academically successful by providing teachers with the instructional resources and professional development to meet this goal. Leaders for today's schools must go beyond purchasing materials, convening committees, reviewing materials, and developing curriculum guides; they must pay greater attention to the total teaching–learning process as the central focus of the school culture.

This chapter discusses the importance of the school leader's role in conversations about curriculum development and alignment. First, the chapter discusses curriculum and curriculum development in general and then in the context of best practices and standards, as they relate to teaching and learning. The chapter also emphasizes the curriculum alignment process by providing both curriculum development and curriculum alignment models that involve the components of planning, implementing, and assessing. Such models are built around assumptions that include (1) learner-centered curriculum, instruction, and assessment; (2) a curriculum of knowledge and skills for all students that forms the minimal foundation; and (3) the mastery of essential knowledge and skills in the curriculum. The section concludes by describing ways school leaders can use student achievement data in the alignment process to modify and adjust the curriculum.

This chapter also describes best practices as they relate to curriculum standards that are learner centered and emphasize (1) developing high cognitive thinking and making connections; (2) addressing varied needs and characteristics of all learners; (3) developing multiple ways of assessing student progress; and (4) establishing learning objectives that are aligned to the essential knowledge and skills in the curriculum. Such a curriculum provides many different avenues for teaching and learning to meet the varied needs and abilities of diverse student populations. School leaders can also support teachers in implementing best practices and curriculum standards as they make decisions about learning for their students.

Curriculum and Curriculum Development

Like the term *leadership*, a commonly agreed on definition for *curriculum* has often been a challenge for educators. Definitions have evolved over the decades, but vestiges of many of the early descriptions still hold. Today's schools, although complex, are in many ways like the one-room schools of the 1800s. Such a typical school might be described as follows.

> On the first day of school eleven students had arrived. . . . 'Little Un' Sams had cried . . . all morning; Jinks Mayfield had gone home, just walked off, because the Baldridge twins announced they couldn't play with her because she had the 'itch,' and Bucy Abernathy, one year older than I, leaned back in his seat all morning as if to say, 'teach me if you can!' (Wood, 2000, pp. 15–16)

While student attitudes and behaviors may sometimes be similar, schools of the twenty-first century also have greater diversity and their complexities present a different and greater challenge for educators.

To understand the term *curriculum*, perhaps the best place to begin is with the earliest definition, the Latin *currere*, which, simply put means "the course to be run." According to Eisner (2002), "this metaphor of a racetrack is not altogether inappropriate. Schools have historically established 'courses' of study through which students pass" (pp. 23–24). Taking specific courses to complete a particular program is still done today. By the 1920s, a more modern definition of *curriculum* was presented as a ". . . series of experiences which children and youth must have by way of attaining [the] objectives" (Bobbitt, 1918, p. 14). Some have described curriculum using mechanistic language such as, a ". . . container (an object with bounded spatial dimensions), [with] references to 'frameworks,' 'standards,' and the flowcharts used to depict planning sequences . . ." (McCutcheon, 1999, p. 50). Others have viewed curriculum as a process rather than a product. Tyler (1957) described curriculum as a plan directed by teachers to achieve a set of educational goals. Others, such as Tanner and Tanner (1995), have defined curriculum as a work plan that includes information and instructional strategies to engage the learner. Reinhartz and Beach (1997) define curriculum as "a flexible plan for teaching that meets the needs of students as well as provides opportunities for teachable moments" (p. 20).

Although curriculum may be viewed as a specific plan of action for teaching, *curriculum development* is a comprehensive process that is continuous in nature. Curriculum development is ongoing as educators monitor the implementation of plans and make decisions to modify those plans to meet the characteristics and needs of students (Reinhartz & Beach, 1997). Four essential questions, originally proposed by Tyler (1949), continue to guide school leaders in curriculum development:

1. What educational purposes should the school seek to promote?
2. What educational experiences can be implemented that are likely to achieve these purposes?
3. How can these educational experiences be effectively organized?
4. How can we determine whether the purposes are being achieved? (pp. 1–2)

A more recent view of these four foundational questions can be found in the context of learning communities. For Eaker, DuFour, and Burnette (2002), the following key questions serve to guide school leaders in making curricular decisions within the school learning community:

- What exactly do we expect students to learn?
- How will we know that students are learning?
- How can we assist and support students in their learning?
- Based on a collaborative analysis of the results of our efforts, what can we do to improve student learning?
- How can we recognize and celebrate improvements in student learning? (p. 19)

School leaders are encouraged to engage in discussions with faculty and staff to generate answers to the original questions posed by Tyler. The first question addresses the goals of the educational program. The second question examines the ways schools can achieve the goals. The third question looks at the scope and sequence of the experiences, and finally, the fourth question addresses assessment or validation of the goals. These questions also address the outcomes, learning strategies, and assessment criteria that will match the needs of the students and lead to greater student achievement. Figure 8.1 presents an overview of the curriculum development process, which involves three major activities: planning, implementing, and assessing. These three components are continuous and should address the characteristics and needs of all students and provide for feedback and modifications. In discussing the nature of the various components, Reinhartz and Beach (1997) suggest that planning involves all of the activities that occur prior to teaching including content analysis, scope, and sequence, and the selection of goals and objectives. While "implementation involves the actual teaching of the material and interacting with students" (p. 21). Assessment is concerned with the degree to which students have mastered the objectives or determine if learning has occurred.

In the curriculum development process, *planning* involves the use of curriculum guides and other resources when deciding on the concepts, or content, and skills to be taught. For Arends (2000), "Deciding what to teach is among the most difficult aspects of teacher planning because there is so much that could be learned and so little time"

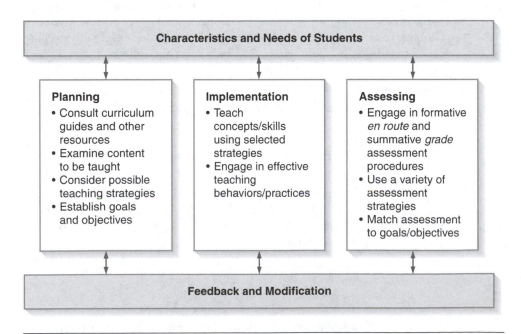

FIGURE 8.1   *Curriculum Development Process*

Source: Modified from Reinhartz, J., & Beach, D. (1997). *Teaching and learning in the elementary school.* Upper Saddle River, NJ: Merrill/Prentice Hall.

(p. 51). Planning also involves scope (what) and sequence (when) so that course material is appropriately presented. In planning, teachers also consider possible teaching strategies to match instructional goals and objectives. In addition to the content and sequence, "Good planning involves allocating the use of time, choosing appropriate methods of instruction, creating student interest, and building [a] productive learning environment" (Arends, 2000, p. 40). Plans are not always written down; they can be in the minds of teachers. But the only way these plans can be assessed is by observing teachers teach (Eisner, 2002).

In *implementing* the instructional plans, teaching becomes the focus as teachers work with students to master learning goals. Teachers must monitor and adjust instruction throughout the lesson by using effective teaching practices. Implementation is an interactive process as students and curriculum come together to create learning.

Assessing involves both formative (en route) and summative (graded) procedures. Teachers use a variety of assessment strategies to match the goals and objectives and to determine if the goals and objectives have been mastered. Assessment is a process that involves collecting a wide range of information and artifact about students and the classroom environment for making decisions about instruction and student performance. Each of these three components of the curriculum development process is discussed in greater detail later in the chapter as part of the alignment process.

School leaders play an important role in the curriculum development process because they facilitate conversations about the understanding and use of each component. Leaders may seek to guide the curriculum development process by securing computer programs that aid in planning by providing templates or formats. When observing teachers in their classrooms and providing feedback, school leaders can also support the interactive nature of teaching and learning. By working with teachers to disaggregate or make sense of their student performance data, school leaders can facilitate the assessment process, which also results in future curriculum modifications.

As the schools have changed, so too have students, and school leaders must work to develop a curriculum that addresses the needs of all students. As Arends (2000) points out, instructional decisions are value laden and influence our points of view. Darling-Hammond (1997) has pointed out that, in a typical class of twenty-five students, "Today's teacher will serve at least 4 or 5 students with specific educational needs that [s]he has not been prepared to meet . . . [S]he will need considerable knowledge to develop curriculum and teaching strategies that address the wide range of learning approaches, experiences, and prior levels of knowledge" (1997, p. 7).

Addressing student needs and characteristics serves as the foundation of the curriculum development process and provides the focus for planning, teaching, and assessing. Eaker, DuFour, and Burnette (2002) have noted a shift in the schools' culture with regard to curriculum development. According to these authors, there is a movement away from each teacher deciding what to teach in isolation from others to a collaboratively developed curriculum focused on student learning. There is also a movement away from a curriculum overloaded with many concepts and programs to a reduced content with more meaningful, in depth learning. Finally, in professional learning communities, assessment is collaboratively developed, and students who are not learning are identified and their deficiencies addressed.

Aligning Curriculum, Instruction, and Assessment

For school leaders to be effective in fostering improved student achievement, they should be well versed not only in the curriculum development process and ways to make links to teaching and learning, but in ways to align the curriculum as well. With an increasingly diverse student population, school leaders need to view curriculum as the infrastructure for implementing the school's mission and vision. Designing a curriculum that intentionally links student strengths and needs to content standards provides the infrastructure that is needed. Through the recursive process of linking standards with planning, teaching, and assessing, the questions of not only "what students should learn and how they are to learn it" are answered, along with how do we know what and how they have learned (Carr & Harris, 2001, p. 58).

Figure 8.2 presents the three domains of the alignment process, curriculum planning, instruction, and assessment or evaluation, which match the curriculum development components. These domains are interdependent and work in concert to meet student needs and promote student learning. Whereas curriculum development refers to the creative process that links goals, outcomes, and curriculum objectives, alignment is designed to determine the degree of congruency and overlap among the three domains. Curriculum development is putting the pieces of the puzzle together, and curriculum alignment examines the *fit* among the piece. Curriculum alignment refers to the *match* that exists between the ". . . content and format of the test and the content and format of curriculum . . . ; the closer the match, the greater the potential for improvement on the test" (English, 2000, p. 6).

Frontloading the curriculum is one method of the alignment process that describes the content and objectives being written first and then matched with instructional strategies. The appropriate assessment strategies are then selected that measure the degree to which objectives are achieved and learning goals are attained. In *backloading* the curriculum, the assessment process drives curriculum development by determining what will be taught and when. According to English (2000), educators are sensitive to the practice of backloading because of the troublesome issue of "teaching to the test."

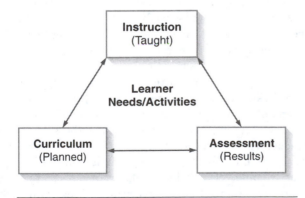

FIGURE 8.2 *Curriculum Alignment Process*

In backloading, the test often becomes the curriculum, and Halayna, Nolen, and Haas (1991) view this type of alignment as "unethical" because it makes the test the curriculum. The following sections provide a more in depth discussion of each domain of the alignment process.

Curriculum Planning

An understanding of student characteristics and needs shapes how and what content teachers select from textbooks and other resources and the strategies they use to present this information. Although curriculum planning is the first domain in curriculum alignment, the process is not linear. Actually as the data become available, school leaders should use data from the assessment domain to modify and adjust the content, goals, and objectives based on the performance of the learners. Reinhartz and Beach (1997) have observed that although research has not provided ". . . solid, empirical evidence as to the single best way to plan, it does provide insights that can be used to understand the complexities . . . [of] planning . . ." (p. 125). Curriculum planning involves the following traits or characteristics (Wiles & Bondi, 2002; Eisner, 2002; Shavelson, 1987; Clark & Yinger, 1987):

- It is viewed as an important step in preparing to teach
- It occurs on several levels, such as district, campus or school, and grade level, as well as in individual classrooms
- It reduces ambiguity and uncertainty in classroom instruction
- It takes many forms
- It transforms thoughts into reality

Curriculum planning involves examining the concepts or content, establishing goals and objectives, consulting materials and resources (curriculum guides, manuals, standards), and structuring learning around instructional strategies. All of these activities occur within the context of understanding the characteristics and needs of the learners to focus and connect within a classroom, school campus, and district. By involving teachers from different grade levels within the same subject field during the planning process, school leaders can help to address the issues of vertical alignment. Discussing the writing process from grades K–6 or from grades K–12 helps teachers see what is occurring at each grade level in order to provide for greater alignment. Alignment of the curriculum is designed to optimize student performance and requires careful reflection and involves the ". . . mindful consideration of one's action [as well as] . . . critical assessment of one's own behavior as a means towards developing one's own craftsmanship" (Osterman, 1990, p. 134).

Curriculum is often defined simply as *what is taught*. This phrase at first appears simple, yet within it there is an element of complexity. Curriculum has many layers of what is taught that may begin with mandates or state standards for each discipline in grades pre-K through 12. These mandates normally include the minimum or essential knowledge and skills that guide and shape the school's curriculum. In addition to state requirements, locally adopted curricular materials may impose guidelines or requirements. Finally, there is the teacher's own professional judgment about the needs of the students. In addressing what should be taught there are many layers of decisions that must be made. Even with state developed frameworks and curriculum standards, curriculum guides and textbooks continue to be primary tools for planning at the classroom and campus levels.

Remillard (1999) examined the knowledge of teacher's curriculum decisions to consider ways that curriculum materials might support change in teaching. Teachers' curriculum decisions are complex and start with textbooks but continue in the classroom as they interact with students. Teachers serve as curriculum developers who not only select and redesign what is taught, but enact those plans in the classroom with students. Even teachers who follow textbook suggestions as closely as possible make curriculum development decisions (Remillard, 1999). The role of the school leader is to assist teachers as they grow from interactions between their beliefs and elements of the curriculum, as well as from the larger context of their teaching by observing and interacting with students

Once the *what* has been determined, the *how* (instruction) comes into play. School leaders encourage curriculum planning by fostering a conversation among teachers with regard to student learning outcomes—the goals and objectives for their courses, subjects, or grade levels. By having teachers regularly reflect on and discuss not only what they teach and why, but also how they teach, school leaders promote curriculum planning beyond the stereotyped lesson plan books. Gross (1997) advocates a joint curriculum design that "is an interactive form of planning that unites teachers and students in a[n] . . . appraisal of curricular components to negotiate goals, content, methods and assessment throughout the various stages of planning, implementing, and debriefing" (p. 6). In promoting a joint curriculum design, school leaders should facilitate teacher dialogue that compares and contrasts the characteristics of a traditional curriculum design with the characteristics of a joint curriculum design presented in Table 8.1. As seen in Table 8.1, the traditional curriculum design relies heavily on

TABLE 8.1   *Curriculum Designs*

Traditional Curriculum Design	*Joint Curriculum Design*
Content mastery focus	Inquiry, process focus
Fixed, competitive setting	Cooperative setting
Teacher-directed learning	Community of learners
Teacher-determined goals and objectives	Negotiated goals and objectives
Isolated content and skills	Integrated content and skills
Standardized tasks	Individualized tasks
Uniform pace	Individual/group pace
Teacher-centered approach	Learner-centered approach
Linear sequential learning	Unique recursive learning

Source: Modified from Gross, P. A. (1997). *Joint curriculum design.* Mahwah, NJ: Lawrence Erlbaum Associates.

teacher-determined and teacher-directed lessons that emphasize standardization of tasks and pace to achieve content mastery. The joint curriculum design focuses on the integration of content and skills and employs a learner-centered focus and inquiry process.

In the View from the Field, the assistant principal, Judd Graves, initiates a conversation among junior high school teachers concerning curriculum design when he asks them to describe their concept of learning and what it looks like.

Implementing Curriculum Plans—Teaching

Equally as important as organizing the curriculum content in an effective way is the implementation of the plans. The implementation of curriculum plans, "as teachers interact with students in the classroom, is . . . commonly referred to as teaching" (Reinhartz & Beach, 1997, p. 151). Teaching, the second step in the alignment process, involves carrying out the plans as teachers and students confront the curriculum and interact with each other. Frieberg and Driscoll (1996) describe the relationship as planning which provides the framework for teaching, but, they note that, "the execution of the plan may require several adjustments along the way . . . [because] the dynamics of the classroom reduce the certainties of the . . . plan" (p. 41). For Gross (1997), "Teaching is a dynamic, ever-changing endeavor. Each success proves to be but a hint of things to come—new challenges, new discoveries" (p. 4). According to Reinhartz and

View from the Field

Recently, Judd Graves, the assistant principal and instructional specialist, attended the mathematics departmental meeting at National Junior High School (7th and 8th grades) math teachers. The teachers had expressed concerns about students' performance on a national achievement test that had been given at the school. Mr. Graves described his role by saying, "To initiate a conversation among the teachers about how students came to know and understand math, I asked them to individually define learning. I then had them get into groups of twos or threes and then had each group draw 'learning,' based on their combined understandings of the process. Their drawings could not contain words, only symbols or drawings."

After each group presented their visual concept of learning to the total group and explained their rationale, some brief discussion occurred within the total group. Judd Graves continues by saying, "I then showed the group the film, *Private Universe*, which discusses how students construct their own mental paradigms to explain their world, even when those mental models are shown to be inaccurate. I then asked each pair to redraw their view of learning based on what they had seen. As the teachers talked and reflected on how their students learn mathematics, I also had them discuss the characteristics of their students as well as the content they taught. During this conversation and interaction, the teachers began to generate a common understanding of what students should learn in 7th and 8th grade math. These conversations have now begun to impact on how the teachers plan instruction for students and have moved the math department toward a more learner-centered curriculum that emphasizes the integration of concepts and skills through an inquiry process."

Beach (1997), as the curriculum plans are implemented, teachers engage in microdecisions that answer the following questions:

- What is the most appropriate order to follow to teach concepts after checking to determine what the students already know?
- What adjustments to the plans should be made after students receive feedback?
- How does the amount of time spent on a concept impact planning?
- What adjustments will need to be made in the instructional act to accommodate individual interests in a topic?

Curriculum is implemented in a variety of ways at the classroom level based on the content, lesson attributes, design, and strategies used. Students have an opportunity to be active learners when they interact not only with the materials provided but also as they share with their classmates. Such interactions among and between students can lead to the accommodation and assimilation of a variety of concepts across the school curriculum, and principles of active learning and collaboration are central to the process particularly in a constructivist classroom. The complex process of instruction emphasizes the importance of both teaching and learning on student performance.

School leaders have an opportunity to shape the teaching–learning process as they conduct formal and informal classroom observations and as they promote peer or cognitive coaching in their schools. Showers and Joyce (1996) found that ". . . teachers who had a coaching relationship—that is, who shared aspects of teaching planned together, and pooled their experiences—applied new skills more frequently . . ." (p. 14). By supporting peer coaching, school leaders can involve teams of teachers, usually from various grades and/or subjects, ". . . who provide daily support and encouragement to each other" (Beach & Reinhartz, 2000, p. 141). The role of the school leader in facilitating this process is to engage teachers in peer coaching so that teaching does not occur in isolation. Costa and Garmston (1994) also suggest that school leaders promote cognitive coaching as a way of enhancing instructional behavior and fostering growth toward both autonomous and interdependent teaching behaviors.

Assessment

What teachers plan and teach is validated through student assessment. The assessment domain determines the extent to which students have achieved the learning goals and objectives. For Gross (1997), "Ongoing assessment clarifies goals, streamlines methods, [and] redirects inquiry. . . . Teachers estimate student progress . . . [by] helping students identify individual strengths and areas for improvement" (p. 139). It is at this juncture that assessment measures help to determine the degree and level of student achievement.

Historically, the term *curriculum evaluation* was used to describe this third domain. Woolfolk (1995) notes that the term *evaluation* connotes judgments and decisions. Assessment is more a process ". . . of obtaining data or information about . . . students, on which teachers then make judgments about teaching and learning. . . . Assessment connotes a broader scope and suggests there are many ways to determine curriculum . . . [and instructional] effectiveness and to measure student learning" (Reinhartz & Beach, 1997, p. 171). Gross (1997) further notes that, "Assessment has broadened from reliance on standardized tests and measurements of discrete, disciplined-linked facts to inclusion of demonstrations and exhibitions of knowledge that evidence individual competence, creativity, interdisciplinary connections, and intellectual growth" (p. 134).

Assessment is a critical piece in the alignment process for it informs decisions made in the other two domains. Based on the assessment data, goals and objectives developed during planning may need to be modified or instructional strategies used in teaching concepts or skills may need to be changed. The data from the assessment process are used to make decisions, not only about the curricular program and instructional strategies, but are used to determine the level(s) of student achievement. Although it is presented as the third domain in the alignment process, Reinhartz and Beach (1997) point out that, "it frequently occurs simultaneously as teachers plan and implement [curriculum]" (p. 173).

Data generated from the assessment process can be used by school leaders to make decisions about the total school program. Chapter 9 provides a detailed discussion of the importance of data-driven decision making, but initially school leaders can assist teachers by examining, not only student achievement on standardized tests, but student performance on other forms of assessment in their classes. One of the key pieces to the assessment puzzle is to make sure that students are assessed in ways similar to standardized examinations. For example, the English faculty members at a high school were asked by the curriculum director to look at their writing curriculum and activities and determine if they were aligned with the objectives of a national examination. They found the objectives were aligned with the content. However, when this same faculty examined the kinds of student work they required and the way that work was evaluated, it did not match the national assessment process. Simply by aligning their classroom assessment of student work with those of the national examination, the school improved student achievement scores. School leaders can facilitate this dialogue and analysis of both classroom and standardized assessment techniques; they must also address the issues of quality and equity.

In recognizing the importance of assessment processes in schools, particularly testing, the American Psychological Association has noted that

> Measuring what and how well students learn is an important building block in the process of strengthening and improving our nation's schools. Tests, along with student grades and teacher evaluations, can provide critical measures of students' skills, knowledge, and abilities. Therefore, tests should be a part of [an assessment] system in which broad and equitable access to educational opportunity and advancement is provided to all students. (2001, p. 1)

In continuing the discussion of the appropriate use of testing, the American Psychological Association (2001) notes that no single test is valid for all situations, and tests vary in their purpose and ability to "provide meaningful assessments of student learning" (p. 1). The potential problem with national and state achievement tests is not the tests per se but the unintended consequences of such tests, which can negatively impact individual students, groups of students, or the school and district. The assessment professionals are clear about one thing: "high-stakes decisions should not be made on the basis of a single test score, because a single test can only provide a 'snapshot' of student achievement" (American Psychological Association, 2001, p. 1).

In recognizing the increased use of high-stakes testing in schools, the American Educational Research Association has adopted a position statement regarding their use:

> Many states and school districts mandate testing programs to gather data about student achievement over time and to hold schools and students accountable. Certain uses of achievement test results are termed 'high-stakes' if they carry serious consequences for students or for educators. Schools may be judged according to the school-wide average scores of their students. High school-wide scores may bring public praise or financial rewards; low scores may bring public embarrassment or heavy sanctions. (2001, p. 1)

With more and more rhetoric regarding high-stakes testing, school leaders are key players in the accountability system. As key players, they provide the mortar for developing an inclusive school culture (Chapter 2), knowing the law (Chapter 4), and being aware of how schools are funded (Chapter 7). And Chapter 9 provides the details about the accountability movement, which will prove extremely valuable.

The three domains of the curriculum alignment process are interactive, and the next View from the Field provides insight into the leadership skills that are needed to foster this interaction.

View from the Field

At Clearfield Academy, teachers regularly meet by grade and subject area to discuss curriculum alignment issues. In determining the success of the curricular program and the school environment, Rosa Gonzales, the assistant principal, has been meeting with teams of teachers as they examine textbooks, curriculum guides, and other resources to make decisions about curriculum and instruction at their school. Rosa has served as the facilitator for the groups: "I generated the following questions for the faculty groups to answer as they reflected on the instructional process."

- Did the students at this grade level or in this subject master the minimal skills established? How do we know?
- What knowledge, skills, and experiences were critical to the students' success?
- Were the goals and objectives appropriate and did they match local and state outcomes?

- Could there be a more appropriate or meaningful sequence?
- Were learning activities meaningful?
- Were assessment procedures adequate to determine students' level(s) of understanding?
- Were the needs, interests, and abilities of the students adequately met?
- Do we need to modify content or strategies based on student learning?

"As a campus facilitator, I seek to not only help teachers answer the questions, but build consensus among the faculty with regard to their answers. I am not as concerned with the answers to the questions as I am in getting the teachers to reflect on the domains of curriculum alignment and make curriculum and instructional decisions based on student performance data."

School leaders may find Figures 8.3, 8.4, and 8.5 helpful as they address the issues of quality curriculum planning, teaching, and assessment taking place in individual classrooms as well as within the school. These documents provide a framework for conversations with teachers, and they can be used by administrators when reviewing teachers' plans, or when making formal and informal classroom observations. The forms can also be used to assess students' perceptions of their educational experience and to determine if employers and colleges are satisfied with their graduates. Figure 8.3 provides a template for addressing issues associated with the curriculum and student learning. This chart focuses on sources of data regarding student performance and the

Criteria	*High Priority (3)*	*Medium Priority (2)*	*Low Priority (1)*
A. What curriculum-referenced test results show significant gains per year (in major subject areas)? Data sources used:			
B. Are students reporting positive feelings about their educational experiences and subjects they are studying? Data sources used:			
C. What do employers and colleges say/report about the general satisfaction of their graduates' skills and knowledge? Types of reports/feedback:			
D. What are parents reporting/commenting on regarding the general satisfaction with the school? (Check Gallup Polls for the past three years in *Phi Delta Kappan*, September issue for topic educational issues for parents) Data sources used, such as parent surveys generated at building level? Types of data:			

FIGURE 8.3 *Issues Associated with Curriculum-Related Learning.* Directions: Read the following items and determine the priority each has in your district to assess student outcomes. Identify the sources of the data.

Did the learners . . .	Yes	No	Did the teacher . . .	Yes	No
1. Seem motivated to learn? Comments:			Seem sensitive to intrinsic motivation by helping students find meaning and purpose in what is to be learned? Comments:		
2. Understand and internalize the learning goal? Comments:			Select an approach that helps students internalize the learning goal(s)? Comments:		
3. Activate their prior knowledge? Comments:			Assist in this process and facilitate it? Comments:		
4. Acquire new knowledge? Comments:			Provide means for acquiring that knowledge that were efficient and effective? Comments:		
5. Relate the new knowledge to prior knowledge and modify knowledge constructs? Comments:			Facilitate the process? Comments:		
6. Construct personal knowledge meaning by organizing, elaborating, and representing knowledge in their own way? Comments:			Facilitate the process? Comments:		
7. Identify a complex problem to be solved and solve that problem by making knowledge generative? Comments:			Facilitate the process? Comments:		
8. Seem to have an appropriate amount of scaffolding and structuring from the teacher in solving the problem? Comments:					

Did the learners . . .	Yes	No	Did the teacher . . .	Yes	No
9. Understand and use the strategies needed to solve the problem? Comments:			Provide the necessary help in this process? Comments:		
10. Learn in a supportive social context? Comments:			Facilitate reflective dialogue, cooperative inquiry, and the social construction of knowledge? Comments:		
11. Use metacognitive monitoring to assess their learning processes? Comments:			Facilitate this process? Comments:		
12. Assess their learning and demonstrate their understanding? Comments:			Make periodic assessments of learning and use assessment data to adjust instruction and remediate when necessary? Comments:		

FIGURE 8.4 *Curriculum Related to Teaching and Learning.* Observation tool: Gaining insights into student learning and facilitating desirable learning practices during teaching.

Source: Modified from Brooks, J. G., & Brooks, M. C. (1983). *In search of understanding: The case for constructivist classrooms.* Alexandria, VA: Association for Supervision and Curriculum Development.

importance of each source in assessing student outcomes. These outcomes relate not only to academic achievement but to positive feelings about school as well. Other sources of data include colleges and universities, employers, and parents. Figure 8.4 seeks imput related to teaching and learning as observed in the classroom and includes several behaviors related to curriculum as implemented in the classroom. Figure 8.5 provides a format to use when examining curriculum materials, especially curriculum guides and other resources that support teachers in planning for instruction.

Best Practices and Curriculum Standards

Decisions about curriculum also need to be made within the context of best practices and standards that present an educational paradigm that transcends content boundaries and grade levels. For Arends (2000), "Best practices are those teaching methods,

Criteria	To a Great Degree	Some-what	Not at All
Emphases 1. Are the values and view of knowledge made clear? 2. Is the content of the guide based on sound research in that field and are their recommendations from experts? 3. Is there depth of knowledge (instead of coverage), acquisition of useful skills in solving meaningful problems? 4. Does the guide contribute to the district's vision of curriculum excellence? 5. Does the guide focus on meaningful outcomes leading to knowledge/skills needed for high education and requisite career skills? 6. Does the guide promote an appreciation of diversity, the value of common heritage, and a concern for equity?			
Placement and Sequence 1. Are the objectives developmentally appropriate? 2. Is there a meaningful sequence of learning experiences?			
Organization and Structure 1. Are the goals clear for that subject area? 2. Do the subject area goals relate to the district's educational goals? 3. Are the grade-level objectives derived from subject goals? 4. Are there resources included for teacher use? 5. Is there appropriate integration of knowledge within the subject and from related subjects?			
Articulation and Coordination 1. Are materials available? 2. Are the mechanisms in place to ensure that what is taught in a particular subject at a particular grade level builds on what was taught at the next grade level, without excessive repetition? 3. Are the mechanisms available to ensure that given grade level subjects that depend on each other are congruent in the skills and knowledge taught?			

FIGURE 8.5 *Issues Related to Curriculum Materials and Resources.* Directions: As you review a curriculum, determine its effectiveness by using the following criteria and rating each item.

Subject Area:

Format: Friendly _____ Not _____
Bound _____ Stapled _____

Date of Publication: _____

Source: Modified from Glathorn, A. (1993). *Criteria for evaluating curriculum guidelines.* Greenville, NC: School of Education, East Carolina University.

processes, and procedures that have been shown to be effective in helping students learn" (p. 4). Such a coherent philosophy of *best practice* is often reflected in integrated learning, thematic units, and interdisciplinary studies. The best practice movement is backed by research that draws heavily on learning theory. Zemelman, Daniels, and Hyde (1998) have identified thirteen principles that articulate the assumptions of best practices that can guide school leaders as they seek to enhance the teaching–learning process:

1. A student-centered curriculum that builds on student needs and interests in all areas;
2. An experiential curriculum that provides students with hands-on, concrete experiences;
3. Holistic learning that presents big ideas, events, and concepts as the framework for understanding the subparts;
4. Authentic learning that uses real-world examples and complex ideas;
5. An expressive curriculum that uses a range of communication skills to help students construct meaning;
6. Reflective learning that involves debriefing after each significant learning experience;
7. Social learning that occurs within classroom environments where interactions *scaffold* learning or support student concept development;
8. Collaborative learning that uses a cooperative system;
9. Democratic learning that includes students in decisions regarding their school or classroom;
10. Cognitive development that fosters higher order thinking;
11. Developmentally appropriate learning activities designed to accommodate differences in student cognitive stages;
12. Constructivist strategies that help students personally interpret and apply content in their own meaning-making; and
13. A curriculum that not only challenges students, but provides them with choices and problems as they take responsibility for their learning.

These thirteen principles may sound familiar because they represent a view of education that has appeared and reappeared over decades. But what is different today is that this educational view is more coherent and has greater support from research. These principles provide the foundation for best practice in schools and guide school leaders in the development of coherent curriculum. By incorporating these principles in the school culture, leaders empower teachers and encourage students to take greater responsibility for their learning. In such a view, the teachers' role is not to provide all the directions and make all the decisions. Using best practices, teachers attend to the needs of individual students and not only foster their ability to take the initiative for their learning, but encourage them to take risks as well.

School leaders need a plan to ensure that the school mission and vision become reality; it is no surprise that standards do not guarantee success for each child. Being a successful school leader requires the local curriculum to be linked to ". . . standards through a purposeful, coherent system of processes and products" (Carr & Harris, 2001,

p. 1). For national, state, and local standards to truly make a difference in the lives of students at the school level, these guidelines must be incorporated into every aspect of the school curriculum.

A standards-based curriculum also helps to define effective practices and seeks to remedy such criticisms as school is boring and irrelevant. National curriculum reports also identify emerging best practices and have many common recommendations. Various professional organizations have identified standards for learning in their respective cognate areas by grade level. Such standards have been developed in mathematics by the National Council of Teachers of Mathematics (NCTM), in reading and writing by the National Teachers of English, and in science by the National Science Teachers Association. Table 8.2 presents a paradigm shift that must occur for more effective teaching and learning as identified in best practices and standards. This shift represents the practices that are increasing and those teaching and learning behaviors that are declining. Teacher-centered instruction is giving way to a more active hands-on constructivist approach, and students, for example, have more opportunities to collaborate with their peers in the pursuit of higher order thinking.

As seen in Table 8.2, the new view of the instructional process has resulted in a decrease in passive learning and memorization and an increase in collaboration and active learning among students with their teachers. It also involves creating a classroom climate that is more student-centered. The goal is to have all students learn, and student

TABLE 8.2 *National Paradigm Shifts in Teaching and Learning*

More	Less
Active learning	Passive learning, silence is prized and rewarded
Experiential, inductive, hands-on learning	Whole-class, teacher-directed instruction
Variety of roles for teachers which include demonstrating and modeling	Classroom instruction devoted to worksheets and seatwork
Higher-order thinking and learning key concepts, principles, and themes	Learning which comes from teacher to student
Depth of study	Superficial learning and memorization of facts
Students working collaboratively in groups	Tracking students by ability
Choices for students	Reliance on standardized tests as measure of performance
Attention given to learning needs and styles using differentiated instruction	Teaching to the whole group

Source: Adapted from Zemelman, S., Daniels, H., & Hyde, A. (1998). *Best practices: New standards for teaching and learning in America's schools.* Portsmouth, NH: Heinemann.

needs form the basis for planning the curriculum. When the *what* and the *how* are aligned with the standards, the results should be greater student learning, and assessment becomes ongoing and more diagnostic in nature.

The process of linking standards to teaching and learning is critical to the success of a campus in promoting learning for all. For Eaker, DuFour, and Burnette (2002), "Approaches are internally validated. Teams of teachers try various approaches and collaborate on how the approaches affect student learning. The effect on student learning is the basis for assessing various improvement strategies" (p. 22). The leader's role is to encourage a dialogue that results in each school determining which of the best practices and standards are appropriate for the school, and how these ideas can be implemented in classrooms. A beginning point might be for school leaders to have teachers review Table 8.2 and then talk about their own classrooms and how they can modify their instruction to move from *less* to *more*.

In the next View from the Field, Mrs. Ramzy, a second grade lead teacher, has been asked to help her principal, Mr. Ford. The goal is to get teachers in grades pre-K through 3 to become familiar with curriculum standards, specifically those from the NCTM and to incorporate these standards in their curriculum planning.

The approach represented in the View from the Field is different from English's (2000) process of *curriculum mapping*, which typically focuses on the question: What topic is being taught and by whom? In this process, step 1 is to obtain a *buy-in* or commitment from the teachers by providing them with opportunities to enrich their knowledge and skills (Loucks-Horsley, Hewson, Love, & Styles, 1998). Steps 2 and 3 directly involve the leader in building learning communities by bringing all levels of the

View from the Field

To better understand the phrase *best practice*, which has become common in the literature, Mrs. Ramzy has been asked to serve as the lead person in working with her second grade level colleagues, as well as those in grades pre-K through 3. Mr. Ford, the principal, says, "I have suggested that the teachers address best practice first in the area of mathematics. I have asked members of the team to complete the following tasks:

- Obtain copies of the mathematics curriculum standards from the NCTM
- Create a chart for each grade level listing these standards in the right column and across the top list the math topics that the school district/state mandates

- Identify areas of agreement in the math curriculum
- Review the chart and determine where the *holes* are in the district/state math curriculum using the NCTM standards as the guide
- Write a summary of their findings
- Investigate other school districts in which NCTM standards form the pre-K through 3 math curriculum

After each grade level has completed these tasks, I have asked Mrs. Ramzy to summarize their findings and suggest recommendations to me."

education system together and then working to develop the leadership capacity in teachers (Lambert, 1998).

School leaders need to ensure that the following characteristics are incorporated in the school's comprehensive view of curriculum: (1) explicitness—learning targets are derived from national and state standards; (2) coherence—content is organized and aligned to promote rigor and connectiveness; (3) comprehensiveness—all disciplines are represented in the curriculum; and (4) manageability—all students are a part of the mission and learning expectations.

Finally, school leaders must recognize that for a curriculum to be effective it must have at least three essential characteristics. A curriculum must provide for consistency (or coordination). It must provide for continuity (or articulation). A curriculum must also provide for flexibility in adaptation as teachers interact with students. Flexibility means that the curriculum must be open to some interpretations concerning how and under what classroom circumstances the content is most effectively taught. The curriculum must continue to evolve by altering the sequencing and pacing of its delivery without fundamentally altering its design fidelity (English, 1992).

Case Study

You have just been hired as the assistant principal at Eagle Middle School. Mr. Jack Anderson is the principal and has three years' experience. On this middle school campus 65% of the faculty are women, and 35% are men. The campus has a highly diverse (many languages) and mobile student population. The school has grown quickly, with enrollment increasing from 450 to 700 students in the past five years.

Although the school district is located in an affluent, suburban community near a large metropolitan area, the school often lacks the needed resources because the district is required to share their wealth with other campuses. Mr. Anderson has worked hard to ensure that a collaborative process is used when making decisions. The teachers at each grade level work as teams to provide input to him and other administrators who then make the final decisions.

The district is ready to adopt a new series for teaching social studies in grades six through eight. The social studies textbook adoption is on the current cycle for consideration. One challenge facing Mr. Anderson is how to make social studies a vital subject because less time has been spent on it in the past few years, with more time spent on subjects with state-mandated tests. Because social studies has been neglected, teachers feel ill prepared to make this curriculum area exciting and meaningful. In fact, Mr. Anderson over the course of the past three years has tried to turn the culture of the school around by emphasizing academic performance on tests, and this has discouraged teachers from allocating time for social studies.

Thus, the teachers are unenthusiastic about the prospect of selecting a textbook and other curriculum materials, much less making time in the school day for social studies instruction when it is not tested. However, the new textbook will be purchased and in the teachers' hands at the beginning of the next school year, leaving only six months for selecting a textbook for this campus.

Mr. Anderson is committed to improving social studies instruction next year. As the assistant principal, you have been enlisted to help rally the faculty and persuade colleagues at the central administration building that social studies is an integral part of the entire curriculum for grades six through eight. To be successful, you will have to (1) generate enthusiasm for the teaching of social studies by recruiting teachers to be part of the textbook selection committee; (2) persuade others to see the value of social studies as a subject in the curriculum; (3) demonstrate to teachers the viability of social studies in supporting other curricular areas; and (4) convince administrators that social studies can contribute to the overall literacy of the student population.

As you assist Mr. Anderson in these four areas, the following questions will help focus your efforts as you develop your action plan.

1. What specific steps will you take to accomplish these four objectives? Indicate the when, where, who, and why that are involved in carrying out your plan.
2. How will you address the issue of teachers' presently wanting to teach only to the areas being tested? What strategies will you use to convince them of the importance of teaching social studies? What types of information and resources will you use to argue for the increased presence of social studies in the curriculum?
3. How can you show a connection between social studies and the tested areas of reading, writing, and mathematics?
4. What activities or events would you recommend to Mr. Anderson that would help to get his message to the teachers?

Summary

As school leaders seek to promote the success of all students through a shared vision of learning, they must advocate, nurture, and sustain an instructional program conducive to student learning. Through curriculum development and alignment, school leaders have the opportunity to impact the teaching–learning process in positive ways by fostering conversations about the what, when, and how of instruction. School leaders can also promote centers of inquiry for teachers as well as students. Leaders in schools must become more than managers as they provide direction for the total instructional program. Issues that can serve to guide school leaders involve educational purposes, educational experiences, organization of learning, and assessment of goals and outcomes.

In the curriculum development process, the focus is on planning, implementing, and assessing. School leaders can use a number of strategies to address these issues of curriculum planning, teaching, and assessment, and strategies can be used to determine the degree to which plans are aligned both horizontally and vertically. School leaders must also assess the degree to which teachers are implementing the curriculum; and determine if members of the community deem the curriculum effective. Strategies include formative procedures that take into account actions along the way and summative procedures that determine the end result.

This chapter presents an overview of the curriculum development process, grounded in the characteristics and needs of students. Although curriculum development is often the primary responsibility of teachers, administrators can support the process by giving teachers time to plan together, observe each other, and then design appropriate assessment instruments to determine the degree of success that has been achieved.

Like curriculum development, curriculum alignment also involves three domains—planning, instruction, and assessment. Planning involves examining the concepts or content, establishing goals and objectives, consulting materials and resources, and structuring learning experiences around instructional strategies. Implementation involves interactions with students in the classroom or simply *teaching* what has been planned. Assessment determines the degree or extent to which students have achieved the learning goals and objectives. The degree to which these three domains overlap determines the amount of congruency or alignment. Congruency is seldom if ever, 100%, but alignment is predicated on development of some degree of congruency in the three domains.

Finally, the chapter discusses the role of best practices and curriculum standards in improving curriculum and instruction. Best practices move schools away from instruction that is isolated and fact based to instruction that is collaborative and process oriented. As school leaders work with teachers in the design and improvement of curriculum, they are helping to shape teaching and learning as reflected in student achievement.

Your Turn

8.1. As a school leader, if someone asked you to define *curriculum*, what would you say? Provide more than words, prepare an artful expression of what curriculum means to and for you and your students. Your *expression* can be mounted or it can stand alone as a piece of sculpture. To accompany your artful expression, prepare a typewritten statement describing it.

8.2. Evaluating curriculum is a task that school leaders are asked to perform. The process of evaluating curriculum, frequently referred to as a *curriculum audit*, is conducted to determine what students are learning, and how they are learning, as well as any gaps in their learning. To get a closer look at a specific curriculum, identify a grade and subject area that you would like to investigate. While a comprehensive curriculum audit can be time consuming, the following steps can be used to engage in a modified curriculum audit. To begin the curriculum audit process, respond to the following questions:

- What grade and curriculum area have you selected to audit?
- What methods will you use to collect data about this curriculum to determine its origin, mission, and role in the overall educational school program?
- Who were the major players in creating this curriculum and who is implementing it?

Data Source	Yes/No	Name of Source (if appropriate)	Comments
Interviews[a] (teachers, students, administrators, parents, school board members, superintendent, professional staff, others)			
Observations[b] (classroom implementation of the curriculum with students)			
Surveys[c]			
Questionnaires[c]			
Products including portfolios, student logs/journals, test scores			
Other documents			

FIGURE 8.6 *Data Sources for Curriculum Audit*

[a]Questions for interview should be developed before; how information will be recorded needs to be decided beforehand.
[b]A guide for observing needs to be developed.
[c]Surveys and questionnaires can be developed or those already prepared can be used.

Completing the chart in Figure 8.6 may prove helpful regarding your data sources as you gather information during the curriculum audit.

• When will you conduct the audit and for how long? Develop a timeline for all key events when implementing the audit.
• Now that you have collected the information including the data sources from Figure 8.1, what did you find? Write a summary of your findings (referring to the documents and questions from the interview).
• On the basis of what the audit revealed, what are your recommendations for actions to be taken?

8.3. Take the opportunity to examine the national standards in one major curriculum area as well as your state's mandated curriculum/standards if appropriate. The following sets of questions may prove helpful in guiding this process.

Name of the Standards Selected: General Overview of the Process
1. What is the rationale underlying the development of the standards?
2. What is the vision for the national standards?
3. What research was used to develop the standards?

4. Why were the standards developed? Why were the state standards developed?
5. What is the *history* of the national standards? What is the history of your state's standards?
6. What are the major assumptions of the national standards? Of the state's standards?
7. How are the national standards organized? Your state's standards?
8. What is the philosophical perspective of the national standards? Of the state's standards?
9. How can the standards be helpful to school leaders?
10. What are the issues related to curriculum in the last ten years? Make a list of terms that are now part of the education vocabulary (jargon) related to the curriculum. Another way to identify curricular issues is to go online and get copies of the Annual Gallup Poll in the *Phi Delta Kappan* for 1990, 1994, 1998, and 2002.

8.4. Maxine Greene argues persuasively for the cultivation of the intellect—the capacity to generalize, analyze, and synthesize concepts—and to achieve this goal requires the cultivation of the imagination. Get online and download an article by Maxine Greene.

1. What does Greene mean when she says that the arts enable "a pluralism of vision" and "multiplicity of realities?"
2. How can the arts contribute to the personal development of children?
3. How do you feel about including the arts in the curriculum and its role in fostering independent thinking, diversity, and the democratic spirit?
4. What does it mean for teachers, school leaders, and policy makers?

References _____

American Educational Research Association. (2000). *AERA position statement concerning high-stakes testing in prek–12 education.* AERA Online: www.aera.net/about/policy/stakes.html.

American Psychological Association. (2001). *Appropriate use of high-stakes testing in our nation's schools.* APA Online: www.apa.org/pubinfo/testing.html.

Arends, R. I. (2000). *Learning to teach* (5th ed). Boston: McGraw-Hill.

Beach, D. M., & Reinhartz, J. (2000). *Supervisory leadership: Focus on instruction.* Boston: Allyn & Bacon.

Berliner, D. (1996). Research and social justice. Presentation at the 76th Annual Meeting of the Association of Teacher Educators, St. Louis, MO.

Bobbitt, F. (1918). *The curriculum.* Boston: Houghton Mifflin.

Carr, J. F., & Harris, D. E. (2001). *Succeeding with standards: Linking curriculum, assessment, and action planning.* Alexandria, VA: Association for Supervision and Curriculum Development.

Clark, C. M., & Yinger, R. J. (1987). Teaching planning. In D. Berliner & B. Rosenshine (eds), *Talks to teachers.* pp. 342–365. New York: Random House.

Costa, A. L., & Garmston, R. J. (1994). *Cognitive coaching: A foundation for renaissance schools.* Norwood, MA: Christopher-Gordon Publishers.

Darling-Hammond, L. (1997). Doing what matters most: Investing in quality teaching. *The right to learn: A blueprint for creating schools that work.* Washington, DC: National Commission on Teaching and America's Future.

Eaker, R., DuFour, R., & Burnette, R. (2002). *Getting started: Reculturing schools to become professional learning communities.* Bloomington, IN: National Educational Service.

Eisner, E. W. (2002). *The educational imagination: On the design and evaluation of school programs.* Columbus, OH: Merrill/Prentice Hall.

English, F. W. (1992). *Deciding what to teach and test: Developing, aligning, and auditing the curriculum.* Newbury Park, CA: Corwin Press.

English, F. W. (2000). *Deciding what to teach and test: Developing, aligning, and auditing the curriculum.* Millennium Edition. Thousand Oaks, CA: Corwin Press.

Frieberg, H. J., & Driscoll, A. (1996). *Universal teaching strategies* (2nd ed). Boston: Allyn & Bacon.

Glatthorn, A. A. (1993). Criteria for evaluating curriculum guidelines. Greenville, NC: School of Education, East Carolina University.

Gross, P. A. (1997). *Joint curriculum design.* Mahwah, NJ: Lawrence Erlbaum Associates.

Halayna, T. M., Nolen, S. B., & Haas, N. S. (1991). Raising standardized achievement test scores and the origins of test score pollution *Educational Researcher, 20,* 5, 2–7.

Lambert, L. (1998). *Building leadership capacity in schools.* Alexandria, VA: Association for Supervision and Curriculum Development.

Lezotte, L. W. (1997). *Learning for all.* Okemos, MI: Effective Schools Products.

Liebowitz, M. (2001). Staying the course. *Education Update, 43,* 1. Alexandria, VA: Association for Supervision and Curriculum Development.

Loucks-Horsley, S., Hewson, P. W., Love, N., & Styles, K. E. (1998). *Designing professional development for teachers of science and mathematics.* Thousand Oaks, CA: Corwin Press.

McCutcheon, G. (1999). Deliberations to develop school curricula. In J. C. Henderson & K. Kesson (eds), *Understanding democratic curriculum leadership.* New York: Teachers College Press.

National Education Goals Panel. (1994). Data volume for the national education goals report, Vol. 1: National data. Washington, DC: author.

Osterman, K. J. (1990). Introduction. *Education and Urban Society, 22,* 2, 131–132.

Reinhartz, J., & Beach, D. M. (1997). *Teaching and learning in the elementary school: Focus on curriculum.* Upper Saddle River, NJ: Merrill.

Reinhartz, J., & Beach, D. M. (1992). *Secondary education: Focus on curriculum.* New York: HarperCollins.

Remillard, J. (1999). Curriculum materials in mathematics education reform: A framework for examining teachers. *Curriculum Inquiry, 29,* 3, 315–342.

Rose, L. L., & Gallup, A. M. (2000 September). The 32nd annual Phi Delta Kappa/Gallup Poll of the public's attitudes toward the public schools. *Phi Delta Kappa,* 41–58.

Shavelson, R. J. (1987). Planning. In M. Dunkin (ed), *The international encyclopedia of teaching and teacher education.* pp. 483–485. New York: Pergamon Press.

Showers, B., & Joyce, B. (1996). The evolution of peer coaching. *Educational Leadership, 38,* 521–525.

Tanner, D., & Tanner, L. N. (1995). *Curriculum development theory into practice* (3rd ed). Upper Saddle River, NJ: Merrill/Prentice Hall.

Tyler, R. (1957). The curriculum then and now. In *Proceeding of the 1956 conference of testing problems.* Princeton, NJ: Educational Testing Service.

Tyler, R. (1949). *Principles of curriculum and instruction.* Chicago: University of Chicago Press.

Weiss, S. (1994 May). Goals 2000. *NEA Today, 12,* 9, 3.

Wiles, J., & Bondi, J. (2002). *Curriculum development: A guide to practice* (6th ed). Upper Saddle River, NJ: Merrill/Prentice Hall.

Wood, J. R. (1987/2000). *The train to Estelline.* New York: Bantam Doubleday Dell Publishing Group.

Woolfolk, A. (1995). *Educational psychology* (6th ed). Boston: Allyn & Bacon.

Zemelman, S., Daniels, H., & Hyde, A. (1998). *Best practice: New standards for teaching and learning in America's schools.* Portsmouth, NH: Heinemann.

9

Accountability: Using Data for School Improvement

ISLLC Standards

Standard 1: A school administrator is an educational leader who promotes the success of all students by facilitating the development, articulation, implementation, and stewardship of a vision of learning that is shared and supported by the school community.

Standard 3: A school administrator is an educational leader who promotes the success of all students by ensuring management of the organization, operations, and resources for a safe, effective, and efficient learning environment.

Chapter Objectives

The objectives of this chapter are:

- Discuss the role of accountability in school improvement.
- Identify and describe components of accountability models and explain how leaders can use them for school improvement efforts.
- Discuss the implications of accountability systems and curriculum development/alignment.
- Identify the kinds of data needed for decision making related to school improvement efforts.
- Explain how school leaders use formative and summative data to develop and revise the campus curriculum and campus improvement plans.
- Identify the five questions that guide data collection and school improvement and discuss their use in the process.

The term *accountability* is frequently used in discussions about education, and it is a term that appears to have many different meanings to different people. The fundamental dictionary definition suggests that being accountable involves being responsible and/or providing explanations (*Webster's New World Dictionary and Thesaurus*, 1996). When the term is applied to educational leadership, it means that leaders must be responsible for all student learning and use data to inform the successes or failures of the instructional process. Accountability simply means that school leaders can no longer be willing to defer to or blame others for school inadequacy and that they must be willing to do whatever it takes to make sure that all students are academically successful. Schmoker (2001) says it is time to acknowledge an ever increasing body of evidence that points to the fact ". . . that accountability promotes higher achievement" (p. 103). He continues by noting that, "It is time [to] reconsider tired, often unexamined notions of accountability—and our knee-jerk propensity to vilify it rather than take on the challenge it presents. . . . Sensible accountability is the price of improvement" (p. 104). Accountability and school improvement are linked because as school leaders take greater responsibility for the successes as well as the failures, their schools begin to improve. Greenlee and Bruner (2001) have observed that, "while many may view standardized testing as just the monitoring piece of accountability, it can raise organizational and instructional capacity when the assessments require higher cognitive levels of performance from students" (p. 2).

As a part of the accountability process, school leaders are becoming increasingly concerned ". . . over how states are addressing the requirements of testing. In fact, success is frequently defined solely on the basis of performance on state-mandated tests. What can be done, they ask, to improve students' scores without making tests the primary focus of education?" (Franklin, 2001, p. 4). However, Greenlee and Bruner (2001) suggest that when aligned with curriculum goals, "standards and assessments do not have to result in just 'teaching to the test,'" (p. 2), but can also serve to influence the teaching–learning process. The dilemma for school leaders becomes one of balance. Although the major focus of accountability may be student achievement as reflected in test scores, other issues, such as dropout rates, other language learners, teen pregnancy, and disenfranchised youth, are also pieces of the larger picture of accountability.

In this new era of accountability, Underwood (2001) notes that, "The only stable aspect of school as an . . . institution is a persistent, constant, repetitive drumbeat of reform" (p. 172). With the publication of *A Nation at Risk* (National Commission on Excellence in Education, 1983), schools began an ever evolving process of change and reform. The school reform measures have embodied changes in assessment and ac-countability strategies that have led to a clearer articulation of what students need to know and be able to do. This increased emphasis on student learning, and student success means that school leaders ". . . must implement better methods and materials, not just [apply] consequences for failure" (Slavin, 2000/2001, p. 23). Systemic and comprehensive reform approaches that are performance based have characterized the process (Comer, Ben-Avie, Haynes, & Joyner, 1999). These approaches provide school leaders with "well-researched, readily replicable whole-school reforms . . . to help improve teaching and learning in underperforming schools" (Slavin, 2000/2001, p. 25).

School leaders must use appropriate and available student data to ensure that systemic reform leads to fundamental changes in the instructional materials and prac-tices in elementary and secondary classrooms. Fullan (1999a, 1993) suggests that, on the basis of his research and observations, an elementary school can make progress in school improvement in three years, a high school in six years, and an entire school district in eight years.

Shifting student demographics is also of great interest and concern to educational leaders and policymakers as an element of accountability. The populations of school districts across the United States are changing, and schools reflect the more diverse and cosmopolitan nature of contemporary society, which has become more diverse and cosmopolitan (Elkind, 2000/2001). As school leaders study the changing nature of their school population, they begin to see why ". . . the field of demographics has become vitally important to education policymakers at all levels" (Hodgkinson, 2000/2001, p. 6). In an attempt to be more responsible for student learning, the following questions may prove helpful to guide school leaders. What student data are needed on a regular basis? What information about students should school leaders know? How can student data enhance learning for all? These questions are central to the process of collecting and analyzing student data because they help track, not only demographic changes, but student performance as well.

Three states, California, Texas, and Florida, are growing rapidly and will experi-ence a significant increase in student enrollments. Demographic shifts have been greatest in cities where one-quarter of the population resides. Decreases in student population are reflected in the eastern part of the United States, with many families fleeing to the suburbs. It is in the *suburban ring*, as Hodgkinson (2000/2001) refers to it, where the greater student diversity can be found. Transiency is also a major cause of student diversity that impacts all schools, and school leaders must track these student shifts. If a classroom starts with twenty-two students when school begins and has twenty-two when school ends, twenty of the twenty-two will not be the same students (Hodgkinson, 2000/2001). Transiency also plays a role in graduation rates; the five states with the highest transient populations have the lowest rates of students graduating and going to college.

The impact of demographics and student data for school leaders cannot be underestimated; this information continues to shape instructional practices in classrooms across the United States. When our society changes so do the schools, and these changes are reflected in the postmodern educational era, which embraces both inclusion and multiculturalism (Elkind, 2000/2001). Inclusion and multiculturalism are more than a matter of curriculum and teaching; their true meaning lies in our respect for one another and a sense of a common humanity. School leaders who understand the implications of these changes will be more sensitive to the demographic changes reflected in the student characteristics. However, Creighton (2001) warns that, "collecting data without purpose is meaningless" (p. 11); or put another way, school leaders should not collect data unless they intend to use it.

This chapter discusses the importance of accountability in school improvement efforts and the use of student data to inform decisions regarding improvement strategies. These data pieces must be ongoing and supportive of a school's accountability efforts. In addition, the chapter describes ways to collect and analyze relevant data in monitoring and tracking student performance. The chapter also provides examples of campus improvement plans and concludes with a discussion of the role of data in making decisions regarding curriculum alignment as a part of the total accountability process.

Accountability Models

The concept of accountability in education is not new; as Pearson, Vyas, Sensale, and Kim (2001) have observed, "Accountability has come . . . and gone . . . and come again. It has assumed many form and guises . . ." (p. 175). In the last two decades, accountability in public education has been the focus of an enormous amount of research (Berman & Gjelten, 1984; Glickman, 1990; Harrington-Lueker, 1990; Darling-Hammond, 1991; Hill & Bonan, 1991; Bryk & Hermanson, 1993). Today, little is left to chance and not only have many states adopted various forms of statewide assessment measures, but recent national legislation has mandated testing in grades three through nine. With the implementation of the *No Child Left Behind Act* of 2001, states will be required to "develop assessments aligned with state standards and to be accountable for students' annual academic progress. States and school districts . . . must develop yearly report cards documenting the success of their students meeting achievement goals" (American Association of Colleges for Teacher Education, 2002, p. 1).

The results by district and campus, usually in the form of student performance, are often reported to the public. Statewide assessment measures are generally aligned with the respective formal state public school curriculum and are designed to assess not only what has been taught, but more importantly what students have learned. The assessment results are normally tied to each state's accountability system, which may involve accreditation ratings or sanctions as well as funding. For Holcomb (2001), the following five questions serve to guide leaders in their efforts to improve educational accountability and ensure learning for all:

1. Where are we now?
2. Where do we want to go?
3. How will we get there?
4. How will we know we are there?
5. How can we keep it going? (p. 7)

When schools are given the results of student performance on either national achievement tests or state-mandated examinations, they can, to some degree, determine how well students have demonstrated mastery of the curriculum. Research suggests that school leaders must not only become familiar with, but know how to use existing school data when making decisions about improving school programs (Fitch & Malcom, 1992; McNamara & Thompson, 1996). For Holcomb (2001), any accountability system must include "three critical aspects of the school's or district's status: . . . student performance, share holder perceptions, and organizational culture and context" (p. 17).

State Accountability Models

Several states have received recognition for their accountability systems based on the level of student achievement on the statewide assessment programs. Alabama, California, North Carolina, South Carolina, and Texas have earned recognition for their strong curriculum standards and accountability systems (Finn & Petrilli, 2000). In addition, Florida's model, which includes the Florida Comprehensive Assessment Test, is not only aligned to the state curriculum standards, but requires students ". . . to demonstrate understanding at higher cognitive levels (application, analysis, or evaluation)" (Greenlee & Bruner, 2001, p. 3).

Two states, for example, California and Texas, have comprehensive accountability models that link student performance to campus and district rating. The California curriculum frameworks have become the blueprint for implementing content standards and were developed by the Curriculum Development and Supplemental Materials Commission. Public school educators, personnel from institutions of higher education, and other stakeholders developed the Texas public school curriculum called the Texas Essential Knowledge and Skills (TEKS). These state initiatives have been adopted by the respective State Boards of Education and illustrate two types of state accountability models.

California, like other states has, "determined to shift the focus . . . from rules and processes to student achievement and accountability" (Hart & Brownell, 2001, p. 183). In California the K–12 Academic Content Standards adopted by the California State Board of Education exist in four curriculum areas for kindergarten through grade twelve and include English-language arts, mathematics, history-social studies, and science. The content standards serve as the blueprints for instruction, and each framework was developed by the Curriculum Development and Supplemental Materials Commission, which also reviews and recommends textbooks and other material to be adopted by the State Board (California Department of Education, 2000a). More information about the California accountability system can be found at the website listed at the end of the chapter. The discipline-based frameworks serve to guide the organization of teaching and learning, ". . . so that every student can achieve high levels of mastery" (Hart & Brownell, 2001, p. 183). This curriculum is also the basis for the state's student performance assessment system, the Standardized Testing and Reporting program.

The California Standardized Testing and Reporting program reports annually the results of the Stanford Achievement Test, Ninth Edition, Form T (Stanford 9), the California Content Standards tests, and the Spanish Assessment of Basic Education, Second Edition. School districts are required to administer the Stanford 9 to all students in grades two through eleven, except for those students whose Individual Education Plan explicitly exempts them, or students whose parents or guardians submit a written request to exempt the student. In grades two through eight students are tested in reading, spelling, written expression, and mathematics. In grades nine through eleven testing is required in reading, writing, mathematics, science, and history/social science. Additional items in language arts and mathematics have been included to address the California content standards that are not addressed by the Stanford 9. Beginning in 1999, Spanish speaking English language learners (limited-English proficient) who had been in California public schools fewer than twelve months were tested using the Spanish Assessment of Basic Education, Second Edition (California Department of Education, 2000c).

The California Immediate Intervention/Underperforming Schools Program (II/USP) is a major provision of California's Public Schools Accountability Act. II/USP grants provide selected schools in California an opportunity to participate in planning and implementing activities for improved student achievement. For example, during the first year, 353 schools received $50,000 planning grants and worked with an external evaluator and a community team to identify barriers to school performance and develop an action plan to improve student achievement. The accountability timeline lists possible intervention strategies to assist schools that do not meet the minimum percentage growth target. The local education agency governing board, in consultation with the external evaluator and the school site and community team, provide a range of interventions for the school, including possible reassignment of school personnel, negotiation of site-specific amendments to collective bargaining agreements, or other changes deemed appropriate, to implement the action plan and meet the school's growth targets.

As an indication of the seriousness of state-wide accountability, participating schools not meeting performance goals but demonstrating significant growth, as determined by the California State Board of Education, are required to participate in II/USP and receive an additional year of funding for implementation. Schools that do not meet performance goals and do not show significant growth are identified as low performing. For these low-performing schools, the Superintendent of Public Education assumes all legal rights, duties, and powers of the governing board with respect to the school. The principal is reassigned, and the State Superintendent of Public Instruction, in consultation with the State Board of Education, is required to develop an intervention plan. Schools that meet or exceed growth targets receive a monetary award and the school receives no additional funding for II/USP (California Department of Education, 2000b).

In Texas, the adoption of the TEKS is another major step toward greater learner accountability. This step was designed to align all aspects of instruction by bringing instructional materials, assessment, and professional development in line with the TEKS. The process involved fifteen writing teams and a connection team to provide interdisciplinary connections. The process included not only state board review committees who edited the drafts, but sought input from educators, the public, and content experts (Charles A. Dana Center, 1997).

The TEKS include both foundation as well as enrichment areas and serve as standards for what students are expected to learn as measured by the state assessment process, Texas Assessment of Knowledge and Skills. Beginning in 2003 this statewide test will be administered to students in grades three through eight in reading, writing, mathematics, and social studies, as well as examinations at the 5th, 10th, and 11th grades in science. The statewide test is a component of a larger accountability process called the Academic Excellence Indicator System (AEIS). The AEIS tracks school performance using data relative to student performance on the test, annual dropout rates, and student attendance rates as the base indicators in determining the district and campus ratings (Texas Education Agency, 2000c). In states and districts where similar data are available, school leaders can use this information to begin the school improvement process and to inform stakeholders of the school's status. Samples of school and district AEIS reports can be found at the website listed at the end of the chapter. The AEIS serves as the basis for all campus and district accountability ratings, rewards, and reports. Currently, the highest rating is *exemplary*, with all groups at the campus having a 90% or greater pass rate on the state-wide test. A *recognized* rating is achieved when all groups have an 80% or better pass rate on all tests. An *acceptable* rating is the result of all groups having a 70% or better pass rate on all areas tested. Schools with lower pass rates are considered *low performing*.

As seen in these examples, school leaders must constantly be aware of the indicators and standards included in accountability systems applicable to their schools. In many cases, school leaders have experienced revisions to state curriculum content standards, an increased level of mastery for students on state assessments, and the inclusion of more students in the assessment process. For Hart and Brownell (2001), "The state's role in the accountability [process] is to monitor the progress of schools and districts, hold them accountable for helping students achieve high standards, allocate resources where they are most needed, and improve educational equity and access for every student" (p. 185). In order for school leaders to be successful in their state's accountability system, they must emphasize academic success for every student.

District Accountability Models

Accountability can also be used at the district level to help eliminate gaps and redundancies, increase student learning, and show measurable accomplishments. For example, in Iowa, the Green Valley Area Education Agency 14 has established an accountability-based curriculum system by combining the following components: mission statement with exit outcomes; subject area mission statements; purpose statements by subject, scope, and sequence; and qualitative assessment rubrics. Without such connections, school districts may have a system that meets minimal state requirements, but provides little or no real change in articulation system-wide and no real application in each teacher's classroom (Green Valley Area Education Agency 14, 2000).

The Greenbriar School District has developed its own accountability-based model. The Greenbriar (2000) Curriculum, Assessment, and Accountability model links accountability with curriculum assessment (see Chapter 10) and contains the following assumptions:

- Interactive learning with curriculum goals is accomplished through interdisciplinary thematic units.
- Some specific tasks that can be efficiently learned through other instructional methods (direct, whole group, small group, large group) must be included.
- Teachers serve as facilitators and resource managers.
- Collaborative teaching teams include various instructional leaders including special service personnel and community members (local/global).
- Problem-based learning uses community resources and institutions.

In addition to these assumptions, which guide the implementation of the model, each domain (curriculum, assessment, and accountability) provides a construct for the Curriculum, Assessment, and Accountability model. The *curriculum domain* includes the following five characteristics: First, learner results, developed according to local, state, and national guidelines are used to identify theme boundaries or conceptual threads. Second, learner results are maintained by entities within a matrix format, and then third knowledge/skill areas within the thematic units are determined collaboratively by teachers and students. Fourth, teachers and students determine the key questions that structure the work within each theme. Finally, projects are developed that enable the student learning teams to answer key questions and report their results.

The *assessment domain* includes six traits. First, formal performance-based assessments are administered by state and national agencies and then, developmental benchmarks are used to assess the needs of individual learners. Third, rubrics are developed based on the learner results identified by school improvement and curriculum teams, and fourth, authentic assessments are developed by the learning teams and become the primary evaluation tool for the thematic units. Finally, knowledge and skill rubrics related to the themes are developed by student learning teams and personal goals are included with each project and thematic unit.

The *accountability domain* includes four components. First, the student is accountable first to himself or herself, and performance is measured according to the knowledge/skill rubrics developed by the learning teams and includes the personal goals that each student committed to at the beginning of the project. Next, each collaborative learning team measures performance based on learner results rubrics and then, the results of authentic and formal assessments are compiled into individual, team, and school portfolios that are maintained. Lastly, the results are evaluated and reported in school improvement plans and then used to enhance or modify learning.

Using and Analyzing Data for School Improvement

As seen from the previous state and district models, results are important in the accountability process. Knowledge of results helps school leaders make decisions that affect the teaching–learning process in their schools. Such an undertaking is a significant challenge, and they should begin by reviewing and analyzing student data by different categories (grade level, program, ethnicity, socioeconomic status, gender). For Glesne (1999), "Data analysis involves organizing what you have seen, heard, and read so that you can make sense of what you have learned" (p. 130). By disaggregating the data, school leaders can begin to identify not only the academic strengths, but also areas of concern, which allows for the development of possible interventions. Fitch and Malcom (1998) note that the effective use of data must play a major role as school leaders develop school or campus improvement plans. Holcomb (2001), however, cautions that, "when we think of data on student performance, our instinctive response is to visualize graphs of test scores and leave it at that. This initial limited scope implies that acquisition of discrete bits of knowledge is the sole and complete function of the school . . ." (p. 17). School leaders know that student learning is linked to a number of variables and is more complex than just knowledge acquisition. Data collection must, therefore, involve more than just test scores.

Lezotte (1992) has suggested that, "school-based plans for school improvement must revolve around strategies for improvement that are data based and results driven" (p. 75). School leaders in concert with faculty must be willing to collect and analyze relevant data so that informed decisions can be made about the instructional process, as well as other factors that impact the school culture. Data collection and analysis do not have to involve complex statistics, but ". . . when used appropriately, allows organizational leaders at all levels, to monitor and adjust the organizational processes, procedures, and systems to assure total quality" (Lezotte, 1992, p. 77).

As school leaders track and review student data, they should keep the following tips in mind:

- Avoid stereotyping; for example, if records indicate, *Hispanic*, a more complete picture would include the country of origin or ethnicity as well as their dominant language.
- Collect information that is *culture fair* not *color blind*, by accurately identifying cultural background rather than *race* or *color.*
- Analyze the number of students on free or reduced lunch; Title I should not be used solely to identify low-income students.
- Identify students who are other language learners when language is part of the assessment.
- Clearly articulate high expectations for success for all and monitor progress.
- Record and publicize student successes by classrooms, schools, and districts.

Creighton (2001) says that, "Data analysis in school involves (a) collecting data and (b) using available data for the purposes of improving teaching and learning" (p. 2). Table 9.1 represents student performance data on the state-mandated exit level assess-

TABLE 9.1 *Liberty High School Student Performance Data*

Groups	Percent Campus Pass All (Reading, Math, Writing)	Percent State Pass Reading	Percent Campus Pass Reading	Percent State Pass Math	Percent Campus Pass Math	Percent State Pass Writing	Percent Campus Pass Writing
All students	63	88	75	86	79	86	72
Males	62	91	75	87	79	70	66
Females	64	94	78	91	79	79	77
Native Americans	6	85	86	82	58	75	71
Asian	19	92	90	95	100	89	90
African Americans	27	84	54	83	46	58	49
Hispanics	57	85	68	84	79	76	71
Low socioeconomic status	45	86	58	80	65	48	56
White	79	82	84	73	77	78	81

ment at Liberty High School in reading, mathematics, and writing. The table is an example of the kinds of state reports that can provide school leaders with the data concerning the performance of the total group as well as subgroups of students. As seen in Table 9.1, the data concern student performance in reading, mathematics, and writing. The report shows the percentage of students who passed each content area test in the state and the percentage of each group that passed the test on the campus. Column one represents the percentage of all students and subgroups on the campus who passed all three areas of the test. The second column represents the percentage of students statewide who passed the reading test, and column three represents the percentage of students on the campus who passed the reading test. Each of the other content areas (mathematics and writing) have similar data represented in columns four through seven. The data for each test are disaggregated for the following groups and subgroups: all students, boys, girls, Native Americans, Asians, African Americans, white, Hispanics, and low socioeconomic status.

As a campus leader, one responsibility is to assist faculty and staff members reading, interpreting, and understanding this report. "As groups review their data, the following questions identify issues that need further examination and suggest possible goals: (1) What do these data seem to tell us?; (2) What do they *not* tell us?; (3) What else would we need to know—for sure?; and (4) What needs for school improvement might arise from these data?" (Holcomb, 2001, p. 48).

As a way of analyzing the data in Table 9.1, the campus leader could have the faculty discuss the following questions based on the information provided:

- What is the campus passing rate for each test?
- Which subgroups perform best on all sections of the test?

- Which subgroups have the poorest performance overall?
- How does campus performance compare with state-wide performance for the total group and for each subgroup?
- Where are the greatest discrepancies in performance between or among subgroups?
- Where are the greatest disparities in performance between campus and state levels?

Each subgroup should be analyzed and addressed with regard to passing rates, and the campus passing rates for each of these subgroups can be compared with the state and the total campus group. To make comparisons between and among subgroups easier, Holcomb (2001) suggests creating histograms or charts to visually or graphically express the differences in the data regarding student performance. Figure 9.1 presents the data concerning pass rates for reading in graph form to illustrate the comparisons that can be made between and among subgroups. As faculty examine the visual representations of data, they can begin to identify subgroups that may need additional assistance to be more successful. School leaders can solicit help from faculty members or departments in reviewing the raw data and then presenting it in a visual comparative form.

Data used by school leaders to make decisions about instructional programs, strategies, initiatives, activities, or other school efforts begins with the data collected. Determining how well students are learning by disaggregating the data helps school leaders to involve faculties and others in the decisions for campus improvement plans, which are discussed in the next section.

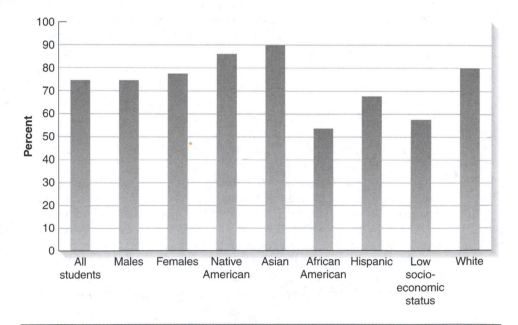

FIGURE 9.1 *Student Passing Rates on Reading Test by Subgroups*

Improving Student Performance: Campus Improvement Plans

As indicated earlier in the chapter, educational accountability occurs at various levels. States have developed systems of accountability and individual school districts have developed or adapted various accountability models. However, it is at the campus level that the greatest potential for school improvement of direct accountability occurs. A recent study discussed by Schemo (2001) found that predominantly black or Hispanic, high-poverty schools can still be distinguished by high achievement when the campus develops intervention strategies that (1) use inventive ways to motivate students, (2) emphasize orderly behavior, and (3) devote more time to reading and math. Effective schools are the result of the school leaders taking the initiative to ensure that students learn. Lezotte (1997) has suggested that effective schools take the necessary actions to make sure that all the students learn the specified curriculum regardless of their backgrounds. As campus leaders work with teachers and support staff to develop a campus improvement plan, it is helpful to remember that:

- Successful students must have successful and effective teachers.
- Successful teachers must have successful and effective leaders.
- When leaders and teachers focus on student success, they produce successful schools.

School improvement and campus accountability most often occur in the form of a campus improvement plan. In developing their strategies for improvement, campus leaders can use both formative and summative data. Formative data come from the ongoing or frequent monitoring activities aimed at documenting progress toward meeting campus goals and increasing student achievement and may include the curricular efforts represented by objectives, skills, and knowledge. Summative data come from student performance assessment, usually given annually, and are represented by national achievement tests or state-mandated tests. This summative data can be used to judge the degree to which the curriculum has been mastered. Other locally generated data such as the number of dropouts or percent retention/failure can also provide summative reference points.

Formative data provide leaders with the opportunity to implement and modify campus goals and take corrective actions. These modifications can be done on a daily, weekly, biweekly, monthly, every sixth week, or other instructional period, depending on the grade level, subject matter, or time available to school personnel. Examples of formative data from the curriculum may include (1) grades for an assignment, homework, project, or test; (2) student portfolios that illustrate the incremental progress of mastering the curriculum objectives; (3) grade distribution; and other (4) performance measures based on the curriculum.

Data used by school leaders to evaluate instructional programs, strategies, initiatives, activities, or other school efforts begin with collecting formative data. Determining how well students are learning using formative data allows for periodic measurement

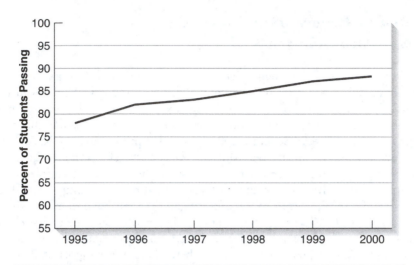

FIGURE 9.2 *Writing Progress: Passing Rates for All Students in Writing 1995 to 2000*

of specific student outcomes related to campus goals and performance objectives. In monitoring student performance and progress, school leaders should (1) include all concerned parties to determine if the curriculum is being taught as it was intended; (2) have stakeholders determine if the curriculum is realistic in its projected expectations and sufficiently supported; and (3) celebrate successes and use this new information to further refine curriculum goals and justify support for additional resources.

Summative evaluation may at times take the form of an annual performance report documenting how well students have learned the required curriculum. When school, district, and state measures exist, these results can be reported in various ways, such as by grade level, gender, economic status, program, and ethnicity, and are often compared with other schools, districts, and/or state measures. These summative evaluation measures condense the school year's results and provide data to be included in the next comprehensive needs assessment to direct the curriculum revision phase for the subsequent school year. These summative data points can be graphed by year to monitor progress over time. Figure 9.2 illustrates the growth in writing over time. As seen in Figure 9.2, writing has steadily improved from 1995 to 2000. Although this figure represents all students, similar line graphs can be done by gender, ethnicity, or socioeconomic status.

The monitoring of the campus performance is the responsibility of the school leaders in collaboration with teachers. Teachers need to take responsibility for initiating and implementing strategies and initiatives in the campus improvement plan and then monitoring how students perform on different types of assessments and making the necessary revisions. These revisions in campus improvement plans should be data driven with the primary goal of improving student achievement.

Common Components

Although states, districts, and schools may have specific formats for developing campus improvement plans, common components include:

1. A comprehensive needs assessment of the entire school based on the performance of students in relation to prescribed content and student performance standards.

2. School-wide strategies that:
   - Ensure that all students meet prescribed performance standards
   - Use effective instructional practices that increase the amount and quality of learning time (i.e., extended school day, extended school year, or summer programs)
   - Provide an enriched and accelerated curriculum
   - Meet the needs of historically underserved populations, such as minorities and girls
   - Address the needs of all students, especially the students of low-performing populations.

3. Commitment of the professional staff to a high-quality instruction.

4. Professional development linked to needs assessment, prescribed content, and performance standards to ensure high-quality instruction.

5. Strategies to increase parental involvement through programs such as family literacy services.

6. Programs that assist students in major transitions from early childhood programs to elementary grades, from elementary school to middle or junior high school, and from middle or junior high school to high school.

7. Involvement of teachers in decisions regarding the use of assessments, both formative and summative.

8. Effective and timely activities for students who have difficulty mastering the prescribed content and performance standards including:
   - Measures to identify the students' difficulties to determine the appropriate assistance
   - Parental conferences to identify what the school will do to help the student meet the standards, what the parents can do to help the student improve performance, and what additional resources are available in the school community.

In the View from the Field, the principal at the elementary school describes developing an action plan for school improvement that is data driven.

As seen at this school, the school leader was able to present the data, involve teachers in the analysis of the data, and then come to some decisions regarding a possible course of action. In many states, campus improvement plans contain performance

View from the Field

Mrs. Marshall is the principal of Midtown Elementary School. At the end of the second six weeks, she noticed an unusual number of failures in reading in the fifth and sixth grades along with a high absentee rate. When she met with her superintendent, she said, "I was concerned that if students were failing reading in their classes, then they probably would not do well on the state assessment test scheduled for February. I was also alarmed by the high absentee rate because not only did the average daily attendance impact funding for the school, it meant that students were not in class to learn. I met with the fifth and sixth grade teachers by grade level and presented the data to them. I reminded them that one of the campus goals for the year was to have 80% of all fifth graders pass the reading part of the state assessment of academic skills. I also noted that we had a campus goal of 95% average daily attendance and that the fifth and sixth grades were just below 90% average daily attendance."

At the meeting the teachers engaged in some initial discussion and brainstorming regarding the data. They wondered if, given this group of students, they had been too ambitious in setting their campus goals. One of the teachers said, "Maybe we need to modify our campus improvement plan before it's too late." Another teacher said, "If the students are not here, we can't be expected to go get them! Many of our parents work two jobs and are gone a lot, so they simply are not home to make sure the kids get to school." After additional discussion, the teachers decided to meet again the next week and review additional data and develop some possible strategies to begin to address the issue, even if it meant modifying the campus improvement plan. Mrs. Marshall told the superintendent she would "keep her posted."

The following week, each grade level met and Mrs. Marshall attended both sessions as a resource person. As she reported to the superintendent, "I was on the sidelines coaching and guiding them and providing data when requested. One thing the teachers wanted was test scores from previous years. In reviewing student performance over several years they noted that the pass rate had been steadily improving and last year 78% of the fifth graders and 75% of the sixth graders had mastered the reading objectives. They did not feel that the 80% pass rate was unrealistic for each group this year. They also looked at the state reading objectives for each grade level. I was very impressed with their ability to analyze and compare the data. As a result of their efforts, we have initiated some new strategies for improving reading as well as contacting parents each time a student is absent."

objectives for appropriate academic indicators for all students, including students in special education or with low socioeconomic status. At the school in the View from the Field, the principal helped to develop strategies for addressing the needs of students who were not achieving their full potential as well as decreased attendance rates. Implied in such a plan is the need for teacher professional development that will assist them in reaching their goal.

Campus improvement plans must also (1) identify the resources needed to implement strategies; (2) provide adequate staffing to ensure strategy accomplishment; (3) develop timelines for implementing and monitoring each strategy; and (4) determine what formative and summative data will be used to ensure that improvement is occurring. It should be noted that no single best model or process for planning exists;

critical components in both the development process and the structure of the plan should be addressed. Also, local district and campus plans should reflect the unique needs of the populations served and should address outcomes for all students. Table 9.2 provides a sample campus improvement plan for Eagle Middle School. As seen in this sample plan, each campus objective includes action steps, resources, responsibility, measurable outcomes, and timelines. Some action steps are a continuation of something started the previous year, whereas other action steps are new this year. As noted in the action plan, numerous people are responsible for the plan's implementation. Few action steps involve a single person. Finally, the action steps must have measurable outcomes to help determine if the action helped the campus achieve the objectives.

Goals should reflect the underlying philosophy that all students can learn and should serve to close the identified gaps in performance existing across various student populations. The goals and objectives should be driven by local, student performance-based needs assessment data. And goals should be based on a long-range vision and developed to reflect multiple-year targeted outcomes for students (e.g., five-year expectations to reach the state standards for each of the academic excellence indicators). Campus performance objectives and district performance objectives should be complementary and mutually supportive. Campus plans should take into consideration innovative structures and approaches and should initiate waiver requests from the state, if needed, to facilitate meaningful improvements in student outcomes.

Campus improvement plans should include measurable checkpoints and incremental timelines to ensure that outcomes are monitored frequently. Formative (or frequent, ongoing) evaluation should provide the opportunity and basis for corrective actions during the implementation of the plans—even if it becomes necessary to redefine objectives and strategies midstream. Summative (or end of year) evaluations should be used to document and celebrate accomplishments, as well as to identify areas for change and modification.

Collecting data is a never ending process in schools that have adopted a work ethic that constantly requires reflection on how they operate, how they go about the business of educating students, and can they do things differently. As Lezotte (1997) says, "School improvement is an endless journey" (p. 70). Some schools describe this process as their continuous improvement process. School personnel see themselves as learners just like their students and seek information regarding the following questions:

1. Do curriculum structures and instructional strategies meet the needs of all students, including students served by the special education program, the bilingual and English as a Second Language programs, Title I, and others?
2. Is curriculum alignment done across grade levels and campuses?
3. Are curriculum offerings linked with the state standards and aligned based on assessment results?
4. Do curriculum offerings not only meet state graduation requirements, but prepare students to enter postsecondary education and be successful?

Data should be reviewed periodically and objectively. In many cases, additional reasons may explain why student performance is not at the desired level. Richardson

TABLE 9.2   Campus Improvement Plan, Eagle Middle School: Campus Objectives

Action Steps	Resources	Responsibility	Measurable Outcomes	Timeline
I. The campus will implement effective strategies for improved achievement for all students and all student groups				
1. Continue the *Making Higher Scores* program a. 3,600 student booklets b. 200 teacher manuals	Supplemental instructional funds from district a. 4,000 b. 500	Administrators, counselors, faculty	Class rolls, pretest/posttest scores, and previous year's scores	Current school year
2. Continue remediation class for math, reading/writing	No additional funding needed (faculty assignment)	Administration, faculty	Class rolls, practice tests Both pretest and posttest, previous year's achievement scores	Current school year
3. Implement training maps a. Training booklets $57/teacher (30) $89/instructor (5) b. Substitute pay c. Three days of training	Facilitator, faculty, counselor, campus instructional improvement funds	Facilitator, faculty, counselor	Results on the HLC question achievement tests and writing scores for organizational structure	First nine weeks of school year
4. Utilize ABCD 2000 Software to diagnose weaknesses in test performance in reading/writing	District/campus supplemental technology funds $250/program	Faculty, technology support	Improvement on test items over previous year	First semester of school year
II. The campus will provide effective staff developmental practices that target teacher needs based on student group needs				
1. Provide diversity training to administrators, faculty, and staff	Regional educational service and support center	Administration campus improvement team	Compare pretest and posttest attitudes and grade discipline referrals	Beginning of current school year

Action Steps	Resources	Responsibility	Measurable Outcomes	Timeline
2. Develop consultation between special service personnel and classroom teachers	Special services personnel, campus staff, development days	Campus improvement team, special services supervisor	Classroom rolls, track grades of special services students	Current school year
3. Implement interdepartmental vertical planning and alignment	Staff development and substitutes for each teacher	Administration, faculty, curriculum director	Previous test scores compared with new test scores based on student subgroups	Quarterly during current school year

III. The campus will improve student attendance rates

Action Steps	Resources	Responsibility	Measurable Outcomes	Timeline
1. Use computer system to monitor student's attendance in every class—three computers needed plus software	Attendance and central offices $7,500 supplemented district/campus technology funds	Administrative staff	Comparison of attendance rates over last three years	Current school year
2. Use computer technology to notify parents of student absences	Attendance office $2,000 supplemental district/campus technology funds	Administrators, counselors, faculty	Comparison of attendance rates over last three years	Current school year
3. Conduct parent conferences of students with excessive absences	Administration, counselors, faculty	Administration, counselors, faculty	Track conferences per year	End of each reporting period
4. Develop a reward system and exemption policy for 100% and 96% attendance	Campus student activity fund $700	Administrators, counselors, campus improvement committee	Increased attendance measured over last three years	End of each reporting period

(continued)

TABLE 9.2 *Continued*

Action Steps	Resources	Responsibility	Measurable Outcomes	Timeline
IV. The campus will increase parental, student, and community involvement in campus improvement efforts				
1. Obtain digital marquees to display all school events for campus	District and campus discretionary funds and private funding $26,000	Administrators, campus improvement committee members	Comparison of attendance rates at school functions compared with last year	Beginning of current school year
2. Provide quarterly mailings to parents regarding students' attendance, progress in class, behavior, and upcoming school events	Mailings: $900 \times 4 = \$3,600$ from campus instructional funds and student development funds	Administration, counselors, faculty	Comparison of attendance rates at school functions compared with last year	Quarterly during current school year
3. Host middle school "First Timers" Camp for incoming 6th graders	Printing, paper, and refreshments $650 from student activity fund	Administrators, counselors, faculty, staff	Comparison of attendance rates of last year with this year	Beginning of current school year

(2000) recommends that in developing and reviewing school plans leaders should (1) examine student demographics and achievement by grade level; (2) examine additional data such as standardized test scores and grades on classroom assessments; (3) break down the data by gender, ethnicity, socioeconomic status, attendance, mobility, discipline referrals, and English language ability; (4) look at the data regarding the lowest performing group; (5) look at gender differences and socioeconomic group differences; (6) summarize the data by describing the meaning of the information; (7) discuss the gaps in learning, curriculum, and instruction; (8) seek additional data that help to reinforce or reject explanations; (9) develop specific goals that are measurable and attainable; and (10) establish a timeline for repeating the process for collecting and analyzing the data.

Finally, school budgets should be developed in coordination with campus plans that include broad-based parameters regarding the allocation of resources. The budgeting process is discussed in Chapter 6. The parameters for the use of the budget should address the use of supplementary funds to which each campus is entitled based on the demographics of the students served. The resource component of the plan should indicate how funds and other resources will be used to accomplish established goals and objectives.

Accountability: Implications for Curriculum Alignment

Student outcomes are closely related to the curriculum as discussed in Chapter 8 and earlier in this chapter. In many states, the public school curriculum is determined at the state level in general terms with the assistance of all stakeholders. In turn, local school districts are then responsible for determining how this curriculum will be implemented at the district and campus level. Key issues for school leaders to consider include the level of involvement by stakeholders, content areas to be included, the scope and sequence of the knowledge and skills contained in the state curriculum, and instructional methods.

Zenger and Zenger (1999) discovered that almost all states report that curriculum development, especially scope and sequence of content at specific grade levels, is left up to local school systems. Most reported, however, that they developed standards, benchmarks, frameworks, goals, or essential learning outcomes to assist and provide guidance for local systems to follow as they develop curricula. According to Greenlee and Bruner (2001), "Teachers connect accountability measures to the curriculum, and become more accustomed to using performance tasks and rubrics in assessments at the classroom level" (p. 3).

Each grade level must consider the unique developmental needs of the students served as well as state requirements or laws. At the high school level, campus personnel must consider the state's minimum curriculum for high school graduation and other graduation requirements, as well as offering instructional programs that focus on technology, science, math, health, liberal arts, performing arts, and others or a combination.

At the elementary level, campus personnel work to deliver a developmentally appropriate early childhood program and seek direction regarding the most appropriate time to introduce a full-scale academic program. The curriculum delivered at the elementary level does not escape accountability either in state-mandated achievement tests or national achievement tests. A few states even have laws prohibiting student promotion if a student cannot read at the third grade level or pass a state-approved assessment.

Accountability for student achievement and curriculum alignment are integrally linked and require that teachers have an understanding of what students need to know and be able to do as they plan the scope and sequence for the school year. In addition, teachers must periodically meet and analyze assessment data to determine the effectiveness and make any needed modifications.

Curriculum alignment, as discussed in Chapter 8, is a process by which the formal curriculum taught to students matches what is planned and tested. The instructional methodology used by the teacher is not mandated, but is usually determined individually or collaboratively by grade level, department, or academic teams. San Miguel (1996) found that when the curriculum is aligned by campus, there are no major achievement gaps between different groups. As Lezotte (1997) has found, "A school can realize a significant gain in student achievement if there is light alignment between the intended, taught, and assessed curriculum" (p. 25). Teachers are the ultimate curriculum developers and must be involved in the curriculum revision process at their schools and districts. Instruction, curriculum, and assessment must receive attention to ensure student learning and success on accountability measures such as state or national examinations.

The ultimate responsibility for school leaders is to monitor student achievement to also ensure that the curriculum is aligned to the assessment instrument so that all students are successful academically. According to Wise (1999), a teacher is the primary determinant of student academic success. School leaders will need to be vigilant in facilitating learning, guiding teachers and students in their learning efforts, supervising their work, and building cooperation and collaboration in the process. School leaders can provide time during the regular schedule for teachers to work on curriculum alignment efforts and serve as a resource by answering questions, monitoring progress, and communicating to all that this work is important and necessary to student success.

Instructional Programs that Address Student Needs

An issue that continues to arise regarding curriculum accountability is the lack of curricular success for all students, especially students of color and those with culturally or ethnically different backgrounds. As Lezotte (1997) has observed, "Intentionally or not, schools often discriminate in how they distribute opportunities to learn . . . [and] the lack of opportunity to learn is often interpreted as a lack of ability to learn" (p. 27).

When instructional programs address the different developmental, special, language, and cultural needs, students can succeed. Ladson-Billings (1995) advocates pedagogy that "empowers students intellectually, socially, emotionally, and politically by using cultural referents to impart knowledge, skills and attitudes" (pp. 17–18). Culturally responsive instructional strategies can serve to change the form and content of instruction. As the principal of one successful school stated, ". . . we try to teach an enriched curriculum for everybody. We feel that all children can learn at a pretty advanced rate if it is presented to them correctly with the appropriate modifications. . . . We feel that they can learn it. And they do" (San Miguel, 1996, p. 78). As Schemo (2001) has indicated, schools that serve predominantly black, Hispanic, lower economic, and other language students can defy the odds and score high on state-mandated tests.

The answer to achieving equity and excellence lies in reforms that reflect a cultural paradigm that emphasizes specific ways in which personal and cultural knowledge can be used to improve education for culturally and linguistically diverse students (Smith-Maddox, 1998). In addition, students' aspirations, homework habits, and participation in extracurricular activities as well as parents' socioeconomic status, involvement, expectations, and regular communication with teachers about classroom activities have a positive effect on students' academic achievement.

To be effective with all students, the school or campus must address the needs of *all* students, and *particularly* the needs of students of target populations that are included in the school-wide program and then determine how these needs are met. The Title I program may include counseling, pupil services, mentoring services, college and career awareness and preparation, such as college and career guidance, comprehensive career development, occupational information, enhancement of employability skills and occupational skills, and personal finance education or job placement services. Innovative instructional methods may include applied learning and team teaching strategies; services to prepare students for the transition from school to work, including the formation of partnerships between elementary, middle, and secondary schools and local businesses; the integration of school-based and work-based learning; and incorporation of gender-equitable methods and practices. All strategies must be consistent with and designed to implement the state and local improvement plans.

Case Study

You have applied for the position of principal at Liberty High School and have been invited to the campus for an interview. The site-based screening committee has provided you with data concerning the campus. Student performance on state-mandated exit level tests can be found in Table 9.1. Additional information regarding dropout rates and attendance can be found in Tables 9.3 and 9.4.

In addition to the data, the committee has provided you with the following information.

- Attendance and dropout rates by ethnic groups are presented in Table 9.3.
- Total enrollment is 1,038; students by grade level and ethnic group are presented in Table 9.4.
- Liberty High School has been loosing an average of twenty-one students per year for the last three years (most of them Anglo students).

TABLE 9.3 *Attendance and Dropout Rates by Ethnic Groups*

	Attendance (%)	Dropout (%)
All students	96	6
Boys	92	16
Girls	94	9
Native American	94	1
Asian	96	0
African American	89	12
Hispanics	84	19
Low socioeconomic status	89	15

- Liberty High School will lose one or two faculty positions at the end of this school year based on the projected number of students next year.
- Liberty High School has had three principals in the last five years (the first retired after being at the school for nine years, the second moved to the central office after a year and half, and the last principal left for a small private high school.
- A parent group has recently been formed to seek additional financial support for instructional materials and programs.
- The average tenure of the faculty is 11.7 years with twenty-one years being the longest and one year being the shortest term.
- Any changes in assignments require approval of the teacher union.

As you prepare for the interview with the site-based screening committee you have been asked to respond to the following questions:

1. What do you see as the school's greatest academic strength?
2. What instructional areas need the most attention?
3. Is the school meeting the needs of all students?

TABLE 9.4 *Students by Grade Level and Ethnic Group*

Group	Grade 10	Grade 11	Grade 12
African Americans	49	54	56
Hispanics	106	121	73
White	211	190	155
Native Americans	1	2	1
Asian	9	7	3
Total	376	374	288

4. Based on your review of the data, why are you seeking the position and what would you propose as a possible course of action?

Develop an outline of your presentation to the site-based committee including possible components of a school improvement plan.

Summary

Up to this point, much of the information has focused on programs, processes, and activities. Attention must also be given to the relationship between the school leader and teachers and the work that needs to be accomplished. Ma and MacMillan's (1999) findings suggest that school administration is important not only to promote teacher's satisfaction with their work, but also to reduce the negative impact of different levels of teaching experience. They believe that a positive perception of their relationship with school administrators may help teachers feel at ease with their teaching and merge quickly and successfully into all aspects of school life. School administrators may consider programs such as information seminars, orientation week, mentor programs, and measures that make newly hired teachers focus on teaching, with less administrative disruption.

The information needed for success starts with conducting a comprehensive needs assessment, and several ideas have been presented, although the list is not exhaustive. Perhaps, the single most effective tool for accountability is the campus improvement plan. This document charts a course to ensure that all students are academically successful. The role of school leaders is multidimensional; they are the catalyst for facilitating the alignment of the curriculum with accountability standards, developing a comprehensive student assessment program, and most importantly creating a safe school where both students and teachers can learn and teach.

Your Turn

9.1. As the newly appointed principal of City Middle School, you have just left a meeting with the Assistant Superintendent for Instruction. Her parting words to you were "We need to improve student passing rates on the state-mandated test." In the interview, you had seen the passing rates for 1998 to 2000. But today you were given the 2001 passing rates (Table 9.5). The last principal, who was at the campus two years, was not an instructional leader. As the principal, you have been charged with improving passing rates on the test.

- What would you say to the faculty and staff?
- How would you present the data?
- What steps would you take to involve teachers in the solution?
- What additional data do you need?

TABLE 9.5   *Comprehensive Test of Basic Skills Score*

Grades	1998	1999	2000	2001
Total math percentiles				
6	42	55	48	41
7	52	56	60	53
8	48	72	59	61
Total writing percentiles				
6	55	69	51	62
7	56	60	59	51
8	46	59	54	50
Total reading percentiles				
6	51	57	45	41
7	57	42	52	38
8	48	60	54	42

9.2. Using the data in Table 9.5 for City Middle School, suggest possible changes that could be implemented to improve performance on the basic skills tests. How does Standard 1 speak to the school leader's role in improving the performance on the tests?

9.3. Describe ways of involving your campus improvement plan team in the development of strategies to address the irregular performance of students on the state-mandated test of basic skills.

9.4. Using the following student data checklist provided, collect the data for each category for at least one grade level at your school. Summarize the findings based on the data collected and present the data in a graphic form.

I. Campus enrollment
   Total number of registered students in grade _____
   Number of students by ethnicity, language group, gender, and other meaningful categories:

African American	_____
Hispanic	_____
Native American	_____
Asian	_____
Anglo	_____
Title I	_____
Bilingual	_____
Talented and Gifted	_____

   Number of students in special programs (e.g., Title I, Bilingual Education, Talented and Gifted Education) by category.

II. Daily attendance

Average daily attendance by school _____
Average daily attendance of students by grade _____
Percent of students tardy for classes for school _____
          by grade _____
Number of students who have been absent from school twenty-one days or more by:
  School _____   Grade _____

III. Mobility/stability and socioeconomic status

Mobility rate of school percent of children who move in and out during the year _____   Mobility rate by grade _____
Stability rate of school percent of students who remain in the same building for the entire year _____   Stability rate by grade _____
Percent of students receiving free or reduced-price lunch in school _____
Average level of parents' education and/or household income by school _____

IV. Student behavior

Number or percentage of discipline referrals or incidents
  School _____   Grade _____
Number or percentage of student suspensions and expulsions
  School _____   Grade _____

IV. What other data could you collect and analyze to assist you in making effective data-driven decisions?

References

American Association of Colleges for Teacher Education. (2002 February). *Governmental relations update.* Washington, DC: AACTE.

Berman, P., & Gjelten, T. (1984). *Improving school improvement: A policy evaluation of the California school improvement program. 2: Findings.* Berkeley, CA: Berman, Weiler Associates.

Bryk, A. S., & Hermanson, K. L. (1993). Educational indicator systems: Observations on their structure, interpretation, and use. *Review of Research in Education, 19,* 451–484.

California Department of Education. (2000a). *Curriculum frameworks and instructional resources.* Sacramento, CA: California Department of Education.

California Department of Education. (2000b). *Immediate intervention/underperforming schools program.* Sacramento, CA: California Department of Education.

California Department of Education. (2000c). *2000 star results.* Sacramento, CA: California Department of Education.

Charles A. Dana Center. (1997). *TEKS for leaders: Leadership development.* Austin, TX: The University of Texas at Austin.

Comer, J. P., Ben-Avie, M., Haynes, N. M., & Joyner, E. T. (1999). *Child by child: The Comer process for change in education.* New York: Teachers College Press.

Creighton, T. B. (2001). *Schools and data: The educator's guide for using data to improve decision making.* Thousand Oaks, CA: Corwin Press.

Darling-Hammond, L. (1991). *Policy uses and indicators.* Paper prepared for the Organization for Economic Cooperation and Development.

Elkind, D. (2000/2001). The cosmopolitan school. *Educational Leadership, 58,* 4, 12–17.

Finn, C. E., & Petrilli, M. J. (2000 January). *The state of state standards.* Washington, DC: Thomas B. Fordham Foundation.

Fitch, M. E., & Malcom, P. J. (1998). *Successful school planning and restructuring: Leadership for the 21st century.* Fort Forth, TX: ISD Publishing Group.

Franklin, J. (2001). Trying too hard? How accountability and testing are affecting constructivist teaching. *Education Update, 43,* 3, 1, 4–5, 8.

Fullan, M. (1999a). *Change forces: The sequel.* Philadelphia: Falmer Press.

Fullan, M. (1999b). *Learning from the past directions for the future.* Alexandria, VA: Association for Supervision and Curriculum Development.

Fullan, M. (1993). *Change forces: Probing the depth of educational reform.* New York: Falmer Press.

Glesne, C. (1999). *Becoming qualitative researchers: An introduction* (2nd ed). New York: Longman.

Glickman, C. D. (1990). Open accountability for the '90s: Between the pillars. *Educational Leadership, 47,* 7, 38–42.

Greenlee, B. J., & Bruner, D. Y. (2001). State assessment rediscovered: Can accountability tests initiate better teaching? *Wingspan, 14,* 1, 2–5.

Greenbriar School District. (2000). Curriculum, assessment and accountability. (Online) http://www.greenbriar.district28.k12.il.us/ifisbe/antarctica/Docs/CAA.html.

Green Valley Area Education Agency 14. (2000). Curriculum core council training overview: Accountability based curriculum. (Online) http://www.ipserv2.aea14.k12.ia.us/edserv/abc.html.

Harrington-Lueker, D. (1990). The engine of reform gathers steam: Kentucky starts from scratch. *American School Board Journal, 177,* 9, 17–21.

Hart, G. K., & Brownell, N. S. (2001). An era of educational accountability in California. *The Clearing House, 74,* 4, 184–186.

Hill, P. T., & Bonan, J. (1991). *Decentralization and accountability in public education.* Santa Monica, CA: RAND.

Hodgkinson, H. (2000/2001). Educational demographics: What teachers should know. *Educational Leadership, 58,* 4, 6–11.

Holcomb, E. L. (2001). *Asking the right questions: Techniques for collaboration and school change* (2nd ed). Thousand Oaks, CA: Corwin Press.

Ladson-Billings, G. (1995). Toward a theory of culturally relevant pedagogy. *American Educational Research Journal, 32,* 3, 465–491.

Lezotte, L. W. (1997). *Learning for all.* Okemos, MI: Effective School Products.

Lezotte, L. W. (1992). *Creating the total quality effective school.* Okemos, MI: Effective Schools Products.

Ma, X., & MacMillan, R. B. (1999). Influences of workplace conditions on teacher's job satisfaction. *Journal of Educational Research, 93,* 1, 39–47.

McNamara, J. F., & Thompson, D. P. (1996). Teaching statistics in principal preparation programs: Part One. *International Journal of Educational Reform, 5,* 3, 381–389.

National Commission on Excellence in Education. (1983). *A nation at risk.* Washington, DC: U.S. Department of Education.

Pearson, D. P., Vyas, S., Sensale, L. M., & Kim, Y. (2001). Making our way through the assessment and accountability maze. Where do we go now? *The Clearing House, 74,* 4, 175–183.

Richardson, J. (2000). *The numbers game: Measure progress by analyzing data.* Oxford, OH: Tools for Schools. National Staff Development Council.

San Miguel, T. (1996). *The influence of the state-mandated accountability system on the school improvement process in selected Texas elementary schools.* Unpublished doctoral dissertation. The University of Texas at Austin, Austin, TX.

Schemo, D. J. (December 17, 2001). School defies odds and offers a lesson. *New York Times.*

Schmoker, M. (2001). *The results fieldbook.* Alexandria, VA: Association for Supervision and Curriculum Development.

Slavin, R. E. (2000/2001). Putting the school back in school reform. *Educational Leadership, 58,* 4, 22–27.

Smith-Maddox, R. (1998). Defining culture as a dimension of academic achievement: Implications for culturally responsive curriculum, instruction, and assessment. *Journal of Negro Education, 67, 3,* 302–317.

Texas Education Agency. (2000). *The 2000 accountability rating system for Texas public schools and school districts.* Austin, TX: Texas Education Agency.

Underwood, T. L. (2001). Reflections on assessment, accountability, and school reform. *The Clearing House, 74, 4,* 172–174.

Webster's New World Dictionary and Thesaurus. (1996). M. Agnes (ed). New York: Hungry Minds.

Wise, B. J. (1999). Vaccinating children against violence. *Principal, 79, 1,* 14–20.

Zenger, W. F., & Zenger, S. K. (1999 April). Schools and curricula for the 21st century: Predications, visions, and anticipations. *National Association of Secondary School Principals, 83,* 606, 49–60.

Internet Resources

www.cde.ca.gov/board
www.cde.ca.gov.iiusp
www.ed.gov/legislation/ESEA/sec4003.html
www.tea.state.tx.us/perfreport
www.tea.state.tx.us/perfreport/aeis/about.aeis.html
www.tea.state.tx.us/perfreport/aeis
www.cde.ca.gov/cilbranch/eltdiv/cdsmc.htm

10

Professional Development for School Leaders: Reflection, Growth, and Change

ISLLC Standard

Standard 2: A school administrator is an educational leader who promotes the success of all students by advocating, nurturing, and sustaining a school culture and instructional program conducive to student learning and staff professional growth.

Chapter Objectives

The objectives of this chapter are:

- Discuss the need for continued growth and development for school leaders.
- Identify and describe various approaches to professional development for school leaders.
- Discuss the need for leader assessment and various models that can be used.
- Develop a personal development worksheet and action plan.
- Discuss the importance of mentoring in leadership development.

Throughout this book emphasis has been on the role of school leaders in supporting teaching and learning so that all students are successful. For Maxwell (1993), "The growth and development of people is the highest calling of leadership" (p. 179). He continues by saying, "Leaders who continue to grow personally and bring growth to their organization will influence many and develop a successful team around them" (p. 180). School leaders, as they continue to grow and develop, influence the effectiveness of others.

Professional development in schools begins with educational leaders, but for Robore (2001), administrators often wonder how they can continue to meet the multiple challenges of their job, when they ". . . are particularly vulnerable because they are on the front line" (p. 181). Like leaders in other organizations, school leaders must continue to grow and learn if they are to maintain their effectiveness, and Levine (1989) has emphasized that "ongoing professional development opportunities . . . are therefore imperative" (p. 269). Hammond and Foster (1987) support the concept of continued professional development by suggesting that like teachers, school leaders ". . . must have effective mechanisms that help inform [them] about their work and provide opportunity for consultation, reflection, self-assessment, and continued improvement" (p. 42). Fullan (1995) adds support to this position by noting that professional development is ". . . integral to accomplishing a moral purpose [and] . . . central to continuous improvements in professional work cultures" (p. 264). School leaders, like others in education, must seek to continuously improve their leadership capacity through professional development.

As the title of this chapter suggests, change is important to leadership development. Maxwell (1993) has observed that, "leaders resist change as much as followers do" (p. 49). Yet leaders must change themselves if they are to continue their own journey of professional development. As school leaders continuously maneuver through what Vaill (1996) calls "permanent white water" they are confronted with the complexities of a demanding job. "All around us the world is changing. Indeed, the existence of change seems to be the most certain element in our experience" (Boy & Pine, 1971, p. 1). But despite a leader's best intentions, "the tradition in education is simply discuss what has happened and move on to new topics" (Costa & Kallick, 2000, p. 62). In this ever changing world, it is critically important for administrators, who often lead stressful lives, to take time to reflect, discuss, and assess their concerns and feelings about their situations. They must be willing to make time in their busy schedules for professional growth and development activities that can help them create a much needed balance. Boy and Pine (1971) refer to this process of growth and reflection as "expanding the self" (p. 1). For Sparks and Hirsch (1997), the emerging view of professional development is one that is decreasing or deemphasizing generic skills transmitted by experts, isolated training events, fragmented and piecemeal activities, and experiences that are isolated from the school context. Professional development is moving toward increasing or emphasizing multiple forms of job-embedded learning, individual development coupled with organizational development, school- or campus-focused and directed activities, and a process that places responsibility on campus leaders.

More than ever, school leaders are being encouraged and even required to sustain their professional development through various activities, including personal assessment and growth plans. According to Levine (1989), such a developmental perspective is crucial to the ongoing renewal of school leaders. For example, the Pajaro Valley Unified School District in California has implemented professional standards for administrators that include a goal-setting and assessment system, along with a professional development support model (Casey & Donaldson, 2001). In Texas, each principal or assistant principal must develop a professional growth plan based on the results of an individual assessment. They must also complete two hundred hours of professional development every five years for certificate renewal. In North Carolina, the Principal Executive Program has school leaders meet regularly to share and discuss experiences. This development process helps principals make sense of their own experiences in school and builds networks to help reduce the feelings of isolation (Norton, 2001).

As school leaders continue to grow and develop, they not only expand their self-awareness, but engage in activities that can enhance their professional skills. In the professional development process, school leaders serve as models to foster the continued growth and development of teachers and students. As Boy and Pine (1971) describe the personal change process, "the expanding self senses an . . . emerging convergence . . . in various areas of human thought; it possesses a deep sensitivity to the psychological, philosophical, technological, and biological [changes] . . ." (p. 104). One reason that continued professional growth is so important for leaders is that "leadership is developed, not discovered" (Maxwell, 1993, p. ix). School leaders must expand their own leadership potential as they continue to learn. It has been said that the way to learn is to lead and the way to lead is to learn; leaders are life-long learners.

This chapter begins by discussing the need for continuous development for school leaders and identifies and describes various approaches and models to professional development. The chapter also describes the nature of reflective journals and their importance for school leaders in recording and analyzing their thoughts. Next, the chapter discusses the role of assessment in leader development and describes several models, including the process of developing a professional growth plan and a suggested format. The chapter concludes with a description of a self-assessment model that puts all the professional development pieces into a framework for continued improvement.

Professional Development for School Leaders

Studies concerning the ever changing role of school leaders have yielded several major themes for leader development (Rebore, 2001). These themes include instruction (teaching and learning); human relations; leadership and management; sociopolitical (cultural) awareness; and self-awareness (understanding). Development activities related to instruction involve not only the more effective supervision and assessment of the teaching–learning process, but a greater understanding of curriculum development and alignment. Developmental activities for leadership and management involve the creation of a campus vision and then developing skills to support collaboration while also diagnosing potential problem areas and generating solutions. Developing skills in budgeting, prioritizing, and allocating resources are also areas of focus. Human relations activities involve improving communication with all constituencies and involving others in establishing a positive work environment. Sociopolitical awareness helps school leaders develop their skills in identifying and involving other leaders within the community in working to meet the needs of all groups in the school community.

Bell (1998) suggests that professional growth comes from three directions: inside, outside, and upside down; it ". . . begins with a look inside that includes a thoughtful examination of strengths, limitations, improvement opportunities, needs, hopes, and fears" (p. 170). Levine (1989) suggests that development for school leaders focuses on active listening, support, and patience. As school leaders begin the journey to look inside, the following questions can provide them with an agenda for growth and development (Heil, Parker, & Tate, 1994):

1. What major area of education have I changed my mind about in the last semester or year?
2. When have my assumptions about something related to schools changed because those assumptions were absolutely wrong?
3. When I compare the way I think this year with the way I thought last year, what is different?
4. What have I learned as a school leader this semester or year that makes my actions last semester or year seem less effective?
5. Who has a different view about teaching and learning than I do and what might I be able to learn from them?
6. How much time have I spent in the last semester or year seriously questioning some aspect of my thinking involving my actions as a school leader?
7. What was the last thing I learned from the teachers, students, and associates on my campus?
8. How long has it been since I had and lost an argument with someone I trust and respect?

Once school leaders have taken a look inside, they are ready to look outside for resources and data that can provide important insights for professional growth and learning. Leaders should ask themselves: What people, tools, supports, and permissions might be needed to be more effective? In gathering information some data or input may be readily available in the form of yearly reviews from district rating forms. Other areas may require leaders to look ". . . in out-of-the-way places, turning things 'upside down,' and squint[ing] to find them" (Bell, 1998, p. 172). As school professionals look outside, it is natural to think in terms of mentoring or coaching with another administrator or cultivating friendships with avant garde individuals who might prompt new perspectives or suggest ideas that disconfirm what were believed to be true. By modeling their own continuous professional learning, school leaders can transform their schools into communities of professional learners (Fleming, 1999).

Reflective Journals

Professional development for school leaders often involves reflection, which has "the ultimate purpose of [getting] us into the habit of thinking about our experiences" (Costa & Kallick, 2000, p. 60). Reflective journals provide a record of events, incidents, and thoughts and by reflecting on these experiences more personal insight is derived (Posner, 1996). Personal learning logs or reflective journals can also provide a ". . . format for gathering information on participants' cognitive learning" (Guskey, 2000, p. 133). The use of such a format prompts individuals to respond at regular intervals by identifying important concepts or behaviors, then describing their understanding of these concepts or actions along with possible implications for and applications to their personal and professional lives. Through journal reflections, individuals have the opportunity to (1) amplify meaning from their experiences based on the input and insights of others; (2) extend meaning beyond the immediate experience to others; (3) make a commitment to change or modify strategies or behaviors; and (4) foster learning and sharing of a rich knowledge base. As Dickman and Stanford-Blair (2002) note, ". . . reflection is the utlimate stringing together of patterns of information through serious consideration . . . of constructed knowledge to proactively explore further configuration, implications, and applications . . ." (p. 95).

Reflection involves hearing both internal and external voices' self-knowledge or *self-talk*. One way to develop this capacity to *hear* is to write a memo or note to self in the journal or to identify and describe the thought process or steps that were used to solve a problem or to address a situation. The external voice of reflection involves sharing thoughts about events, dates, problems, or situations with others. In sharing thoughts with others, leaders are provided the benefit of their insights through response or feedback.

Reflection involves mental processes that include drawing forth cognitive and emotional information from visual, auditory, kinesthetic, and tactile sources (Costa & Kallick, 2000). In addition, reflection links information to previous learning by providing opportunities to compare current results with those that were anticipated and intended. By linking previous learning with new results, school leaders can search for effects and find connections between and among causal factors through analysis, synthesis, and evaluation. *Thinking about thinking* or conducting a *personal internal audit* by comparing what has been experienced with what has been uncovered, becomes part of the action plan for moving forward with complete satisfaction (Costa & Kallick, 2000). As described by Dickman and Stanford-Blair (2002), "the reflective nature of intelligence can be interpreted as the conscious bending back of information patterns to discern potential relationships . . . [The] reflective brain is not content to . . . accept what is immediately revealed [but] rather in its reflective mode . . . is moving information at will to generate alternative images" (p. 96).

Journals provide school leaders with opportunities to analyze and reason through dilemmas or situations and to build a greater understanding by writing about what has been observed or learned. The journal can take many forms, but should be left to the personal preference of the individual; it may include notebooks, binders, bound books, or even computer files. The individual records his or her personal thoughts, ideas, and feelings, which are the most important dimension. Sentence structure, spelling, grammar, or punctuation should be of little importance because the key to journaling is to get the main thoughts and ideas recorded.

Journal entries should be dated and reflect thoughts and feelings that immediately come to mind. The journal entries may be chronological and include a description of the sequence of events for each day, along with reactions to those events. Using a split-page format may prove helpful; half of the page records the events and the other half records the reactions. Box 10.1 provides an example of a journal entry using the chronological sequence of daily events. As seen in this example, the school leader has recapped the events of the day along with the feelings and thoughts that were triggered by the events.

BOX 10.1 • *Reflection Journal: Chronological Sequence*

A Week in the Life of an Assistant Principal
Thank God It's Here—spring break. We have been swamped with registration and grant proposals here this week. Once the teachers were validated by winning three of the last twenty grants awarded, other teachers then seemed eager to pursue the challenge as well. It has been very rewarding this year . . . they all need your help at the last minute, nonetheless, we finished them and took them over a whole hour before the deadline.

Then there were those *daggum* politics again. What a deal! We had to chat about job descriptions once again today and the ubiquitous *they* expected me to help counselors with registration . . . but, I had to do the grants—an actual part of my job.

We received the formative results back from the district today. Yuck! We had a 58% in math, 70% in writing, and 72% in reading. Data cannot be broken down by objective or subgroups . . . so, it really does not provide a *pinpoint* on which to focus. Nonetheless, they are dismal statistics. Math does not want to broach this at our SBDM meeting on Monday because they do not feel it accurately reflects the students' performance . . . with their not having any geometry background. However, I am doing the English portions because SBDM should have both the "good, bad, and the ugly" in order to make necessary adjustments/improvements.

BOX 10.2   •   *Reflection Journal: Critical Incident*

Family math night was held last week. I was the point of contact for the vertical math team that planned the family math night program. I had to oversee and facilitate the meetings that were held in preparation for the big event. It was difficult to facilitate a discussion that led the team to develop consensus from various ideas. Delegating responsibilities was difficult as well. I was tempted to take care of all the items that needed to be done so that I knew that they are completed properly. However, I know that I could not handle all the details; and the teachers wanted and deserved to be involved as well. As I began to let go of the reins of the event, the teachers began to take ownership in the events they were involved in. They were a vital part of the function of the school and I began to realize that they should be treated as such.

Over the last week as plans for family math night were finalized I realized what a resource the teachers could be as they drafted letters to parents, purchased food and planned games, and then decided where to put the 6-foot python one of them brought in. I now realize that by letting go of handling all the details, not only do I empower teachers, I empower myself as well.

Another form of journaling involves a detailed description of one or two incidents or critical situations and includes a discussion of reactions to such incidents, possible explanations for the incidents, issues raised, and strategies that were used to handle the situation(s). Box 10.2 provides an example of a journal entry based on the analysis of a critical incident.

As seen in this example, the school leader's reflections focus on an episode that happened at school and include reactions and insights. For Costa and Kallick (2000), as we ". . . reflect on our actions, we gain important information about the efficacy of our thinking . . . [and] practice the habit of continual growth" (p. 62).

Leader Assessment and Professional Development

School leaders can use a variety of assessment models to provide direction for constructing their own plans for professional development. The use of these assessment models varies from state to state, and only a selected sample are described here to illustrate the kinds of assessment opportunities that are available to support school leaders in their professional development efforts.

According to Robore (2001), "a growing number of school districts are taking a more personalized approach to . . . development for [school leaders]. This . . . type of program emphasizes acquiring skills that either help . . . with their job or enhance their professional development" (p. 182). These personalized approaches often begin with some form of assessment that focuses on job-embedded skills or those behaviors that are specific to school leaders. Ultimately, these assessments are designed to provide feedback that can be used as the basis for a professional growth plan for school leaders.

Rather than relying solely on personal perceptions of strengths and weaknesses from a self-assessment inventory, objective feedback from others regarding job-related activities can yield additional data. Each assessment model that is described in this section involves assessment activities that are viewed by others, and data are provided to the participant based on the participant's behavior in identified job-related skills.

Selecting and Developing the 21st Century Principal is one assessment program that has been developed by the National Association of Secondary School Principals. This model assesses the presence and strength of specific school leadership skills through participation in a series of interrelated simulations that closely mirror the work of the campus leader or principal. The data generated from these simulations are related to job-specific skills and give the participants feedback about their strengths as well as areas for improvement in developing a personal growth plan. Specific strategies for continued growth are also included as a part of the assessment report.

The Professional Development Inventory is another assessment model for school leaders that has been developed by the National Association of Elementary Supervisors and Principals. This assessment program uses twelve simulations that reflect the reality of a school setting. Thirteen skills are assessed by a team of assessors and a computer-generated profile is provided for each participant. The Professional Development Inventory identifies strengths as well as areas for improvement and can provide the basis for generating individualized professional development plans.

School Administrator Skills Assessment is a one-day developmental assessment process with job-like activities designed for campus leaders (principals and assistant principals) in the early stages of their assignments or who have not participated in previous assessment activities. This model is also appropriate for those aspiring to be school leaders. The assessment occurs in one day at a center that brings participants and assessors together in a central location. A structured feedback component provides the participants with a written report and a conference with the assessment center director. This feedback provides the data that can be used to develop a personal professional growth plan. Feedback is based on (1) an in-basket activity requiring participants to use skills in prioritization and communication; (2) a problem analysis and resolution activity that focuses on instructional direction, vision development, ethical responsibility, problem analysis, judgment, and organizational ability; and (3) a group activity that emphasizes skills in facilitation, human relations, oral communication, problem analysis, and organizational ability.

The *Developmental Assessment Center* model was developed by the National Association of Secondary School Principals to provide input for the professional growth and development of school leaders. This model engages participants in several activities to assess job embedded behavior. The model begins with the behavior exhibited and incorporates assessor notes and participant reflections for each exercise. The process does not focus on adequate skills of leadership, but instead is designed to identify areas of significant strength and any potential *derailers*. The leadership skills assessed include interpersonal skills (leadership, sensitivity, motivation of self and others); administrative skills (problem analysis, judgment, organizational ability); communication skills (oral and written); and knowledge of self. The participant receives a summary report that is based on an integration of all of the activities. The participants also receive feedback about possible developmental strategies to improve or enhance their leadership skills.

In selecting an assessment model, school leaders should pick one that will give them the best feedback regarding their current job-related skills and their sense of efficacy. According to Monk (2002),

> A meaningful mix of activities will give a quality read on skill levels from a variety of perspectives. Through an assessment process which includes primary job alike activities, other job-related activities as appropriate, detailed feedback, and meaningful suggestions for growth, campus leaders will receive a quality snapshot of ability to 'walk the walk' of the principal. (p. 21)

Developing a Professional Growth Plan

In developing a professional growth plan, the school leader should focus on enhancing strengths and managing weaknesses. For Rebore (2001), "whatever an individual . . . identifies as the area of need, a prerequisite for success is commitment. Therefore, it is advantageous to write down such personalized programs in a document that includes a personal needs assessment and a plan of action" (p. 182). This written document is generally referred to as a *professional growth plan*.

A professional growth plan for campus leaders is primarily for development purposes and should be shared with others on an as needed basis. If the campus leader is working with a mentor or coach, sharing some information might be helpful in the relationship dynamics. The growth plan should be generated based on input from various sources including (1) reflective journals; (2) formal assessment models; (3) feedback from others in a variety of forms; and (4) district personnel evaluations of school leaders. In developing the growth plan, the campus leaders should focus on maintaining and enhancing perceived strengths, while addressing and improving identified weaknesses. For Monk (2002), "One suggested process for developing goals is for the individual leader to create a vision of himself/herself at his/her 'best' as a campus administrator. This vision should be written in the present tense as if it exists. . . . The goals should be important and attractive enough to ensure continuing commitment and include a personal needs assessment and plan of action" (p. 25).

A beginning point for a professional growth plan is the creation of a vision of the ideal self—the best leader for a campus. The vision statement should be written as if the ideal self already exists. Using this vision, and other data sources, the leader should then begin to develop goals that will ensure continuing enthusiasm and effort to achieve them. The development plan should also include strategies, people, and resources that are necessary to achieve the goals, along with a timeline for completion. Figure 10.1 provides sample general guidelines to follow in developing a professional growth plan for school leaders.

As seen in the professional development planning guide, not only does the growth plan include a *personal best* vision statement, goals, strategies, people, resources, and a timeline, but it should also include such items as anticipated problems or potential roadblocks, benchmarks for completion of tasks, and ways to document and celebrate completion of the goals. Determining a personal course of action for professional

1. Identify one of the ISLLC Standards or a state standard that relates to an area you want to

   ISLLC Standard/State Standard: _____

   _____

2. Identify behaviors associated with the appropriate standard that you want to develop.

   _____
   _____

3. Describe the sources and kinds of data related to the identified standard that provide evidence of current performance level.

   _____
   _____

4. Identify at least three strategies or activities that you feel will help you address your targeted area.

   Possible Strategy/Activity   Desired Outcomes

   _____   _____

   _____   _____

   _____   _____

5. Locate additional resources you can consult to help you address the need you have identified.

   _____
   _____

6. If desired, identify one primary and two secondary mentors who can also assist you by providing guidance and insight.

   Primary Mentor: _____

   Curriculum Mentor: _____

   Resources Mentor: _____

   Other Mentor: _____

7. Either with your mentor(s) or on your own, identify potential barriers or roadblocks that can impede your progress toward the desired goal and then identify possible ways to overcome the barriers.

   Roadblocks to Implementation   Suggestions to Overcome Barriers

   _____   _____

   _____   _____

   _____   _____

8. Discuss how you will know that you have made progress in achieving your desired goal. Match your expected results with measurement or documentation data along with target dates.

   Expected Results   Measurement/Documentation Data

   _____   _____

   _____   _____

   _____   _____

9. Identify a target date for completion of the plan. _____

10. Identify at least three ways to celebrate the completion of the growth plan.

    A. _____

    B. _____

    C. _____

FIGURE 10.1 *Professional Development Planning Guide*

growth requires campus leaders to (1) clarify the purpose, meaning, and function of their work; (2) focus on the learning-based concerns of their schools; (3) identify appropriate goals for their learning; (4) assess their current level of understanding and expertise; (5) seek out appropriate mentors and others in collaborative activities; (6) continuously engage in reflection concerning their progress; and (7) share and celebrate their learning outcomes. School leaders who are able to see their own professional growth as a priority will be able to use what they learn as they engage in school improvement efforts.

Self-Assessment Model for School Leaders

As school leaders engage in professional development and develop a growth plan they are engaging in self-assessment. Reinhartz and Beach (1993) have suggested a self-assessment model that incorporates the various professional growth activities to provide for a comprehensive development plan. This model is appropriate for instructional leaders as they ". . . assess and reflect on their performance, using input and assistance from teachers and other school personnel . . . to address professional development" (Beach & Reinhartz, 2000, p. 287). Figure 10.2 identifies the steps in the self-assessment model as school leaders assume responsibility and development.

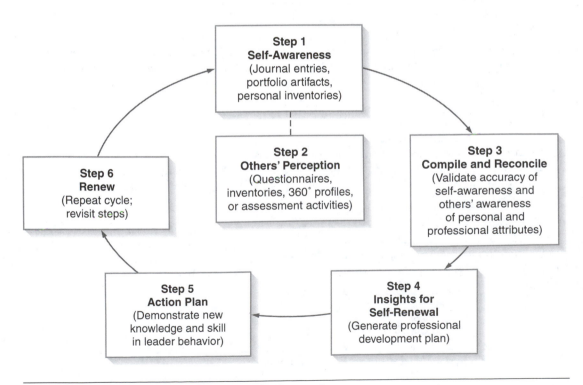

FIGURE 10.2   *Leader Development: Model for Renewal*

In the self-assessment model, leaders begin the process by collecting data from their own journal entries or selecting artifacts from their portfolios as they begin building their professional profile. As indicated earlier in the journal section, journal entries are useful to prompt leaders ". . . to reflect on specific situations, interactions, and behaviors they experience over time as they perform their job" (Beach & Reinhartz, 2000, p. 288). Leaders may also complete personal inventories or answer questions similar to those posed earlier in the chapter. Step 1 produces a summary or general sense of the leader's own perceived professional strengths and weaknesses. Take a moment and complete the Self-Report: Skill Evidence of the ISLLC Standards, Figure 10.3, and assess yourself on each of the categories.

Step 2 in Figure 10.2 involves seeking input from others (colleagues, teachers, staff, and perhaps parents and students) regarding the use of questionnaires, invento-

Superintendent	_____
Asst. Superintendent	_____
Principal	_____
Asst. Principal	_____

Rubric Scoring Tool	0 No Evidence	1 Some Evidence	2 Outstanding Evidence
Standard 1: Learner-Centered Vision			
Facilitates improvement and change through research and best practice			
Facilitates the implementation of sound, research-based instructional strategies (see professional development)			
Uses formative and summative data to develop and improve instructional strategies and goals			
Standard 2: Learner-Centered Campus Culture			
Creates a culture of high expectations			
Ensures that parents and others are an integral part of the campus culture			
Uses strategies that promote collegial relationships and collaboration			
Facilitates collaborative development of campus vision			
Establishes process to assess and modify the plan to ensure achievement of the vision			
Supports innovative thinking and risk-taking efforts			
Recognizes and celebrates the contribution of all			

(continued)

Rubric Scoring Tool	0 No Evidence	1 Some Evidence	2 Outstanding Evidence
Standard 3: Organizational Leadership and Management			
Gathers information from a variety of sources for decision making			
Frames, analyzes, and creatively resolves campus problems			
Develops, implements, and evaluates change processes			
Uses planning, time management, and work organization to attain goals			
Standard 4: Communication/Community Involvement			
Demonstrates effective communication			
Implements strategies to systematically gain input from all stakeholders			
Establishes partnerships with parents, businesses, and other groups that support campus goals			
Standard 5: Values/Ethics/Integrity			
Models and promotes continuous development of all learners including self			
Promotes awareness of all diversity issues			
Articulates the importance of education in a free democratic society			
Standard 6: Learner-Centered Political Context			
Uses emerging issues and a variety of data sources for planning			
Facilitates planning, implementation, monitoring, and revision of curriculum			
Ongoing Professional Development			
Engages in ongoing, meaningful professional growth			
Collaboratively develops and implements professional growth for staff in alignment with campus goals			
Total			

Comments:

FIGURE 10.3 *A Self-Report: Skill Evidence of the ISLLC Standards.* Using the ISLLC Standards for the School Leaders, assess yourself on each of the following categories.

ries, or 360-degree profiles to obtain data and insights from others. The school leader may also choose to participate in an assessment center to get feedback regarding specific job-embedded skills (see examples of assessment models identified in this chapter).

In step 3, leaders begin to compile and reconcile the data they have collected as they analyze, evaluate, and reflect on what they see. By bringing these data to a level of consciousness they discover more and more about themselves and ". . . become connoisseurs and self-critics and they learn to look at their behavior more objectively" (Beach & Reinhartz, 2000, p. 288). Step 3 is critical as each individual seeks to reconcile any discrepancies in perceptions or any conflicting data. This step represents the moment of truth as each person looks at himself/herself in the mirror of the data and begins to *see* not only the strengths, but the areas for possible professional growth and development. This introspective process coupled with job-related criteria and skills gives focus and direction for developmental activities.

In step 4 the school leader begins to develop a plan of action, usually in the form of a professional growth plan as suggested in the chapter. The professional growth and development activities should be viewed from a learning perspective. For Vaill (1996),

> the learning perspective is essential for it involves 'discovery,' 'recognition' . . . [which] are process words. They are names for ways of working, thinking, and feeling. They are all qualities of learning as a way of being. They apply to every subject, not just to things that a[n educational] leader needs to know. Anyone who knows something about discovery, cultivation, and recognition is in command of his or her learning processes and knows how to engage in learning as a way of being. (pp. 191–192)

As leaders continue their own professional journeys, ". . . they need the freedom to determine their own direction and growth, to interact with other [leaders] in a cooperative manner, and to discuss new ideas and break the feeling of isolation" (Beach & Reinhartz, 2000, p. 288).

In step 5, leaders begin to implement their professional growth plans. Growth activities may involve additional training that is job related, seeking or becoming a mentor, participation in study groups (book study) with other leaders, creating a community of learners in their schools, or engaging in cooperative action research (as discussed in Chapter 5). Step 5 involves taking action as leaders become risk takers and step out on groundless ground. Although step 6 begins the self-assessment cycle again. However, in reality, once self-assessment begins, it should become a continuous, ongoing process.

Professional development for leaders is a lifelong process and takes time and effort. Daresh (1986) has noted that leaders must continue to grow personally and professionally if they are to be effective administrators. Alvarado (1998) says that "Thinking about our work and improving what we do—these things are professional development. So is . . . talking about [our] practice and how to make it better" (p. 23). Scherer (2002) notes that good professional development:

1. Sheds light on how students learn in the classroom
2. Inspires collegiality
3. Improves student achievement.

For us, self-assessment is critical to leader development, and leader development is essential for school improvement as campus leaders examine who they are, what they are doing, and why they are doing it.

Guskey (2002) has provided five levels to use in evaluating professional development. Level one assesses participant's reactions regarding such areas as likes and dislikes, will it be useful, and was their time well spent. The second level assesses participant's learning through simulations or demonstrations. Level three determines the degree of organizational support and change and examines the degree to which implementation was facilitated and supported. The fourth level of evaluation seeks to determine the degree to which the participants used the new knowledge and skills through structured interviews, participant reflections, and direct observations. Level five looks at the impact on student learning outcomes by examining student records, conducting interviews, and disaggregating school data. These five levels of information about professional development evaluations are offered as evidence of success, not proof. As Guskey (2002) notes, "in the absence of proof you can collect good evidence about whether a professional development program has contributed to . . . gains in student learning" (p. 50).

Case Study

You have just completed your first year as an assistant principal of an elementary school. Following your assessment from an independent source, you have been given the following feedback based on the assessment activities you completed (in-basket activity, case study, and role playing).

In your reflections you wrote: As I reflect on my first year as an assistant principal, the one area that I feel I need the greatest assistance is in human resource development. Throughout the year, I felt that I was ineffective in supporting teachers because I was so concerned with my own survival I did not fully support others in their professional growth, especially the new teachers. Often my discussions with teachers focused on what seemed to be trivial items or on particularly troublesome students, rather than on the teacher's own developmental needs. If I had a chance to *do over*, I would spend more time addressing the broader issue(s) and would continually bring the conversation back to the teacher's own insights. Only when needed would I add my observations to the proceedings.

Activity Challenges

1. Based on your responses to the *in-basket* activity, challenge yourself to involve others in collaboration.
2. Based on your participation in the case study, challenge yourself to work with various teacher populations in supportive roles and shadow administrators on other campuses to observe their interactions and leadership styles.
3. Based on your participation in the role-playing activity, challenge yourself to validate others who do not think in an organized manner and be willing to let others express alternative views or solutions.

Using this information and information from Figure 10.1, develop a professional growth plan for yourself. Consider where you are now regarding your career goals and where you want to be in three to five years. Discuss your plan with a mentor or friend to get feedback.

Summary

This chapter has focused on the professional growth and development of school leaders. As leaders continue to grow and develop, they bring growth and change to their organizations and model learning for teachers and students. As Dickmann and Stanford-Blair (2002) note, such ". . . leadership engages the collective capacity of a group to think, learn, and achieve important purposes" (p. xviii). The continuous growth for school leaders is essential in the ever changing environment of schools.

Although leaders often resist change as much as followers, they must be willing to make time in their busy schedules to *expand the self*. In many states, school leaders are being required to sustain their professional growth and development through various activities, including personal assessments and growth plans.

The chapter discusses the role of professional development in the continuous growth of leadership potential. As leaders begin the journey, they can reflect on a series of questions posed for them that causes them to take inventory of their own learning and leading behaviors. The chapter also discusses the role of reflective journals in the leaders' professional development. Reflection is the ultimate form of personal and professional growth and development because such a practice causes leaders to examine experiences, thoughts, implications, and applications. Examples of journal entries are provided for leaders to use in constructing journal entries.

The chapter concludes with a discussion of the role of leader assessment in the development of professional growth plans. Sample assessment models are described along with a professional growth plan framework for leaders to use in developing their own plans. The chapter concludes with a self-assessment model that brings all the different professional development activities together in a continuous renewal cycle.

References

Alvarado, A. (1998). Professional development is the job. *American Educator, 22*, 4, 18–23.

Beach, D. M., & Reinhartz, J. (2000). *Supervisory leadership: Focus on instruction*. Boston: Allyn & Bacon.

Bell, C. R. (1998). *Managers as mentors: Building partnerships for learning*. San Francisco: Berrett-Koehler Publishers.

Boy, A. V., & Pine, G. J. (1971). *Expanding the self: Personal growth for teachers*. Dubuque, IA: Wm C. Brown.

Casey, J., & Donaldson, C. (2001). Only the best. *Leadership, 30*, 3, 28–30.

Costa, A. L., & Kallick, B. (2000). Getting into the habit of reflection. *Educational Leadership*, 60–62.

Daresh, J. C. (1986). Principal's perceptions of the quality of administrative inservice models. Paper presented at the annual meeting of the Mid-Western Educational Research Association. Chicago, IL: [Mimeographed].

Duckmann, M. H., & Stanford-Blair. (2002). *Connecting leadership to the brain*. Thousand Oaks, CA: Corwin Press.

Fleming, G. L. (1999). Principals and teachers: Continuous learners. *Issues About Change*, 7, 2, 9, ED 447565.

Fullan, M. G. (1995). The limits and potential of professional development. In T. R. Guskey & M. Huberman (eds), *Professional development in education: New paradigms and practices*. New York: Teachers College Press.

Guskey, T. R. (2002). Does it make a difference? Evaluating professional development. *Educational Leadership*, *59*, 6, 45–51.

Guskey, T. R. (2000). *Evaluating professional development*. Thousand Oaks, CA: Corwin Press.

Hammond, J., & Foster, K. (1987). Creating a professional learning partnership. *Educational Leadership*, *44*, 42–44.

Heil, G., Parker, T., & Tate, R. (1994). *Leadership and the customer revolution: The messy, unpredictable and inexplicably human challenge of making the rhetoric of change a reality*. New York: Van Nostrand Reinhold.

Levine, S. (1989). *Promoting adult growth in schools: The promise of professional development*. Boston: Allyn & Bacon.

Maxwell, J. C. (1993). *Developing the leader within you*. Nashville, TN: Thomas Nelson Publishers.

Monk, B. J. (2002). *First time Texas campus administrator academy: Resource guide*. Austin, TX: Texas Principals Leadership Initiative.

Norton, J. (2001). Sharing the mystery. *Journal of Staff Development*, *22*, 51–54.

Posner, G. J. (1996). *Field experience: A guide to reflective teaching* (4th ed). White Plains, NY: Longman.

Reinhartz, J., & Beach, D. M. (1993). A self-assessment model for supervisors: Increasing supervisor effectiveness. *Record in Educational Administration and Supervision*, *14*, 35–40.

Rebore, R. W. (2001). *Human resources administration in education* (6th ed). Boston: Allyn & Bacon.

Scherer, M. (2002). Perspectives. *Educational Leadership*, *59*, 6, 5.

Sparks, D., & Hirsch, S. (1997). *A new vision for staff development*. Alexandria, VA: Association for Supervision and Curriculum Development.

Vaill, P. (1996). *Learning as a way of being*. San Francisco: Jossey-Bass.

Author Index

Subject Index